The Sick Chicken Case

LANDMARK LAW CASES & AMERICAN SOCIETY

Julie Novkov and Victoria Woeste
Series Editors

Peter Charles Hoffer
N. E. H. Hull
Founding Series Editors

For a complete list of titles in the series go to www.kansaspress.ku.edu.

Published by the University Press of Kansas (Lawrence, Kansas 66045), which was
organized by the Kansas Board of Regents and is operated and funded by Emporia State
University, Fort Hays State University, Kansas State University, Pittsburg State University,
the University of Kansas, and Wichita State University.

Library of Congress Cataloging-in-Publication Data

Names: Hoffer, Williamjames, author.
Title: The Sick Chicken case : the US Supreme Court and the new deal /
Williamjames Hull Hoffer.
Description: Lawrence : University Press of Kansas, 2025. | Includes
bibliographical references and index. | Contents: The Great Depression
and the New Deal – Litigating a "Sick Chicken" – A Unanimous Court –
Kritocracy – Court Packing? – Aftermath
Identifiers: LCCN 2024028962 (print) | LCCN 2024028963 (ebook)
ISBN 9780700638154 (cloth)
ISBN 9780700638161 (paperback)
ISBN 9780700638178 (ebook)
Subjects: LCSH: United States. National Industrial Recovery Act of 1933. |
Constitutional law–United States–Cases. | United States. Supreme
Court–Cases. | Poultry industry–Law and legislation–United States. |
United States. National Recovery Administration. | Competition, Unfair.
| Depressions–1929.
Classification: LCC KF6011 .H64 2025 (print) | LCC KF6011 (ebook) | DDC
343.7307/6365–dc23/eng/20240626
LC record available at https://lccn.loc.gov/2024028962.
LC ebook record available at https://lccn.loc.gov/2024028963.

British Library Cataloguing-in-Publication Data is available.

The Sick Chicken Case

The US Supreme Court
and the New Deal

UNIVERSITY PRESS OF KANSAS

CONTENTS

ACKNOWLEDGMENTS

The author owes a debt of gratitude to many. My editor at the press, David Congdon, played a pivotal role. The copyeditor, Stephanie Marshall Ward, in particular, as well as the staff at the press made this manuscript into a book. The readers for the press provided vital corrections, suggestions, and editing. My parents, the founding co-editors of this series, Peter Charles Hoffer and Natalie Hull, edited drafts, supported me financially, and contributed in countless ways. Seton Hall University awarded me a yearlong sabbatical and financial assistance to complete the project that proved essential. Both the Seton Hall University Libraries and the University of Georgia Libraries supplied research assistance. My colleagues at Seton Hall University and elsewhere assisted with the work. My students at Seton Hall University over the years have had a substantial impact on both the work and its author. The staff in the Dean's Office and elsewhere at Seton Hall University have made this book possible. To all of them and those I have forgotten, I thank you. For the errors that remain, I take full responsibility.

Colloquially known as the "Sick Chicken Case," *A.L.A. Schechter v. U.S.* (1935) is cited routinely throughout the constitutional literature of the twentieth century. At first glance, one might wonder why. Its two findings, that chicken slaughtering was not interstate commerce, and so not open to congressional regulation under the interstate commerce clause of Article I, and that Congress could not delegate (the "non-delegation doctrine") open-ended discretion to the executive branch (a variant of separation of powers doctrine) or to private parties, are no longer the landmarks of doctrine they once were. But the doctrinal importance of *Schechter* remains. It is a loaded case in two ways. The reasoning of the Court is still controversial, and the two grounds for reversal of the lower courts' conviction of the firm are the subject of an armada of academic legal scholarship. As a part of our political history, rather than as constitutional law, *Schechter* is even more important. Just why will become apparent as the reader progresses through the following pages.

It is conventional in constitutional casebooks and law review articles for an author to lay out their thesis at the outset. After all, they know where they are going with the lesson. History narratives like the one below follow a different pattern—a kind of jigsaw where all the pieces are there, but one has to wait for their assembly to see the full picture. This book is such a narrative, and I ask the reader to be patient until the end. Such an approach does, however, require a deft touch—for at places in the narrative one has to stop and explain points of law. As law students discover in their first weeks, law is a language as well as a body of knowledge, and learning law requires learning to use that language. Thus, lay readers may thus find some of the terminology herein difficult to follow. On top of this, as we have already seen, constitutional law is full of "doctrine"—"prudential" judicial reasoning (or more bluntly, judicial inventions). I have tried to simplify the terms of art without doing too much damage to them.

The Landmark series ordinarily focuses on a single case or a group of closely related cases, but the narrative arc of this book starts with the beginning of the Great Depression and ends after that crisis had passed. The importance of *Schechter*, seen in this long view, becomes clear, for

Schechter stood at a defining moment in that narrative, and no one at the time could tell how that story would conclude. This is a book about the New Deal, with *Schechter* at its center.

———

Our story begins in the midst of the Great Depression. On May 25, 1935, a day New Dealers would later lament as "Black Monday," the US Supreme Court handed down a series of decisions that dealt mortal blows to New Deal legislation and presidential initiatives. Thus, one branch of the three in the federal system appeared determined to thwart the New Deal in its entirety. In the most significant decision on Black Monday, *A.L.A. Schechter Poultry v. U.S.*, which National Recovery Administration (NRA) director Hugh Johnson reportedly derisively labeled the "Sick Chicken Case," the Court declared the National Industrial Recovery Act (NIRA) unconstitutional, thus abolishing the NRA and all of the hundreds of codes it had enacted.

The NRA was part of a broader attempt to deal with the underconsumption that supposedly caused the Great Depression. President Franklin D. Roosevelt swiftly denounced the Court's attempt to limit the United States to the "horse and buggy age." Later, he would unveil a plan to ease the aged Court justices' burdens with new appointments—what critics called a "court-packing plan." With a so-called Second New Deal arriving on the Court's docket, including Social Security and the National Labor Relations or Wagner Act, in the coming year, the United States seemed on its way to a constitutional crisis.

But appearances can be deceiving. *Schechter Poultry* did not result from the machinations of the far-right wing of the Court, a last gasp of judicial conservatism. It was a unanimous decision, with the liberals on the Court agreeing with the conservatives and the chief justice, Charles Evans Hughes, aged but no reactionary (he had been a Progressive governor of New York), writing the opinion of the Court. What is more, it was not the only case in which the Court struck down key New Deal legislation. For many on and off the Court, it was hard to quarrel with skepticism of laws like the NIRA that tried to do too much, delegating such broad authority to local codes so minutely the justices could laugh about some of the rules during oral argument. *Schechter Poultry* is still worth studying—raising important questions about federal regulation of the economy, religion, and public safety and how far the political branches, the executive and legislative branches, should be allowed to go in service to any particular partisan view.

But most important for the tale worth telling, the Sick Chicken Case is about the Great Depression and the New Deal—a look at 1930s America before World War II and the Cold War, a nation in the age of radio and movie palaces, and a time of experimentation with government that some likened to fascism or communism, maybe both. Through this landmark law case, which threatened, but ultimately did not undo, the New Deal, we can arrive at a deeper understanding of both American law and society. *Schechter Poultry* is, thus, not just about a sick chicken; it is about a sick nation trying to heal itself.

In retrospect, one might say the major background constitutional issue in *Schechter* embodies a conflict between individual rights and government authority, basic in our democratic republic. It is not liberal or progressive versus conservative. Instead, one side is that individual rights should not be abridged whether these are framed as economic or political, public or private. Government should operate under severe restrictions. In a federal system like ours, this stems from a natural law theory relegating the national government to limited powers and the creed that the states hold the rest, although they are also held to the bare minimum. The other side posits that government has an obligation to police society on behalf of the entire society, with some individual rights sometimes acquiescing for the greater good.

Aside from the points of law arising in *Schechter*, historians of the Great Depression have long cared about the overall impact of New Deal agencies like the NRA. Initial scholarship during the 1950s and 1960s considered the New Deal an experiment with liberal democracy that was largely a success and praised President Franklin D. Roosevelt (FDR) for his leadership, though court packing went too far. Later, historians were largely unimpressed by a reform effort that not only did not go far enough but also left out people of color and women. Such scholarship also criticized efforts like the NRA, largely on the grounds that it homogenized, then replaced, diverse community-based institutions in favor of a faceless federal bureaucracy. More conservative critics of the New Deal concluded that FDR's New Deal had deepened and prolonged the Depression rather than helped.

Nevertheless, present-day emanations of *Schechter* live on in countless conversations about government power, an alleged administrative or "deep" state, and what constitutes the rule of law in a democratic society. One could find legislative precedents (like the Confiscation Acts in the Civil War and the Espionage and Sedition Acts in World War I) for almost untrammeled executive discretion during an emergency like the COVID-19 pandemic. One can find similar hints of President Roosevelt's suggestion, in his first inaugural address, that if Congress did not act to solve the Great Depression, he would use his inherent powers to do so. One historian of the New Deal reported that some in the audience cheered at those remarks. Today, with mere enabling legislation, governors can place the population in lockdown, impose curfews, and mandate face coverings and social distancing. It poses a fundamental question about executive power and separation of powers.

Nor has the "New Deal" as a rallying slogan disappeared from public consciousness. Since climate change theory has centered on carbon dioxide and other "greenhouse gases" starting in the 1990s, those concerned with fossil fuel use—a key source of those gases—have called for a "Green New Deal." Not coincidentally, the most recent proposal as of this writing, from Representative Alexandria Ocasio-Cortez (D-NY), also calls for green equity—a redistribution of wealth to traditionally underserved groups. New Deals seem to encompass far more than addressing a limited set of problems. Rather, they tend to aim at wholesale reform on a national scale.

It is understandable that more radical proposals of this type might run afoul of the US Supreme Court, an institution that has frequently posed a roadblock to the political branches (and to the states—what Justice Louis D. Brandeis described as "laboratories of democracy"). The justices are appointed for good conduct tenure, not elected. They are selected for their qualifications as well as their political connections. The nominees pointedly emphasize the nonpolitical, nonpartisan nature of their reasoning. At their confirmation hearings they tell members of the

Senate Judiciary Committee that they do not have an overt political agenda. They have a jurisprudence, a philosophy of law—they "interpret" the law (merely calling "balls and strikes" as one nominee explained)—they do not make law. Though many have questioned some, most, or all of these distinctions, there is little doubt of the Court's role in frustrating attempts at change.

When the Court is seen as an obstacle to the democratic will ("the counter-majoritarian problem," in the words of Alexander Bickel), one hears the occasional call to place additional (supposedly more friendly) justices on the Court. The object is a political one: to remake the majority into a favorable one to keep whichever government agenda is being derailed on track. At the time of writing, a whole host of issues is subject to this concern. Hence, there are now several calls from members of Congress and the public to enlarge the Supreme Court in order to reverse its positions on the law. It was the same in the 1930s when the Court began overturning significant elements of the New Deal, including the NIRA at issue in *Schechter*. The same important questions arose. What is the right balance between the popular will as embodied in the presidency and Congress as opposed to the reserved legalism of the Court? Should the Court give way to the polls? If so, how much?

Finally, similarly controversial and relevant today, *Schechter* concerned religious faith, specifically Jewish observance of kashrut or kosher butcher rules in a secular society. Though religious freedom under the First Amendment did not arise during the litigation (it did not become prominent in First Amendment jurisprudence until *West Virginia Board of Education v. Barnette* in 1943), the Schechter brothers' ability to practice their faith played a major role in their desire to overturn their prison sentences and fines, and their guilt. In *Masterpiece Cakeshop v. Colorado Civil Rights Commission* (2018), the Supreme Court divided over whether a baker could be compelled by an anti-discrimination law to create a wedding cake for a same-sex couple's marriage, which violated the baker's religious beliefs. Society wants to eliminate adverse discrimination, but what happens when anti-discrimination ends up discriminating against minority religious views? The Schechters' Jewish practices came into conflict with the national government's health standards and desire to improve the overall economy. Whose rights should prevail? Whose values should triumph? These are not easily answered questions.

Like other books in the Landmark Law Cases in American Society Series, this volume addresses two groups of learners: students in classrooms and a lay audience with an interest in US legal history, but who are not experts. This does not mean, hopefully, that scholars in the field will find this account without merit. The author, the series editors, the readers, and the press have endeavored to produce a responsibly written, well-researched, and high-quality rendering of this complex topic. The bibliographic essay at the end details the sources for this volume in place of notes. I have leaned toward explaining instead of formulating a unique jurisprudential take or attempting to revolutionize the field or coin new terminology. In short, this is not a standard monograph, and I hope the scholarly reader will not view it as such.

Chapter one offers an overall background for the case. It provides a depiction of US society, government, and economy at the time as well as the immediate progress of events that led to President Franklin D. Roosevelt's New Deal, in particular the NIRA, which set up the NRA. In addition to covering the First New Deal, it then lays out how the NRA created the codes, one of which governed the New York metropolitan area's poultry butchers. Finally, the chapter meets the Schechters, follows their prosecution for violating the code, and introduces the court test.

Chapter two lays out the trial court and appellate court cases that led to the US Supreme Court. The chapter reviews the wealth of cases that affected the litigation in *Schechter*. It concludes with a detailed analysis of the briefs, oral arguments, and machinations behind the scenes for both sides. Chapter three analyzes the *Schechter* decision, the cases that accompanied it, and those that immediately followed. It also tells the story of the reception of the case; the political reaction, both favorable and unfavorable; and what happened to the Schechter brothers.

Chapter four covers the contest between the US Supreme Court and the New Dealers in the second half of FDR's first term, under the title "Kritocracy"—rule by judges. Though the Court upheld some pieces of the First New Deal, they also decided against many aspects of it at both the state and national levels, with increasing divisiveness between the conservatives and the progressives on the Court. The chapter lays out the Second New Deal and the New Dealers' mounting anxiety about its prospects before the Court, heavily under the influence of *Schechter*'s blow on "Black Monday." In what he may have believed was a referendum on his New Deal, Roosevelt won a resounding reelection victory for himself and the Democrats in 1936, and he made plans to deal with the Court.

Chapter five tells the story of the fight over FDR's plan to reorganize the judiciary in 1937, a piece of legislation its opponents viewed as "court packing." Alongside that battle is the US Supreme Court's change from a supposedly conservative majority to a progressive one, with Justice Owen Roberts considered the swing vote—the "switch in time that saved nine." This chapter analyzes that supposed shift in jurisprudence as well as the demise of FDR's scheme to receive more appointments to the Court. *Schechter* loomed over this fracas as both a cause of and a potential threat to the Second New Deal.

Chapter six concludes the story with the aftermath of the controversy, including the New Dealers' ultimate reshaping of the Court. The chapter outlines further developments with the non-delegation doctrine, and the reach of congressional authority under the interstate commerce clause versus federalism—the two bases for the decision in *Schechter*. Much of what is known as the administrative state followed the Court's decision in *Schechter*, for good and ill. It is a history worth recounting so that we may better understand our world.

CHAPTER I

The Great Depression and the New Deal

Like every other US Supreme Court case, *Schechter Poultry v. U.S.* did not happen in a vacuum. To fully understand it, we need to look at the environment that produced it. In 1935, when the Court announced its decision in *Schechter*, the United States had been suffering from the effects of the Great Depression for nearly six years. At its height, one-quarter of the workforce had been unemployed, but unemployment had come down to 20 percent. It would decline to 14 percent in 1937, only to rise to nearly 20 percent again the next year, and it would not decline into single figures until US entrance into World War II. Those who were employed were largely struggling with wage cuts, and many had lost much of their savings in the bank panics that had struck the financial services sector after the collapse of the stock market in October of 1929. Then there were those who had only found part-time work, and, therefore, did not count toward the unemployed. Economists estimate that up to 50 percent of the workforce struggled at or below the poverty line during this catastrophe.

If anything, international affairs were even worse. Not only had Benito Mussolini and his black shirt–clad Fascists taken control of Italy after their "march on Rome" in 1927 but they were being hailed as a success story. The trains ran on time. There was full employment. The birth rate was good. Industry had never been better. In 1934, they won a World Cup Championship in a World Cup competition they had hosted. Italy seemingly had found a solution to its doldrums amid a newly found unity. After all, the fascist symbol—an ancient Roman bundle of sheaves around an axe—meant strength through forced combination. Their Fascist state arranged its industries into cartels, often known as syndicates, which in turn were managed by the state. Markets still existed, but the supposed chaos of competition had been transformed into a predetermined order. The goal was efficiency at the cost of liberty.

Further north, in Germany, Adolf Hitler's National Socialist Workingmen's Party, derogatorily called Nazis, had taken power in 1933 when the soon-to-die President Paul von Hindenburg had given the decorated veteran of the Great War the chancellorship of democratic Germany. Soon thereafter, a lone Communist agitator set fire to the national legislature's building, the Reichstag. Blaming all Communists and sympathizers, the Reichstag gave Hitler emergency powers to root out the threat. When his Gestapo (national police) and SS (stormtroopers under Heinrich Himmler) did so with murderous efficiency, the democratic government of law that was Weimar Germany began to suffer the death of a thousand cuts that was the installation of Hitler's fascism, Nazism, in Germany.

While Himmler's SS rounded up Jews for torture and murder, their atrocities hidden from view, Hitler's Germany emerged from its own Great Depression with the same vigor as Mussolini's Italy, in much the same way. Massive public works projects, including the autobahn, a mass of wide concrete superhighways exclusively for automobiles, helped revive the economy and lower unemployment. And during rearmament, conscription finally took care of the remaining unemployed. Women were encouraged to marry early, give up potential careers, and dedicate themselves to motherhood. Boys and men were enrolled in Nazi youth camps. With the 1936 Olympic Games in Berlin, the capital of the old and the new Germany, the Nazis had a showcase for their "reich" (empire) and the alleged superiority of their Aryan blood (a perverted kind of Nordic race theory). Though US athlete Jesse Owens and others showed that people of color could be superior to Hitler's would-be "supermen," the Olympics put the Nazi state center stage—a place the Nuremberg rally–loving regime adored. After all, much of the revival was spotlights and showmanship anyway. In fact, the Nazi state was a hodgepodge of inefficiency, corruption, incompetence, waste, and theft.

To the east soared another alleged model of efficiency, Josef Stalin's Communist utopia, the Soviet Union. There was no doubting the achievements Western visitors saw firsthand and reported back. From its bloody birth in the Russian Civil War, after the Great War, through the early 1920s, to Stalin's current five-year plan, the Bolshevik (majority) state had modernized, urbanized, industrialized, educated, and provided health care to much of the population across that vast empire. The

Soviet Union's population was greater than that of the United States, and the tsarist congeries of ill-clad, ill-housed, and ill-educated serfs had the appearance of a Western country, but with none of the inequality of wealth and status and without the bigotry. Civil rights leaders, reformers, and journalists marveled at what had happened under a planned state. The liberal reformer and journalist Lincoln Steffens reported of his visit: "I have seen the future, and it works."

However, like fascist Italy and Nazi Germany, the Soviet Union was not what it appeared to be. As some of the less starry-eyed visitors noticed, there was no freedom in Stalin's utopia. The Bolsheviks had created a vicious police state where lives were cheap and individual rights gave way to the "greater good" of the collective. Sometimes, this took the form of Stalin's forced collectivization of largely Ukrainian agriculture in the late 1920s and early 1930s. Millions died from disease, starvation, and execution. Beginning in 1933, Stalin initiated the first of his Great Purges. Hundreds of thousands were tortured, executed, or forced into slave labor—a system that came to be known as the gulag—in the east, the frozen wastes of Siberia. The amazing centralized economy that had so enthralled the reformers was actually a charnel house of death, degradation, and environmental destruction. This hellscape of human suffering escaped popular notice. This is partly due to the success of Stalin's propaganda machine, but also because of a need to believe in an alternative to the miseries of "capitalism" (adherence to a market-based economy) and its disturbing relation, fascism.

In a world of Italian-, German-, and Soviet-style states, the central question was what path the United States would follow in order to emerge from its Great Depression. Both President Herbert Hoover and Franklin D. Roosevelt had answers, but neither could promise success. Hoover, "the Great Engineer," came to the office with the most promise. US prosperity during the 1920s was just short of miraculous. Electrification enabled the widespread adoption of electric appliances. The automobile industry became a mass production behemoth with the states and, to a lesser extent, the national government providing roads for a new kind of freedom—the freedom of the open road. Visionaries like New York's Triboro Bridge Authority pioneer, Robert Moses, initiated a movement to remake the American landscape for the automobile. Charles Lindbergh's world-famous solo flight across the Atlantic in 1927 heralded a new era in plane transportation. Hollywood moved from the silent period into the age of sound with grand movie palaces, many of which featured the revolutionary technology of air conditioning.

In cities like New York, home of Schechter Poultry, a vibrant metropolitan scene sponsored the new movie palaces, jazz clubs, and an underground economy of drugs and alcohol. The United States had begun a great social experiment in the 1920s—Prohibition. National and local law enforcement waged its first major drug war, sometimes with disastrous results. Demonstrating the rule of unintended consequences, scholars estimate that drinking actually increased with Prohibition, the quality of beer and spirits decreased, and crime replaced legitimate sellers. Also, the national government tried to keep industrial alcohol away from the public by poisoning it. Industries knew how to remove the poison, but bootleggers often did not—countless people died from government-poisoned alcohol. It was not the first foray into policing drugs. (Marijuana and cocaine had led the way early in the century.) And it would not be the last.

Herbert Hoover, international engineer, food relief administrator during the Great War, and highly active secretary of commerce under the Harding and Coolidge administrations just prior to his own landslide victory in 1928, symbolized the optimism, the can-do spirit, and the solid reputation of American government and business during this period. Unlike the presidents he served, Hoover believed in the benevolent power of an active government. However, Hoover's voluntarism and Quaker-inspired collective action were not the basis of a command-and-control government. The national government fostered self-help, whether it was sponsoring industrial associations, having companies bid for radio frequencies the Federal Radio Commission (later the Federal Communications Commission or FCC) allocated, or promoting the benefits of standardization in individual industries. His calm, dispassionate demeanor combined with his considerable confidence to produce a leader of exceptional quality. Yet these characteristics did not prove equal to the crisis of the 1930s.

The Great Depression

Black Tuesday and Thursday, October 24th and 27th, 1929, respectively, certainly constituted cause for concern among investors and lay observers. The Dow Jones Industrial Average lost most of its value, wiping out the gains of a decade in a week. Cooler heads called the Crash a necessary correction of an inflated market, and that may well have been right except that the glamour of the Jazz Age had concealed major problems with the US economy. First, agriculture was still suffering from the multiple ills of overproduction leading to low prices; the Dust Bowl covering much of the Great Plains, from Texas to Nebraska; the boll weevil and locust destroying cotton and grain crops, respectively; and its perpetual financial crisis of indebtedness followed by bankruptcy in bad times. Although electrification, sanitation, and road building had proceeded apace in urban and suburban areas, much of the country's workforce was rural and lucky to have a telephone in town, let alone electricity and indoor plumbing. Rural America was in distress everywhere, not just in the Dust Bowl or the sharecropper South. Housing construction had also leveled off as consumers reached the limit of their credit. And, finally, the entire financial system was a series of dominoes ready to fall due to faulty business practices, new corporate forms like Samuel Insull's Chicago-based electric utility company, and the aftereffects of the Versailles Treaty, which formally ended World War I.

To pay off their loans to US banks, the other Allies, Britain, Italy, and France, imposed enormous reparations on defeated Germany. But Germany was in no position to pay. When it defaulted in 1923, French and Belgian troops occupied the Ruhr—Germany's industrial heartland. The impasse ended when Charles Dawes, an experienced Republican lawyer and future vice president under Coolidge, negotiated the plan that bears his name. American banks would lend the Weimar Republic moneys that it would then use to pay the reparations to the Allies that they, in turn, would use to pay their debt to US banks. It was an intentional circular system of payments that benefited all concerned, especially the bankers who received their fees and interest on the loans at each stage. The flaw in the system was that if there was a contraction in the credit system, the entire arrangement would collapse, taking the world economy with it.

Making the financial situation even worse, investors in the United States had bought a significant amount of stock on the New York Stock Exchange on margin. That is, the anticipated rise in the stock's price constituted the bulk of the collateral for their loans to buy the stock. If the stock went down in price, the purchaser owed the bank out of pocket. Therefore, the collapse of the stock market did not remain confined to the Wall Street community. It soon spread throughout the country in the form of defaults and bankruptcies. To remain solvent, banks throughout the nation had to call in their loans and restrict credit. This created a general contraction in the money supply, leading to a condition known as deflation—a decrease in prices and an increase in the value of the dollar.

Although the United States was not dependent on foreign trade, foreign trade changes impacted the US economy greatly. The increase in the value of the dollar made US-made goods more expensive and boosted US assets on world markets. International exchange rates adjusted to these new conditions with a rush to the US dollar. Because the United States was on the gold standard, international gold deposits flowed into the US Treasury with a corresponding outflow of dollars.

Hoover tried to manage these developments. He gathered business leaders together to ensure no cuts in wages. He arranged for a settlement of a coal strike with better wages for the miners. As employers compensated for the loss of consumer confidence and subsequent decrease in sales with job cuts, Hoover sought to rectify the farm crisis and the financial crisis in one fell swoop—a revision of the tariff. The resulting legislation, the Smoot-Hawley Tariff of 1930, not only failed to end the economic downturn; it may well have turned it into a depression that struck the entire world. The increase in tariffs was one of the largest ever enacted, and it included not only agricultural goods but also manufactured goods. It spurred foreign governments to retaliate, and the subsequent reduction of worldwide trade diminished everyone's markets. For example, Weimar Germany's turbulent recession turned into a chaos-filled breakdown with the Nazis the most substantial beneficiaries.

Similar problems beset Japan, giving rise to a militarism that, in 1931, set it on a course for a wider war with its invasion of Manchuria.

Hoover tried again with the Reconstruction Finance Corporation. The RFC used federal seed money to spur private investment in manufacturing plants and equipment. It was meant to be a constrained and targeted intervention, but one he expected to have a major impact, because business was the largest purchaser in the economy. However, the funds were too small to make up for the downfall in private credit after the Crash, and Hoover would allow it to give money only to highly sound firms. This restricted its customer base and encouraged potential customers to cut their workforce in order to meet the requirements for credit. The rumor that it was a slush fund for Republican-owned businesses did not help the situation, not if the idea was to restore confidence in the economy.

One might consider this lackluster response to the growing calamity affecting the United States to be heartless, incompetent, or some combination of the two, but it was actually consistent with the consensus of economic thought at the time. Almost all economists in the country believed government intervention in the economy, especially policy meant to influence the size of the money supply, to be doomed to failure. Under Say's Law, the supply of money was immaterial; only the production of goods mattered. Any government intervention would interfere with the functioning of the markets, exacerbating economic problems.. This foundation for classical economics became known as the general policy of laissez-faire, French for leave well enough alone, roughly translated.

Though Jean-Baptiste Say had formulated these ideas in the early nineteenth century, they seemed commonsensical enough when scientific discoveries like Charles Darwin's theory of evolution reinforced ideologies reliant on supposed natural laws. Another age-old doctrine, Gresham's Law, held the same view concerning government attempts to increase the money supply. "The bad will drive out the good" as the less valuable money will cause people to hoard the more valuable money such as gold or silver. Thus, any attempt to stimulate the economy through deficit spending or lowering the central interest rate was doomed to fail as businesses and consumers withdrew valuable currency from both investment and prospective purchasing.

This set of beliefs is what likely drove the Federal Reserve Bank of

New York—the most important one in the Federal Reserve System, due to its size and position in the financial capital of the United States—to raise interest rates in 1930. All of this runs afoul of modern thinking based on the IS-LM (Investment Savings Liquidity Money) Model, a.k.a. neo-Keynesianism, named after its originator, English economist John Maynard Keynes. In his book *The General Theory of Employment, Interest and Money* (1936), Keynes argued that government did have a role in managing the economy. If there is too much demand for the supply of goods, there will be inflation, and the central bank will raise interest rates, restricting the supply of money in the economy. If the supply is large enough, the government might also cut back on spending to achieve the same result. If deflation, recession, or depression is the problem, the authorities will do the opposite. Because this theory emphasizes the demand side of the economy—business and consumer spending—it is known as demand-side economics. However, this well-developed theory, which would earn Keynes a Nobel Prize for Economics, did not exist in recognizable form for any of the policymakers in the Great Depression.

As shantytowns, called Hoovervilles, spread throughout urban America; banks started to close their doors at record-setting rates; and Dust Bowl migrants, derisively labeled "Okies," went west seeking a better life; Hoover seemed stultified by the increasing strain. With Republicans losing their majority in the by-election of 1930, his ability to influence events shrank even further. More and more, a state of despondency hung over the nation. Its population decreased for the first time in its history. The optimism of the 1920s had dissipated along with the country's faith in its business leaders. Former titans, like Samuel Insull, who had built an electricity behemoth in and around Chicago, were now facing bankruptcy. They turned into the shady villains who had recklessly brought down the country with their financial evil-doing. Hoover's use of the US Army to clear the Bonus Marchers—World War veterans seeking in vain early payments of their bonuses—from the Anacostia Flats in Washington, DC, cemented his reputation as a villain, if not a callous incompetent. In terms of political storytelling, this meant his opponent in 1932's presidential election was the hero—provided the Democrats did not self-destruct.

That nominee turned out to be a consummate unifier, the successful governor of New York, Franklin Delano Roosevelt. A distant cousin of

Theodore Roosevelt and the husband of TR's niece, Eleanor, FDR did not have much of a political platform on the campaign trail except that he would do the opposite of Hoover. That proved enough to give him and the Democrats a landslide victory. His "new deal for the American people" sounded good in his nomination acceptance speech, with its resemblance to cousin Teddy's "Square Deal," but its details remained murky at best all the way up to his inauguration in March of 1933. In the meantime, a second, larger wave of bank panics swept the nation, threatening to bring down the entire financial services sector. Hoover wanted his successor to steady the economic ship by pledging to uphold the gold standard and back an international debt solution to the Great Depression. Unwilling to be saddled by anything his unpopular predecessor wanted, FDR politely declined. The nation would just have to wait until after the inauguration to find out what the "New Deal" program would be. Yet this was not the only challenge he faced. The new leader was hiding something from the public.

In the summer of 1921, the future president-elect, tall, handsome, and charming, with a bright political future—former New York state legislator, assistant secretary of the navy, and vice presidential nominee in 1920—visited a boys' camp. Shortly thereafter, he became paralyzed by the summer scourge of America—polio. Though he regained his bodily functions, the disease left him unable to move his legs. From that point until he gave the nomination speech for his mentor, Governor Al Smith of New York, for president in 1928, he attempted to regain a measure of functioning so he could keep his long-standing presidential ambitions alive. This meant he had to conceal his state from the American public. Believing, probably correctly, that America would not elect a "crippled" president, he managed to conceal the full extent of his paralysis by using heavy braces on his legs and having someone to support him when he needed to "stand" or "walk" for long periods. He also cultivated the press so that they would cooperate in the deception. Fortunately for FDR, his charm plus the condition of the country won their support. Several years after his death in April of 1945, the vast majority of Americans still had no idea that he could not use his legs.

Political scientists have coined the term "rally 'round the flag effect" to describe why the public, including the news media, tends to view the president positively in times of crisis, at least initially. Mass psychology is beyond the scope of this work and its author's expertise except to note that something appears to be hardwired into human beings in larger groups that makes them want to cooperate under strong leadership when confronted with a threat. This partly explains why even Republicans were muted as the US Congress vastly expanded presidential power and the national government's scale and scope and dramatically altered the state of the American economy during Roosevelt's first one hundred days, and, to a lesser extent, thereafter, in what became known as the New Deal.

The New Deal

There was, and is, a general debate about what kind of political program the New Deal was. Was it socialism? Was it fascism? Was it revolutionary? Was it conservative? A wit might well answer: "Yes." FDR had no set political program when he uttered the term at the Democratic National Convention in Chicago in 1932, and it remained so after his inauguration in March 1933. What he did have was a group of advisers he referred to as the "Brain Trust." The Columbia-educated lawyer was referring to a legal instrument in which a financial asset or assets is held sacrosanct, looked over by a trustee or trustees for the beneficiary. Professors Rexford Tugwell, Raymond Moley, and Adolf Berle of Columbia were among them. So was Professor Felix Frankfurter of Harvard Law School, or at least he was trying to be. Harry Hopkins and a host of other progressive reformers, all on the left, rounded out the group. Only one thing knitted them together: the US economy had to change for there to be a return to prosperity. They just did not agree on how to do it.

But there was another adviser, advocate, and brain that played a pivotal role in the New Deal, and that was the First Lady, Eleanor Roosevelt. With the discovery of her husband's affair while he was assistant secretary of the navy, Eleanor separated from Franklin in their private lives, but she remained his partner to further his political career. While they worked on his mobility and his mood, she branched out—giving speeches, networking, and going where her husband could not. In this role, she forged a new identity, in effect, as a public issue lobbyist. She publicized the woes of working mothers, impoverished children, and blue-collar oppression and the reality of racism and sexism throughout America, not just in the Jim Crow South. She overcame the abuse of her childhood, her awkwardness, and her husband's betrayal to transform the role of First Lady into a more visible outlet for the presidency. Her discreet interventions also compensated for her husband's occasional lack of fortitude.

Legislation in the first hundred days began with banking, giving the president unprecedented, perhaps unconstitutional, power to deal with the crisis. FDR exercised it to impose a "bank holiday," in effect shutting down the financial services sector. It was meant to calm the panic and save the remaining banks, but it was also an ominous signal of popular support to violate traditional restraint in the exercise of presidential authority. Most significant legislation FDR signed into law during this period, as well as thereafter, breaks down into three general categories: relief, reform, and rebuilding. The relief agencies, usually under the Federal Emergency Relief Agency, took up where the state agencies and charities had left off before exhausting their funds. The Roosevelt administration attempted to avoid the dreaded "dole"—mere government handouts to the destitute—because of its debilitating aspects. Men were to work for their relief on public projects. The Civilian Conservation Corps, for example, built roads, cleared land for development, built nature trails in public parks, and created soil preservation landscaping to prevent further erosion.

The reform efforts are not easily categorized because they ranged widely and often contradicted each other. FDR wanted to move quickly, but he also did not want to alienate any person or constituency. This meant he would say "yes" to one person or group then give support to an opposing viewpoint as well. As a result, what came to be known as the First New Deal constituted a hodgepodge of programs stemming from multiple philosophies. The Public Works Administration (PWA) spent conservatively on a host of infrastructure projects like massive hydroelectric dams, including Hoover Dam, the Grand Coulee Dam, and the Muscle Shoals project in Alabama. By design, however, the National Industrial Recovery Act (NIRA), which created the PWA, also contained new taxes to partially cover the expense. At the same time, financial reform under the Securities and Exchange Commission (SEC) regulated the public stock exchanges with a lighter touch, emphasizing disclosure, openness, and standardized accounting. The Federal Reserve System received centralized, overarching governance with a national committee and chair, all of which was intended to be nonpartisan. Agriculture got its subsidies from the Agriculture Adjustment Act's Agricultural Adjustment Administration.

At the same time, there were more radical exercises of federal power in the interest of reform. The national government separated commercial banking from investment banking, in the Glass-Steagall Act, in order to prevent buying on margin, among other alleged causes of the Great Depression. The Roosevelt administration set up a government-run utility company for much of the Southeast in the form of the Tennessee Valley Authority (TVA), supplanting private utilities in the region. The dams were modeled after those built in the Soviet Union, with similar goals. The national government planned to remake the region, not through the use of markets or even market incentives, but through expertise. This harkened back to the Progressive Era in the United States (roughly 1890 to 1920), when college-educated would-be reformers took power away from elected officials and gave it to nonpartisan commissions. They believed their educated views would root out corruption in elections. This unparalleled faith in supposedly scientific governance had achievements as well as failures. There were subway trains, cleaner water, and safer places for work and home, but there were also gross abuses of human rights, including the eugenics movement, supported by some progressives, which forcibly sterilized men and women deemed "unfit" for having children.

FDR's New Deal also attached reform to a "modern" way of life, as opposed to the old, local, traditional ways of working and living. Federal highway construction moved the United States away from mass transit and railroads to a society, economy, and landscape based on the automobile. The vast expansion of the federal income tax redistributed wealth under its highly progressive system while, at the same time, requiring every wage earner to file a tax return with the Internal Revenue Service regardless of whether they owed taxes or not. Law enforcement agencies like the Bureau of Investigation, under J. Edgar Hoover within the Justice Department, became substantial organizations. In 1935, Congress renamed it the Federal Bureau of Investigation and made it an independent division within the Justice Department. Under J. Edgar Hoover's unscrupulous direction, it became similar to a national police force, albeit one with several rivals in Treasury. The Food and Drug Administration emerged with considerable power over the pharmaceutical industry, while other permanent agencies increased their scale and scope in American life.

But the New Dealers did not stop with relief and reform. Per FDR's instructions, they also set about to rebuild America in such a way that there would be no further depressions. While the SEC, the Federal Deposit Insurance Corporation (FDIC), the centralization of the Federal Reserve, and investments in infrastructure fixed the financial services sector, and the AAA (Agricultural Adjustment Administration) buoyed the agricultural sector, other projects aimed to boost consumption—as insufficient consumption was supposed to have been a major cause of the crisis in all sectors. For example, the FDIC guaranteed deposits up to a certain amount in all member banks, which could display a label stating the accounts were "FDIC Insured." This label created customer confidence and largely prevented bank panics without exposing the fund to actual runs on banks. The mere label was enough in the vast majority of cases to ensure faith in the bank. In exchange, the Federal Reserve gained regulatory authority over those member banks. The New Deal's economy would be governed from Washington, DC, the physical location of the newly created governorship of the Federal Reserve.

After the first hundred days, new laws subsidized rural America, not just through road construction but with taxes and fees on telephone service and electricity. Profitable, efficient urban dwellers paid for the work of the Rural Electrification Administration and American Telephone and Telegraph's (AT&T) near monopoly on telephone service, under federal supervision, to agricultural, rural, and, though it was staggeringly unprofitable, rural dwellers. Railroad companies simply could not counter the long history of anti-rail sentiment among farmers, other small-scale shippers, and anti-monopolists, who were now largely Democrats, nor could they lobby as well as the automobile industry and its labor forces.

FDR would never lose his conviction that the US economy had matured, but rural America, labor, and middle-class urban dwellers had not kept up with the modernization. The Brain Trust had only reinforced a set of ideas the gentleman farmer from Hyde Park, New York, had already conceived. Government needed to intervene, redistribute wealth, and spur consumer spending if the United States was to emerge from the Depression. Instead of the cycle of boom and bust that had governed the economy since its inception, the catastrophic downturn resulted from market failure of a singular kind. Interestingly, this cycle-opposing viewpoint recurs throughout US history as an analysis of the current day's ills. Coxey's Army and William Jennings Bryan had argued in a similar vein during FDR's youth in the 1890s. Regardless, much of the New Deal legislation, including the NIRA, propped up prices in order to put money into the hands of rural dwellers as a solution to the supposed under-consumption.

Anti-monopoly laws, progressive taxes, and FDR's manipulation of gold signaled to Wall Street that the earlier coalition to rescue the country no longer held firm. Hoover had rigidly adhered to the gold standard as the best way to revive the economy and foreign trade. Under the influence of a variety of professors, FDR had no such commitment. Though even John Maynard Keynes wrote to the new president that his daily gold purchases were causing volatility, thus destabilizing markets worldwide, FDR paid no attention. A great rift had begun that would eventually break out into open disputes. As it developed, the New Deal coalition had little use for what FDR increasingly referred to as the "malefactors of great wealth."

While he initially gave his support to the World Economic Conference in London, in the spring of 1933, the president killed the international attempt to reestablish stability through the gold standard with his message on June 6th. The United States would go its own way to solve its purely domestic economic problems. Though his inflationary policies remained, FDR was not committed to advancing them through deficit spending. In fact, one of the first laws he pushed through Congress in the first hundred days cut salaries and raised taxes to cover the budget deficit. Even the spending of the PWA was to be offset with new taxes. Why he enacted this series of contradictions is anyone's guess. No one factor was likely paramount. A Columbia-trained lawyer, FDR may have been adhering to the principle of safeguarding client money, which was a pillar of an attorney's professional responsibilities. It may have been the doctrines he learned at Harvard or at his finishing school, Groton. Childhood instruction emphasizing thrift may have also influenced his thinking. Even President Barack Obama, long after Keynesian demand-side economics had become accepted practice, called for balancing the federal budget during the Great Recession of 2008 to 2010. Regardless, FDR's policies likely had little ability to end the Great Depression, only ease it.

The National Industrial Recovery Act

The goals of relief, reform, and rebuilding came together in the first hundred days in the form of the National Industrial Recovery Act. If anything, the NIRA symbolized the First New Deal. Democrats and Republicans supported it. Business leaders, labor, and consumer advocates joined to write its codes. The news media and academics agreed that it was necessary, given the emergency. Finally, the legislation was a massive social experiment, potentially far more ambitious than even Prohibition. It had several sections, which included the PWA (later assigned to Secretary of the Interior Harold Ickes); a labor provision—section 7(a)—that allowed for collective bargaining, a.k.a. unions; section 9(c) for the "hot oil" problem; and the National Recovery Administration, under former army general Hugh Johnson, with Donald Richberg as its general counsel.

Everything except section 9(c) concerned ending the Great Depression. Section 9(c) dealt with the separate but related matter of the discovery and exploitation, in 1930, of one of the largest oil fields in the world: the East Texas Reservoir, also known as "the Black Giant." Besides its sheer magnitude, the East Texas Reservoir's discovery near the start of the Great Depression could not have come at a worse time. With wildcatters creating wells faster than consumers were buying oil, the price of oil dropped from $1.85 to fifteen cents a barrel. The Texas state government tried to establish a monopoly over the Black Giant but found the "hot oil"—the illegal oil outside of the monopoly—easily found a market once out of the state's jurisdiction.

Desperate to stem the tide of hot oil, oil producers and state governments whose revenues depended on maintaining the price of oil lobbied the national government for help. Section 9(c) of the NIRA was the answer to their pleas. It allowed the president to enforce state monopolies like Texas's in interstate commerce with up to six months imprisonment and/or one thousand dollars in fines for violators. Notably, it did not restrict the president's power in this matter. FDR promptly delegated almost all of it to the secretary of the interior, Harold Ickes, who had been the point person for the federal government's investigation into what to do with hot oil from the Black Giant.

In the meantime, the NIRA legislation was a rushed affair. Worried by Alabama senator Hugo Black's proposal for a pro-labor thirty-hour-week bill in the Senate, FDR replied with a counterproposal. Brain Trust members Rexford Tugwell and Raymond Moley, as well as Johnson and Richberg, played a part in drafting the legislation. Tugwell's desire to create a World War I–style war industries board, Moley's vision of a justice-oriented economic order, and Richberg's progressive lawyer's approach found their way into the law. At the same time Tugwell, Moley, and Richberg, with an able assist from Johnson, worked in the executive branch on a draft, FDR asked pro-labor senator Robert Wagner (D-NY) to formulate his own. Wagner drew upon his own group of luminaries, including lawyer Jerome Frank, general counsel of the Agricultural Adjustment Administration; John Dickinson, assistant secretary of commerce; and Harold Moulton, president of the Brookings Institution, a think tank in Washington, DC.

On May 10, 1933, FDR brought the two groups together to create a single draft with organized labor, business, and their representatives largely excluded. The House passed it with a massive majority nine days after its introduction. The Senate had a more lengthy debate but gave its consent by a substantial majority. Progressives in the Senate objected to the suspension of the anti-trust laws. Senator Huey Long, "the Kingfish" from Louisiana, sought to stake out a position more southern Democratic and left-leaning than Roosevelt's and denounced the NIRA as a gift to the plutocrats and a swindle of the common man. Some astute maneuvering by Wagner in the legislative process, however, brought a majority on board with the experiment, at least temporarily. (After all, the NIRA was scheduled to terminate in two years.) FDR signed the reconciled bill into law on June 16, 1933, declaring it "one of the most important and far-reaching legislation ever enacted by the American Congress."

The president's address on signing the legislation spelled out its complexity, the theory behind its creation, and its callback to World War I. He called that effort "the great cooperation." Once again a national emergency, this time the Great Depression, had aided a complete reworking of the American economy. In his words, "We are putting in place of old principles of unchecked competition some new Government controls." To reassure those who might think this was Soviet- or Fascist-style economics, he noted, "Their purpose is to free business, not to shackle it," something the criminal penalties in the law contradicted. He closed this address with the maxim that is widely regarded as the governing idea of American liberalism, his permanent contribution to American politics: "Must we go on in many groping, disorganized, separate units to defeat or shall we move as one great team to victory?" It was an odd juxtaposition of war and sports given one's bloodiness and the other's usual lack of severe consequences, but it did give a Harvard crimson touch for someone who had never seen actual combat in either venue.

Its few critics objected to its very breadth. Conservatives in the Senate like Carter Glass of Virginia denounced it as unconstitutional. Quietly, a few lawyers within the bill's National Recovery Administration (NRA) came to share this view. Concerned about the NRA's ability to write codes that would allow for cartels, Senator William E. Borah of Idaho, a progressive maverick and Republican, successfully proposed an amendment forbidding monopolistic practices. The reconciliation process sharply reduced it in order to allow for the planned corporatism. The news media, advocacy groups, and prominent commentators reflected on the urgency facing the nation and endorsed the massive federal oversight of the economy as a necessary emergency measure.

Although the code written for the trade associations was the provision that snagged the Schechter brothers and led to the US Supreme Court case overturning section 1, there were other sections likely to attract the attention of the courts. Foremost among these was the ability to create hour and wage restrictions on all interstate businesses, potentially all businesses in the United States. Limitations on work hours and a minimum wage had been goals of labor advocates, reformers, and politicians since the Progressive Era, though some labor organizations, including the American Federation of Labor, opposed minimum wage laws because they allegedly limited employment. American labor's gains had possessed a mixed record since the arrival of factories and mining in the early nineteenth century. Common law inhibited workers' ability both to sue their employers for compensation and to organize. State litigation and legislation had eroded some of these obstacles but not all of them. The prevailing ideas concerning private property, individualism, and entrepreneurship also placed the onus on labor to behave in such a way as to maintain public sympathy. The federal courts had often been hostile, particularly in the area of anti-labor injunctions. Previous attempts to ban child labor, limit working hours, and allow for collective bargaining had run afoul of the US Supreme Court on multiple occasions.

The NIRA's sections assisting labor constituted a direct challenge to that anti-labor environment. Section 7(a) provided for collective bargaining units, a.k.a. unions, for the industries agreeing to be part of the NRA effort. Unions prevented employers from negotiating contracts with individual employees. With this ability, employers could play one worker against another. The result would be maximum power for the employers and little to none for workers, even those that had banded together in a union. Especially in times of economic stress, employers could simply hire replacement workers, known to the unionists as "scabs," given their resemblance to the tissue that temporarily covers wounds, and break the union. Employers then fired the replacements and rehired their old, experienced workforce under the new contract. Section 7(a) allowed workers to form unions under the "closed shop" where only the union representatives could negotiate for the workforce, although this provision was hotly contested. Still, the union could now compel negotiations with a much stronger position against the employer. Often denounced as socialism or, worse, Communism, it was technically neither. (Socialism is worker-owned enterprise and government programs displacing private industry. Communism is the collective owning everything and there is little to no private property of any kind.) Unions were now more powerful, at least potentially.

Johnson and Richberg immediately set to work creating the NRA after FDR signed the legislation in June of 1933. Hugh Johnson certainly had the credentials for such an ambitious agency. He had graduated from West Point Military Academy and distinguished himself in various commands in the western United States before creating the Selective Service System to draft soldiers for US participation in World War I. In the interim he earned an undergraduate degree and law degree at Berkeley and, during World War I, earned a promotion and national acclaim as one of the youngest generals in US history. After the war, he served as general counsel for Moline Plow Company under future New Dealer George Peek, first administrator of the Agricultural Adjustment Administration, then he replaced Peek as head of the company. It was in this capacity that he joined the Brain Trust along with Donald Richberg, his successor as chief administrator of the NRA.

Both Johnson and Richberg believed that the Great Depression had proved that classical capitalism had failed and needed to be replaced by Mussolini-like Fascism (Labor Secretary Frances Perkins was certain it was fascism), though without the police state and political assassinations. Under what Johnson called "government supervision," the NRA would arrange for various industries and trades to form syndicates, a.k.a. cartels, with representation from labor and consumers, to organize their field for maximum efficiency, eliminate harmful competition, and promote worker and consumer safety. Through these syndicates, market share and prices would be prearranged, ending "wasteful competition." In addition to exercising command and control over large swathes of the American economy, this all assumed that the American economy was fully developed, the Depression would be cured by arranged price inflation, and that small businesses, derogatorily known as "mom and pop stores," were obsolete, deserving of elimination because Johnson believed that the NRA needed to end the previous system's "murderous doctrine of selfish individualism."

Richberg had become general counsel largely due to his reputation as a labor lawyer. In addition to representing Chicago-based railroad unions in the 1920s, he had largely written the Norris-LaGuardia Act of 1932 ending the use of the union-abhorred labor injunction. Along with Harold Ickes, Richberg had litigated the case against Insull's utility company. With Felix Frankfurter, their mentor at Harvard Law School, as the key organizer, Richberg and Ickes became part of the Brain Trust, with Richberg as the author of the NIRA's section 7(a). Richberg's key job as general counsel for the NRA was to implement this provision. It did not go well. Labor strife, increasing management hostility, and Richberg's gnawing sense that the codes would not survive Supreme Court review dimmed his hopes for the NRA's renewal in 1935.

As for the fair practice and competition codes, they followed swiftly in some areas while others lagged. At a minimum, all of them required a forty hour weekly maximum and a minimum hourly wage with the right to organize. Codes for specific industries set prices and standardized practices and ensured worker and customer safety. The poultry business in the New York City metro area received special treatment. Its trade association had a long history of small businesses undercutting the larger suppliers. While the minimum wage and maximum hours provisions would cut into large businesses' profits, they could write a code that would prevent smaller, nimbler businesses from "cheating" with lower prices. Their oligopoly would control the industry under the guise of policing the health and safety of the poultry business. With President Roosevelt's signature on April 13, 1934, the "Code of Fair Competition for the Live Poultry Industry of the Metropolitan Area in and about the City of New York" came into effect.

According to the code, chickens had to be killed a certain way, in groups, a practice known as "straight killing." That is, the customer could not select their live chicken for slaughter. There had to be inspections and proper paperwork, and all chickens sold had to meet the minimum standards or criminal penalties would ensue. Like all regulations, the codes favored larger businesses that did not specialize in a certain market. These smaller units included privately owned slaughterhouses that adhered to the strict Jewish rules, known as kashrut, for chicken butchery. They allowed their customers, whether individuals or retailers, to pick which chickens they wanted killed and prepared. These businesses would be in violation of the codes.

Though the textile code adopted with such fanfare seemed to herald Johnson's new order for capitalism, the rest of America's economy did not yield so easily. For example, the poultry code, which had done largely the same thing, had taken nearly another year after the passage of the act to be implemented. Therefore, like its model, the War Industries Board from World War I, the NRA's workforce grew in both sheer numbers and complexity. By 1934, it was in the thousands, producing hundreds of codes with thousands of interpretive rulings with many of them overlapping in several industries. By one estimate, the codes had created ten times as many pages as the whole Federal Register—the official record of US legislation and regulations. The labor and consumer board representatives were largely absent as larger industry associations wrote codes for their businesses. This was not the first example of industry "capturing" a governmental regulatory authority. (That would be the Interstate Commerce Commission, which regulated or attempted to regulate railroads.) And it would not be the last, but the consequences for small business were dire. Price competition through not having to invest in lots of fancy equipment and procedures was the way they stayed in business. The codes, like all business regulations, did not care.

At the start, Roosevelt, Johnson, and the NRA's sponsors emphasized that the associations and codes would be consensual, as expressed in FDR's message on its establishment, like a "guild." Although the law gave the authority to the president to issue licenses for businesses, the lawyers Johnson, Richberg, and Roosevelt all agreed that would incur the wrath of the courts. In order to encourage membership, compliance with the NRA's objectives, and consumer confidence in the NRA, Johnson inaugurated a massive public relations campaign over the summer of 1933. There were parades, advertising, and marches all centered on the blue eagle, the symbol Johnson had chosen for the NRA, with the slogan "We Do Our Part." Businesses that adhered to the codes (or signed a Reemployment Agreement authorized by section 4a of the NRA) could display the NRA blue eagle in their windows, and the public was encouraged to buy only from businesses with this NRA seal of approval. A similar approach had worked to encourage buying war bonds in the Civil War and World War I, for Hoover's Food Administration, and for conscription during World War I, with the famous Uncle Sam pointing at the viewer stating "I Want You" for the American Expeditionary Force.

And, for a time, it worked well. FDR's optimism in fireside chats on the radio, newsreels at the movies, and the initial enthusiasm spurred an immense participation among businesses, labor, and consumers alike. There were even signs that the NRA's efforts were spurring a recovery. Hugh Johnson became an international celebrity with his face on the cover of *Time* magazine as its "Man of the Year" for 1933. However, the upward movement soon faded. There was too much of an incentive to cheat.

We now know it as the prisoner's dilemma. Two thieves are imprisoned and accused of working together. The police give each one an offer: the first one to confess to both criminals' involvement gets a lighter sentence, but the second one to confess or the one who does not confess gets the harshest sentence available. Both prisoners know that if neither confesses, they will get out of jail time altogether. What will they do? The answer most likely is that both will confess, betraying each other, because each cannot trust the other to stand by him. It was the same with the voluntary codes, particularly those fixing prices. Anyone who cheated had the chance to make immense gains. Thus, everyone had an incentive to cheat and cheat quickly. By the fall of 1933 various businessmen around the country were calling for government enforcement to stop the rampant cheating.

In part because of the rampant cheating, in 1934 Johnson directed the NRA to create an enforcement bureaucracy. Regional offices had inspectors, investigators, and support staff. US Attorneys were directed to prosecute offenders. According to the NIRA, though officially misdemeanors, penalties included fines of up to $500 and/or jail sentences up to six months per offense per day of the violation. This kind of government operation was not unique or new. For quite some time in the Progressive Era, the state, local, and national governments had become concerned with a broad legal category called "public safety." The states and localities focused on water, sewage, violent crime, vice, and, after fires devastated urban areas, building codes, while the national government increasingly intervened in immigration, monopolistic practices, and labor strife. The "great experiment" with Prohibition, which FDR cheerfully helped to end through constitutional amendment, was only the most notorious attempt at government-sponsored social improvement. As noted above, other efforts also led to increasingly powerful government agencies, like Hoover's FBI. But the NRA was an entity unto itself.

Johnson, however, did not see his term through to its conclusion. Though the reasons are somewhat murky, FDR fired Johnson as head of the NRA in September of 1934 and replaced his directorship with a board of overseers. Secretary of Labor Frances Perkins, the first woman to head a cabinet-level department, had become increasingly alarmed at Johnson's open support of Mussolini's fascism. Reports of Johnson's abuse of his staff, use of alcohol, and overall lack of organizational skills probably also played a role. His failure to make a substantial dent in the Depression loomed even larger. Richberg returned from his duties as the overseer of the White House's special committees supposedly coordinating the New Deal to head the board. It was certainly a step down for Richberg, who had become extraordinarily powerful, the so-called assistant president. Richberg almost immediately began scaling back the enforcement mechanisms. He later recalled that they "had gone far beyond the original intentions of those sponsoring the law." But it was already too late for those caught in that machinery.

A Small Poultry Business

In the borough of Brooklyn, New York City, the Schechter brothers operated a poultry slaughterhouse that bought from wholesalers and sold to retailers. Joseph ran the financial side of the two corporations that constituted the business, while Martin, Alex, and Aaron managed the workforce. Because they were Jewish and operated under kashrut, the religious rules for keeping kosher, the killing of the chickens had to be done by *shochtim*—specially trained workers who had to adhere to the strict religious code. The Schechter brothers were immigrants and served their locality, a Jewish area in a time when clubs, universities, and whole neighborhoods were restricted—in other words, they banned Jews.

The Schechters and many of their customers were not German Jews, who had immigrated in the mid-nineteenth century. The Schechters were part of the great second wave of immigrants, largely from eastern and southern Europe, who had crossed the Atlantic during the late nineteenth and early twentieth centuries. They were not alone. During its height, one in eight Americans was an immigrant or the child of an immigrant. New York City was at the heart of this demographic transformation, with a large majority of its population either immigrants or children of immigrants. It was also the largest city in the nation, its financial, publishing, media, and, arguably, cultural capital. Radio, newspapers, banks, and merchants of all kinds among others largely took their cues from this city of immigrants.

The Jewish population of New York played a large role in the city. Not allowed into Wall Street banks or law firms, they formed their own, becoming a who's who of both fields, particularly investment banks. Because of the persecution they faced, they formed a tightly knit community that nevertheless frequently divided over certain issues. The old joke went that if there were two Jews, there would be three different arguments at any one time. Businesses like the Schechters' and ALA Poultry Corporation sprouted like weeds in New York as peddlers and tradesmen tried to establish themselves. Some, like R. H. Macy, founder of Macy's department stores, succeeded. Countless others did not. From the records, we can guess the Schechters were somewhere in between by 1933: not failures, but not great successes either. Though the courts described their operation as the largest in the city, the business did not yield a significant income for the brothers.

Despite their support of FDR and the New Deal throughout the proceedings, the Schechter brothers' relationship with their local NRA officials deteriorated rapidly over 1934. At first, the NRA inspectors were unobtrusive, and the Schechters gave them full access to both the facility and their records. The cooperation ended when the agents started questioning the customers, then correcting them for not complying with the NRA code when they did not order "straight killing" or "straight pull." The agents subsequently raided the facility seizing poultry and records. The Schechter brothers' English was poor, and they were not as intimately familiar with US law enforcement as their larger competitors, thus they probably did not realize that the NRA had decided to make an example of small businesses. In any case, they were routinely violating several provisions of the code.

The "special assistant to the US attorney general" who prosecuted their case, and then argued it all the way to the US Supreme Court, Walter L. Rice, came from Minnesota via Harvard Law School. Before taking on the Schechters, he had successfully brought cases against the "poultry trust" in New York City. As the chief justice of the Supreme Court, Charles Evans Hughes, detailed in his summary of the case for the Court, New York City was the largest poultry clearinghouse in the United States. He could have noted that it was also probably its most corrupt. A largely Jewish group of poultry business owners, not including the Schechters, who had cooperated with authorities, had conspired to restrict trade and set prices for the entire market. Rice had not only broken this ring but successfully argued to the US Supreme Court that the Sherman Anti-Trust Act applied. Interestingly, he now pursued a case for the US government that created a code-mandated cartel, effectively a monopoly. And he selected the Schechters as his examples of wrongdoers.

The grand jury indicted the Schechter brothers and their two companies on over sixty counts of violations of the poultry code and the NIRA. Facing fines of thousands of dollars and years in prison, they were charged with not paying the minimum wage or limiting the work week to forty hours, underselling their competitors, allowing customers to pick their chickens for slaughter instead of "straight killing," and selling unsafe poultry to a customer. As it turned out, the unsafe or "sick" chicken was not actually diseased but had eggs in it, something no one could have known unless they had fully processed the carcass before selling it. Nevertheless, as a local story of national importance, it made the cover of the *New York Times* on August 27, 1934, with an emphasis on the "diseased" poultry and the threat to public safety.

After they largely lost their appeal of the indictment, the trial that followed turned out to be more of a tragic farce than a contest of titans. Rice and the presiding judge in the Eastern District Court, Brooklyn, Marcus B. Campbell, had difficulty understanding the Schechter brothers' accents and their local expressions. The influential and well-known anti-Semitic columnist Drew Pearson mocked the Schechters' lawyer, Joseph Heller (not the novelist), another Brooklyn Jew and a graduate of Brooklyn Law School, in his column. Heller had stated in court that he had known the Schechter boys since they were children together and they would not sell tainted merchandise to the public. After several days of witness testimony, largely from NRA agents, and incisive examinations of the brothers, there was an extensive trial record of code violations.

In October 1934, after a two-and-a-half-week trial, with a warning from Judge Campbell not to be sympathetic to the defendants, "Decide on the evidence, not some views that you have," the jury convicted the brothers on all counts, including conspiracy to violate the laws of the United States. Judge Campbell sentenced them to $7,425 in total fines (equal to $164,456 in today's dollars and several times their annual salary) and three months, two months, and one month each for Joseph, Alex, and the other two respectively. Individual violations might have been minor, but the cumulative counts per day of each violation made the punishment more like a felony than the intended misdemeanor.

In some ways it was very much a David v. Goliath story. The Schechters were relatively small business owners, barely scraping by, and were adhering to an ancient code of standards that was now subject to the modern, secular, and heavily bureaucratized state. Who were they to stand in the way of progress? Who were they to challenge the wisdom of authorities who were trying to revive the nation's economy and look after public health? They served a small minority, albeit an over-represented one, in poultry in New York City, along with finance, entertainment, medicine, and law, in a country of over 125 million, which did not share their views. Nevertheless, despite these odds, the Schechters appealed their sentences to a higher authority as well as the appellate courts.

———

On occasion small things become extremely important. *U.S. v. Schechter Poultry* was one of those things. With a conviction in hand, Walter L. Rice, later joined by the US Justice Department, represented the US government in its prosecution of the Schechter brothers and their two companies for violations of the NIRA and the codes enacted under it that bore President Roosevelt's signature. According to the US Attorneys, the Schechters were criminals, a danger to public safety, and part of the cause of the Great Depression. For the Schechters, this was a matter of basic liberty—the goal they had sought when they left Tsarist Russia with their parents. For the country at large, this constituted a case of complications, which happened to have collected a silly name, "the sick chicken case."

CHAPTER 2

Litigating a "Sick Chicken"

The US legal system was complex in 1934 and 1935. Even if the Schechters had prevailed against the odds, they would not have regained their court costs, and it would not have undone the pain and suffering they and their families went through, nor would they have been made whole. They would have had to pursue an entirely different path in order to approach that with even greater odds against them. However, until 1946's Federal Tort Claims Act, the US government possessed something known as "sovereign immunity," a holdover from the colonial period. The concept meant that a government could not be sued without its consent. Its origin was in the principle that the king could do no wrong. Today, in certain specific kinds of cases, the federal government and various state governments have allowed themselves to be sued. The Schechters had to be satisfied with merely escaping fines and imprisonment. Even so, their lawyers had a difficult course ahead.

Initial Appeals

Joseph and Jacob R. Heller, the Schechters' attorneys, needed to show that the law, their conviction under it, and/or the procedures used to arrive at that conviction were themselves unlawful. Because this was a federal criminal case, the subject matter was almost entirely the US Constitution and the appellate courts' interpretations of it. The jury's verdict had determined the facts, and that factual record could not be reviewed except under extraordinary circumstances. If there was a legal defect, their trial would either disappear or have to be redone. This meant the Hellers had to make constitutional arguments, hopefully, with a lot of precedents—previous court decisions—in their favor and to distinguish those that were not. As the appellees, they also possessed the burden of persuading the courts they were correct, while the US government's lawyers only had to raise reasonable counterarguments. If the Schechters' side won on appeal, the government lawyers, in turn, had the burden, and so on, until it reached the highest appeals court in the federal system, the US Supreme Court, if it went that far.

While the Hellers represented the Schechters, Leo J. Hickey, the US Attorney for Brooklyn; Harold M. Stephens, the assistant attorney general, who headed the Antitrust Division in the US Department of Justice; and Walter L. Rice, special assistant to the attorney general; argued for the national government, continuing their role from the trial. Hickey was a recent appointee but had practiced law in his native Brooklyn since 1919. In December of 1937, he succumbed to pneumonia at the age of forty-seven. Stephens hailed from Nebraska with a law degree from Harvard and undergraduate studies at the University of California–Berkeley and Cornell. After his stint as head of the Antitrust Division and the Second Circuit's ruling in the *Schechter* case, FDR appointed him to the United States Court of Appeals for the District of Columbia Circuit, known as the DC Court of Appeals, in 1935. President Truman later nominated him to be chief judge, where he served until his death in 1955. There can be little doubt the Roosevelt administration gave this case its full backing.

While the Schechters appealed their convictions, on February 5, 1934, a unanimous US Supreme Court ruled, in *Local 167 of International Brotherhood of Teamsters, Chauffeurs, Stablemen & Helpers of America et al. v. U.S.*, that the interstate commerce clause, in the form of the Sherman Anti-Trust Act of 1890, applied to a would-be conspiracy of poultry dealers in New York City. Justice Pierce Butler wrote that the "interference . . . , the transportation, the sales . . . , the prices charged, and the amount of profits exacted operates substantially and directly to restrain and burden the untrammelled [*sic*] shipment and movement of the poultry while unquestionably it is in interstate commerce." Besides the fact that this case stemmed from Rice's prosecution at the trial level, its facts very closely conform to those of the *Schechter* case. Jewish poultry merchants in New York City were held to be violating federal law. At the very least, it did not bode well for the Schechters' appeal.

Prior to the trial, on August 28, 1934, the Schechters and their attorneys received their first defeat. The presiding judge, Marcus B.

Campbell, issued his largely adverse ruling denying them their appeal of the indictment. He grouped their arguments into three main areas: the constitutionality of the NIRA regarding the commerce clause in Article I of the federal Constitution, the constitutionality of the NIRA concerning the non-delegation doctrine, and the constitutionality of the indictment and charges under due process. Congress's power to regulate under the commerce clause (Article I, Section 8) had a number of limits including not extending to commerce within a state. Non-delegation was a prudential (judge-made) concept that barred Congress from giving its law-making powers to either the executive or judicial branch. At this time, due process largely meant whether the rules governing the prosecution's conduct were in accordance with the rights guaranteed under the Constitution.

In order to review these three areas, Campbell needed a standard on which to evaluate the constitutionality under the Fifth Amendment's "due process" clause. Analogizing to a review under the Fourteenth Amendment's due process clause for when a state action is suspect, he used the following: "because there is an unreasonable, arbitrary, or capricious regulation, or if its provisions bear no real or substantial relation to the object sought to be obtained," it would be unconstitutional. This is a form of the rational basis (a.k.a. relations) test.

The rational basis test is the lowest level of scrutiny a court can use to judge a government action. Arguably, it originated in a *Harvard Law Review* article, "The Origin and Scope of American Constitutional Law," by Harvard Law professor James Bradley Thayer, which inspired Justice Oliver Wendell Holmes Jr. to use it in his dissent in *Lochner v. New York* (1905). In *Lochner*, the US Supreme Court invalidated New York State's bakeshop law limiting the hours and days bakeries could employ their workers, ostensibly for the workers' and the customers' safety. For Holmes, the state's objective—public health and safety—was legitimate, and the law was reasonably related to that objective. For the rest of the Court, it was an unwarranted interference under the due process clause of the Fourteenth Amendment's inherent guarantee of liberty—the right of workers to negotiate the contracts under which they work.

However, as Judge Campbell cited, the Court, in an opinion by Justice Owen Roberts in *Nebbia v. New York* on March 5, 1934, some four months before Campbell issued his opinion in *Schechter*, upheld New York State's

Milk Control Board, which set minimum and maximum prices for milk. Using the exact same language as Campbell had, the Court deployed its first explicit application of the rational basis test. Campbell was nothing if not up to date. The Schechters were among the first to discover a substantial shift in the Court's jurisprudence. The rational basis test was and is the lowest level of scrutiny because it reflects Justice Holmes's judicial conservatism. He believed strongly in judicial restraint: courts should not act unless their intervention is necessary. Unfortunately for those like the Schechters, facing jail and financial ruin due to the government's policy choice, the courts did not particularly care about either their liberty or their ability to make a living in their chosen trade. That was a matter for the political branches to decide.

The *Nebbia* decision also presented something of a contradiction for those wishing to portray the Court as the tool of the old regime. The state of New York was taking over the market's function of determining prices and production under a milk board. Under the conservative view supposedly expressed in *Lochner*, which had also concerned New York State, the Court might well have declared this a deprivation of property and/or liberty without due process of law or in violation of the compensation clause incorporated against New York through the due process clause of the Fourteenth Amendment. Yet Justice Roberts had agreed with the progressive wing of the Supreme Court, Justices Louis D. Brandeis, Benjamin Cardozo, Chief Justice Charles Evans Hughes, and Harlan F. Stone, instead of what were known as the "Four Horsemen"—Justices Pierce Butler, James McReynolds, George Sutherland, and Willis Van Devanter, the conservatives. The label was taken from the Four Horsemen of the Apocalypse (famine, war, pestilence, and death).

By 1935, the four were also all over seventy, reinforcing the view among some of their opponents that they were recalcitrant old fogies who did not appreciate the new world that confronted the nation. Besides possible ageism, there was also a fundamental disagreement about what the prevailing jurisprudence of the Court should be—one favoring conservation of unchanging principles or one favoring adaptation. It was a very old argument that one could find in various forms, from the speeches and writings of Edmund Burke, in the eighteenth century, for conservatives, and Jeremy Bentham, active in the late eighteenth and early nineteenth centuries, for the progressives, right up to the present day. At the time of writing, we use "left" and "right," "liberal" and "conservative," but the dispute remains very similar if not the same. Judge Campbell was siding with the progressives, and all that that implied.

After dismissing rather quickly a claim that the fines violated the Eighth Amendment's prohibition on "cruel and unusual" punishments without even considering the jail time, Judge Campbell explained why the NIRA did not violate the non-delegation doctrine. Oddly, his entire analysis hinged on Congress's delegation to the president the ability to approve the code. "The only delegation of powers involved in this case is the President's approval of the code, and we are not concerned with any delegation of powers which include order, regulations, and rules suggested by the defendants." Given that the entire code for poultry came not from Congress but from an executive branch agency, the NRA, this was either a misunderstanding of the non-delegation issue or a judicial choice.

Campbell next laid out a very well-researched argument for why Congress's delegation of code-making authority to the president withstood reasonable scrutiny. There were several Supreme Court cases, cases heard by the Second Circuit (the federal appeals court that included New York), and lower court decisions that allowed the president, or his subordinates, to make decisions, rules, and other judgments that further codified statutes. We know them today as regulations, and they are a vital part of how the US government, as well as state governments, functioned starting in the second half of the nineteenth century. This was most notable at the federal level with the formation of the Interstate Commerce Commission (ICC) under the Interstate Commerce Act of 1887. By the 1920s, Professor Felix Frankfurter of Harvard Law School and his co-author and former student, James Landis, had written a book on the *Business of the Supreme Court* (1928), including materials on administrative law, and Landis wrote *The Administrative Process* (1938), both growing out of Frankfurter's original course on "administrative law" at Harvard Law School.

The key US Supreme Court case on the non-delegation doctrine, *J.W. Hampton, Jr. & Co. v. United States*, had been recently decided, in 1928. Chief Justice William Howard Taft, the former president, wrote the opinion for the Court upholding Congress's delegation of tariff rate–making power after consideration by the Tariff Commission under the Fordney-McCumber Tariff of 1922. "If Congress shall lay down by legislative act an intelligible principle to which the person or body authorized to fix such rates is directed to conform, such legislative action is not a forbidden delegation of legislative power." As to what exactly an "intelligible principle" was or what standard the legislation needed to meet, Taft did not specify. One may suppose a Republican-dominated high court trusted a Republican president, in this case Calvin Coolidge, to carry out the will of a Republican majority in Congress. What is clear is that the Court was deferring to the other two branches. In other words, the imposition of a tariff on business determined by political appointees having little to guide them except Congress's desire for it to make foreign goods' production costs equal to that of American goods was not worth further consideration.

Though it was not the province of the US Supreme Court to consider the wisdom of any law Congress passed, the impact of the Fordney-McCumber Tariff was as predictable as any other piece of protectionism. Other countries raised their tariffs in response. American farmers lost about three hundred million dollars in exports per year. Consumers in both countries paid more for their goods. And, finally, world trade fell back, paving the way for the Great Depression. None of these arguments could come before the Court though, because it outwardly rejected a "takings clause" litigation strategy. The national government was not obliged to compensate the victims of a tariff law for the alleged violation of the Fifth Amendment, whereby "nor shall private property be taken for public use without due compensation."

Though Judge Campbell's argument for rejecting the Schechters' claims was a sound one, he gave judicial notice to the precedents in the Hellers' brief, but his swift disregard of them is noteworthy. Campbell seems to have confused "code" with "power" in rendering his opinion. Because he found a sound basis for Congress delegating "power" to the executive branch, they were authorized to grant "code" writing authority to the extent employed by the NRA. The nature of those codes was the very topic under review, not whether Congress could authorize the president to act. Yet Campbell did not think to examine the codes for whether they went too far toward legislating the poultry industry for metro New York, nor did it matter that the "Live Poultry Code" applied only to metro New York and nowhere else.

Proceeding to very rapidly apply the rational basis test to the NRA, he moved into the most substantial part of his opinion—the reach of the interstate commerce clause. Again, Article I, Section 8 of the US Constitution grants Congress the authority to regulate commerce among states, with Indian Tribes, and with foreign nations. This interstate commerce clause was and is the basis for much of the US government's ability to govern the US in such diverse fields as sex trafficking, drugs, food safety, and, eventually, civil rights. Yet the clause has limits due to the restriction to "interstate" and "commerce." As with other interpretations of US law, the devil is in those details. For instance, Judge Campbell had to find that the NRA codes derived from the NIRA were in total a proper exercise of Congress's constitutional authority to regulate interstate commerce, specifically concerning the Live Poultry Code for Metro New York.

Campbell listed each violation in the indictment and concluded that the offense either was interstate commerce or "affected" interstate commerce as Congress had provided in the NIRA. He certainly had enough evidence that some, if not all, of the poultry might have come from Pennsylvania. What he did not have was an argument that the sale and kosher killing of chickens constituted interstate commerce. Therefore, he had to rely on the phrase "affecting interstate commerce" for most of the violations. He also ran into problems with the case law on interstate commerce power. The cases never used the word "affecting." It was either "intermingled with," "inextricable from," or "related to" interstate commerce. Ultimately, he admitted as much: "Congress has never before legislated as to general trade practices merely 'affecting' interstate commerce."

In order to overcome this major problem, Campbell placed this "change in social theory," as he called it, with the "emergency" that Congress had declared and the expiration date of 1935 it had given the NIRA. Apparently, if urgent and temporary, the Constitution allows Congress to override it. Given that this was taking place at the exact same time Germany, Japan, and the Soviet Union were using the exact same logic to overthrow their rule of law, we might be tempted to call Judge Campbell's reasoning questionable. However, it was well within the US Supreme Court's jurisprudence for there to be exceptions to the guarantees of the Constitution during strenuous times. Lincoln's (temporary) suspension of habeas corpus (an appeal of unjust imprisonment) during the Civil War, World War I's Espionage and, later, Sedition Act's violation of several clauses in the Bill of Rights, and the balancing tests the courts had been using since time immemorial to judge whether government authority could be excused or justified in violating civil rights for their higher purpose of public safety all demonstrated precedent for the NIRA overriding normal restrictions, including federalism as embodied in the restriction to "interstate" commerce.

Federalism is the idea embedded in the Constitution of 1787 that the national government is one with limited powers. Everything else is left to the state governments or the people. If the original document did not make this clear, the Tenth Amendment did: "The powers not delegated to the United States by the Constitution, nor prohibited by it to the States, are reserved to the States respectively, or to the people." This guiding doctrine had become controversial by the time of the New Deal. The national government had become far more capable, powerful, and ambitious in its scale and scope since the late eighteenth century, when the Tenth Amendment was ratified. Wars, national economic developments, new technologies, and the attitudes that went with them had long since presented an alternative view. The New Deal may have been the culmination of this development, an original contribution, or some combination of the two, but, regardless, Judge Campbell held that the NIRA required forbearance, at least for the time being.

In order to discover whether the interstate commerce clause should be read to include "substantially" "affecting" interstate commerce, Judge Campbell turned to all of the significant US Supreme Court cases interpreting the interstate commerce clause. Although this field of law is important, historically significant, and relevant to deciding *Schechter*, whole books have been written about Chief Justice John Marshall's opinion in *Gibbons v. Ogden* (1824) (defining interstate commerce to include navigation on rivers); its gutting in *E.C. Knight & Co. v. U.S.* (1895), when the Court eliminated manufacturing from the clause; and its limited revival in *Swift & Co. v. U.S.* (1905) under the "stream of commerce" concept. They all reflected their respective time periods, but together they told the story of the expansion of government power after the American Civil War.

For Campbell and current investigators of the reach of the interstate commerce clause, the only topic was the NIRA's reach into New York

City's poultry market. Did the subject of the regulation have a direct impact on commerce as per the *Swift* standard? Campbell decided the violations were "substantial" and the law met the rational basis test under *Nebbia*. Congress had the ability to grant to the president the authority to regulate the New York metropolitan area poultry market. Implied was that the president could have issued a code for the poultry industry nationwide. As for what would happen to the federalism concept should this ruling hold, Campbell did not discuss it.

Judge Campbell's decision was not a total loss for the Schechters. Despite upholding enough counts of the indictment and convictions to merit substantial jail time and fines, he voided the sixth through the twenty-third and the fortieth because they did not specify a particular act, but instead alleged a whole series of them. As he stated, "you cannot charge eighteen crimes in one count by simply giving that count eighteen numbers." Prosecutors under the federal code had to separate out each violation by time and place. Otherwise, the defendants could not refute any of the charges. This would be a denial of a fair trial. Prosecutors must prove beyond a reasonable doubt individual acts or a systematic pattern of wrongdoing. Having voided these counts, he ended his involvement in the case. Still facing substantial penalties, the Schechters now had to make the difficult decision of whether to mount the onerous process of an appeal.

Before the Second Circuit Court of Appeals

As noted above, the Schechters would not be able to gain compensation for their legal expenses. However, there might well have been something of the spirit of an immigrant who was the child of immigrants in the Schechter brothers' decision to seek justice of some kind. Though they were vocal supporters of FDR, the Democrats, and the New Deal, in interviews with the *New York Times*, they strongly opposed the idea they had sold tainted goods, cheated, or acted criminally. The ins and outs of constitutional law were probably beyond them—as it is today for almost all but the specially trained, and sometimes even then—but they did seem to have potent convictions as to what was right and what was wrong. For whatever reason, they appealed to the Second Circuit

Court of Appeals, which covered New York as well as Connecticut and Vermont.

Though they had lost at the lower level, the list of charges had shrunk from sixty to eighteen, and the political winds were shifting. By the time the Second Circuit handed down its opinion on April 1, 1935, the NRA seemed more like an albatross around the neck of the administration than a savior. Initially, the NRA had been popular, along with the other New Deal programs. American voters liked the New Deal and gave the Democrats a resounding victory in the by-elections of 1934. Contrariwise, by this time, the national experiment that was the NRA seemed to be failing. Organized labor had swung against the increasingly adverse treatment NRA rulings had dispensed to them. Consumers were frustrated at the higher prices. Unemployment remained stubbornly high. Civil rights advocates documented the racism of the codes toward Black Americans in the South, who were paid less than half of what their white co-workers earned for working under terrible conditions. Progressives in both parties denounced the anti-trust violations at the same time the conservatives denounced the pro-labor provisions. All attempts at salvaging the cornerstone of the First New Deal, including open forums for criticism, only made things worse.

In an attempt to assuage criticism of the NRA, on March 7, 1934, FDR appointed a National Recovery Administration review board with the eminent people's lawyer Clarence Darrow as chairman. Unfortunately for Roosevelt's purpose, they undertook their task with vigor, including holding open hearings. Johnson tried to manage the overwhelming tide of hostile complaints to no avail. Labor, consumers, and small business owners gathered en masse to deride the codes. Senator William Borah, who had opposed the suspension of the anti-monopoly provisions of the NIRA in the Senate, was blunt in a personal comment to *Time*'s former "Man of the Year": "Hugh, your codes stink."

Even Johnson's resignation or dismissal (depending on the source) at the beginning of 1935 and Richberg's return did not stem the tide of opposition. Al Smith, in some ways FDR's former mentor, joined an anti–New Deal opposition group called the American Liberty League. As FDR's predecessor as governor of New York, and before that a popular mayor of New York City, the Roman Catholic Smith had been the quintessential progressive Democrat. Instead of a triumphant career in the

White House, Hoover had dealt him, but not FDR, a humiliating defeat, with a great deal of anti-Catholic, anti-Irish, anti-immigrant slurs slung his way. He had wanted a redemptive renomination in 1932, and he felt his former pupil had betrayed him by seeking the nomination for himself.

From an office in the relatively new Empire State Building, Smith and other spokespeople denounced the tyranny of the NRA and FDR's New Deal's excesses in advance of the 1936 presidential election. Because they were funded by wealthy lawyers and representatives of large corporations like DuPont, the New Dealers and their supporters used the criticism to portray themselves as working on behalf of the common people. If the goal of the American Liberty League was to mount a meaningful challenge to Roosevelt's reelection bid, they failed badly, yet the personal insult from his former mentor still hurt.

A more serious threat came from Senator Huey Long, former governor and "Kingfish" of Louisiana. In a radio address in February 1934, he mounted an alternative program called the "Share Our Wealth Plan," which would have taxed wealth and income up to 100 percent over one hundred million and one million dollars respectively. The national government would then spend the revenue on a universal basic income of $500 a month (approximately $11,450 in today's dollars, adjusted for inflation), public works, senior pensions, free education, veterans' benefits, and medical care for everyone. When Long failed to get US congressional support for his challenge to the New Deal, he created the Share Our Wealth Society with Reverend Gerald L. K. Smith as its chief organizer. A year later the Society had grown to seven and a half million members in twenty-seven thousand clubs around the nation. An assassin cut short Long and Smith's challenge to Roosevelt by killing the senator in Baton Rouge, Louisiana, on September 8, 1935. Smith later allied with the defrocked anti-Semitic radio sensation Father Charles Coughlin, in 1936, but it was short-lived. Then, there were those within the FDR administration who worried that the US Supreme Court would soon dismantle all they had achieved or planned to achieve. They did not have to wait long.

Although there will be a detailed examination of the Hughes Court, its justices, and its jurisprudence later, we must consider one more of its rulings here because, before the Second Circuit could even consider the Schechters' appeal, the US Supreme Court struck down section 9(c), the "hot oil" provision, in *Panama Refining Co. v. Ryan* on January 7, 1935. The rationale of the Court was that "nowhere in the statute has Congress declared or indicated any policy or standard to guide or limit the President when acting under such delegation." Chief Justice Hughes wrote the opinion with only Justice Cardozo dissenting. Because the Petroleum Code and the orders under it had become irrelevant to both parties (the enforcement provision was excluded), the justices took no notice of those provisions of the law. The interstate commerce implications would have to wait for another case. In his opinion for the Court, Hughes found that section 9(c) violated the non-delegation doctrine with its granting of unlimited authority to the president over any state actions regulating the production and distribution of petroleum and petroleum products. His review of the Court's precedents led to this conclusion—a separation of powers existed, and the Court had a duty to enforce it. This refers to the Constitution vesting the legislative, executive, and judicial powers in the US Congress, the president, and the Article III courts, emphasizing the use of the definite article "the" as part of his reasoning

While he did not elaborate on the political theories or origins of the topic in the colonial and early national periods, Chief Justice Hughes did state that this division was "an essential part of our system of government." In short, section 9(c) did not specify a policy for the president to enforce or any standards the president was to use in deciding whether to enforce a state's decision. "There is no requirement, no definition of circumstances and conditions in which the transportation is to be allowed or prohibited." Thus, section 9(c) violated the non-delegation doctrine and was, therefore, null and void. Interestingly, it did not matter to the Court that FDR had dedicated that authority in its entirety to Harold Ickes, the secretary of the interior and the one person who had been behind the formation of the section. Apparently, the president's complete delegation of his authority, specifically granted to him by Congress, did not rate a mention.

In his dissent, Justice Benjamin Cardozo argued that there were standards throughout the NIRA, and it was perfectly legitimate for Congress to allow the president to choose among them with the overall goal of aiding the recovery of the US economy. The opening paragraph alone was sufficient for this, but the section itself gave the reason for the delegation of power as the promotion of industry. Cardozo used a method for statutory interpretation, first proposed in Francis Lieber's hermeneutics and common in contract law, where the judge is to look at the whole document, its overall goal, and its essence in order to discern the meaning of any particular provision within the contract.

The other rule of statutory construction he cited is to read the statute in such a way as to avoid finding it in conflict with the Constitution. To summarize, "There must be sensible approximation, there must be elasticity of adjustment, in response to the practical necessities of government, which cannot foresee today the developments of tomorrow in their nearly infinite variety." If he had gone on to emphasize the "dignity of the human person" as one of the goals of the Constitution, this would have been the earliest formation of Justice William Brennan's "living Constitution" jurisprudence in the late twentieth century. Yet Cardozo did not seem to realize the evils of unfettered discretionary authority in an executive branch officer, let alone the president of the United States. Like Hughes, Cardozo cited a great deal of precedent to support his interpretation. Still, the eight other justices disagreed.

There were other cases that term and before it relevant to the New Deal, yet this examination of *Schechter* will have to wait to analyze them later. For now, it is sufficient to note that the Court had already indicated its concern with FDR's New Deal, though Congress solved the Court's objection to 9(c) with the Connally Hot Oil Act of 1935, which was never challenged in court. But the Second Circuit Court of Appeals did not receive that message as far as the Schechters' appeal was concerned. The judges unanimously rejected both the non-delegation and the interstate commerce claims. Martin T. Manton wrote the opinion for the court. A Columbia Law School graduate and Wilson appointee to the federal district court in 1916, then the Second Circuit in 1918, he resigned in disgrace in 1939 and served nineteen years in federal prison for conspiracy to obstruct justice after being accused of taking bribes.

Manton was joined in the opinion by Judge (Billings) Learned Hand, Manton's successor as chief judge. An honors graduate of Harvard and Harvard Law School, Hand is often regarded as one of the foremost legal thinkers to serve on the federal bench. His opinions, writings, and phrasings are reputed to be the most cited of any judge not on the US Supreme Court. He supported civil liberties, judicial restraint, deference to legislatures, and general tolerance. The third and final judge to join in the opinion was Vermont's Harrie B. Chase, a conservative who gained a reputation as a solid though indifferent judge. None of the three had much regard for the Schechters' appeal.

Importantly, Manton gave a reason, for the first time, why there was a poultry code solely for the New York metropolitan area and for no other part of the country. New York's was the "largest in the country and dominates the industry" and was "beset with evil trade practices." It was highly unlikely that "evil" had been proven beyond a reasonable doubt in the Schechters' criminal trial, but at least someone stated for the record why New York had a poultry code handed down by the national government and no one else did. According to Manton, New York was not only the center of the nation's poultry industry but also a magnet for "diseased" birds. Given that no disease was proven at trial, one has to wonder about the judge's proclamations in this case. He had been a practicing lawyer in New York City for over a decade before becoming a judge. Perhaps he was speaking from experience. The problems of America's largest city were well known and, perhaps, like Batman, Manton decided he was going to clean up Gotham.

Once again, the two main issues were the interstate commerce power and the non-delegation doctrine. Manton disposed of the interstate commerce question quickly. The "emergency" of the Great Depression in the form of overproduction and a collapse of prices impacted all of interstate commerce. Congress was merely addressing this limited, special emergency. This was understandable. The immensity of the supposedly temporary problem required deference to the political branches' more finely attuned powers. Putting aside Manton's support of the national government attorneys' economic theory without evidence in the form of economists' testimony or widely accepted analyses, there remains his general contention that emergencies give Congress leniency in the exercise of its powers rather than the opposite. One of the possible flaws in the judicial restraint philosophy, made popular by Justice Oliver Wendell Holmes Jr., and continued by Judge Learned Hand, Justice Louis D. Brandeis, Justice Benjamin Cardozo, and others down to the present day, is that legislatures, government, and people in general are less trustworthy with power in an emergency. Emotions run hot. Reason, temperance, and moderation retreat. Panicked thinking is frequently, if not always, poor thinking governed by instinct rather than higher mental functioning. Manton did not acknowledge this. He had more urgent matters to address.

Panama Refining had created a substantial obstacle to the government's case. Yet, because that decision had been limited to section 9(c), Manton could distinguish it from the rest of the NIRA that governed the Schechters, specifically section 3. Using the same precedents Campbell had used and likely provided in the government's brief for the Second Circuit, Manton found ample standards, limitations, and policy choices to restrict the president's authority to promulgate codes that governed almost all sectors of the economy. "The delegated power, if confined within proper limits, if the circumstances calling for its exercise and restraint are adequately confined, is lawful." *Panama Refining* applied, but section 3 met the test.

In fact, the very weakness of the restraint was its virtue. "That the standard is broad, that the limitations are not too confining, that the scope of power invested in the President is of great magnitude, is a necessary and essential factor if the results sought to be accomplished by Congress are to be attained." Fairness, price supports, increased productivity, and industrial rehabilitation were too complex for Congress to legislate. It had to be left to the president. Manton did not bother to ask whether Congress was allowed to act when the solution was too complex for them to master. The nature of the emergency demanded flexibility.

The Court of Appeals for the Second Circuit did chip away at the charges somewhat. Manton's opinion held that the wages and hours provisions of the code did not involve interstate commerce. Therefore, those counts went away. Interestingly, this was wholly consistent with another line of cases, which declared similar legislation unconstitutional at the state and national level. Because they followed the US Supreme Court's decision in *Lochner v. New York* (1905), these cases were part of the so-called *Lochner* era. In effect, what had been happening was the justices looked very closely, in other words scrutinized, the legislation to determine whether it violated either the due process clause of the Fourteenth Amendment, if it concerned a state or local government, or the Fifth Amendment, if it concerned the national government.

Under the idea of "substantive due process," a judicial reading of the due process clause's protection of "life, liberty, or property" in both the Fifth Amendment (applying to the federal government) and the

Fourteenth Amendment (applying to the states) could be used to incorporate a certain number of rules and standards or a particular right. In the case of *Lochner*, it was liberty of contract—the supposed ability of workers to negotiate their own terms of employment, including days and hours worked. In subsequent years, only a few pieces of legislation passed the *Lochner* standard. This made it very difficult for the national and state governments to regulate the economy as they wished during the Progressive Era (1890–1920) and afterward. In the *Schechter* case, it helped another business, though this one was considerably smaller and impotent compared to the large, well-connected corporations that usually benefited from the Court's heightened scrutiny.

A Skeptical Court

The Schechters, still facing jail and fines for the remaining counts, appealed to the US Supreme Court. In addition to the substantial political shift against the NIRA, and the NRA in particular, the Court had also begun to turn against certain elements of the New Deal even before *Schechter*. Despite the ruling in *Nebbia*, the justices were almost all Republican appointees, with the Democrats, like McReynolds, being even more conservative, thus more hostile to the New Deal, than the Republicans. FDR and his supporters may well have concluded that the judiciary needed reform as much as the rest of the national government. This reasonable suspicion turned into substantial evidence with a series of cases that preceded the decision in *A.L.A. Schechter Co. v. U.S.*

Decided on February 18, 1935, a group of cases that came to be known as "The Gold Clause Cases" caused concern. Chief Justice Hughes along with the progressives on the Court overruled the Four Horsemen and validated almost all of FDR's and Congress's machinations over the gold standard. The background was that the Depression had undermined the US gold reserve, thus destabilizing the currency. Congress and FDR had responded with various laws and executive orders to take the United States off the gold standard by invalidating gold currency and exchanging it for dollars as well as invalidating the gold dollars the government owed on World War I Liberty Bonds. Because business contracts often had provisions, known as a "gold clause," to protect against currency fluctuations, these contracts interfered with the new policy by drawing on the US gold reserves. The Gold Clause Resolution voided them. The national government's attorneys argued that Congress had the power to do this. The various parties whose property and contracts were adversely affected asserted, through their lawyers, that this was arbitrary, capricious, and a violation of due process.

While the majority of the Court supported the administration's view (with one exception that Congress later swiftly resolved through a subsequent enactment), the Four Horsemen stuck to the traditional view of cases like *Lochner* that, even concerning the currency, the government possessed limited powers to contravene private contracts. In an opinion by McReynolds, they distinguished the present cases from the adverse precedent set by the Court in *The Legal Tender Cases*, which concerned debts and obligations by Confederates. The gold clauses were entirely private, not public, and thus beyond the scope of Congress's authority over the currency. Interestingly, they did not seem all that perturbed by FDR's use of discretionary power, seemingly at a whim, to play with the dollar's value. Nevertheless, Justice Owen Roberts's swing vote for Chief Justice Hughes's opinions caused the New Deal Democrats grave foreboding about the Court's tolerance for the national experiment. Winning by just one vote did not reassure them.

Unbeknownst to the American public, the FDR administration had been working feverishly over the preceding month to create a series of actions they would employ if the Court did not rule in their favor. Assistant attorney general and future US Supreme Court justice Robert H. Jackson suggested sovereign immunity—refusing private citizens the ability to sue the government. Attorney General Homer S. Cummings proposed again a plan to enlarge the Court. FDR agreed it might well come to that. Special legislation and a fireside chat dedicated to addressing the emergency stood ready for that purpose. Chair of the Securities and Exchange Commission (SEC) Joseph Kennedy, father of the future political dynasty, recorded in his diary that the radio address might well lead to crowds burning the justices in effigy. Thus, there is ample evidence to show that the administration had already entered into a bunker mentality with an echo chamber substituting for any grounded views of what the public thought was appropriate. This is understandable given the pressures they were under to deliver economic miracles in an increasingly disturbing geopolitical environment.

On May 6, 1935, a little more than three weeks before their decision in *Schechter*, Justice Roberts's opinion for himself and the Four Horsemen seemingly justified the foreboding. In *Railroad Retirement Board v. Alton Railroad Co.*, the Court voided the Railroad Retirement Act passed on June 27, 1934, as a violation of the due process clause because it exceeded Congress's authority to regulate interstate commerce. Once again using the rational basis test, the Court found that requiring all railroads in the country to contribute to a pension fund, which paid a pension regardless of length of service, reason for dismissal, or the company's ability to pay, did not serve the efficiency or promotion of commerce goals stated in the legislation and constituted deprivation of property. The dissenters agreed with the administration's attorneys that it was the exact opposite. The disagreement officially centered on the reach of the interstate commerce clause. Unofficially, the decision hinged on the use of a tax to fund the retirement of railroad workers so that the industry would hire more, but not at general taxpayer expense.

It is not hard to understand why this case's outcome worried New Dealers. The plan the act created bore an incredible similarity to the Social Security bill making its way through Congress, in which general taxation would provide for old age pensions in amounts dependent on, but not limited to, how much people had paid into the system. FDR had sold it as old age insurance. You received what you paid into it. That was simply not true, as was easily demonstrated when retirees received Social Security checks starting in 1940, after the establishment of the Social Security Administration. It was largely a pay-as-you-go program, in other words, a redistribution of wealth from the young and employed to the elderly. There was also a disability component that worked the same way with the same purpose. Taxes on wages that were barely progressive (based on ability to pay) would alter the income and wealth of the nation based on a moral or ethical judgment. The unemployable needed help from the employed. Therefore, the government commanded it. What we would later call the social welfare safety net hung in the balance.

The decision in *Railroad Retirement Board v. Alton* appeared to threaten this grand design. The desire to help retirees and encourage people to retire, to open up employment for the young, may seem ageist, but it was a popular sentiment that promised a win for both sides. Arguably it had started with retired doctor Francis Townsend's letter to his local California newspaper in 1933. In it, he proposed a 2 percent sales tax that would fund two hundred dollars a month to every retiree in the country over the age of sixty with the requirement that they had to spend the money. According to his economic theory, the tax would pay for itself because the boost in retiree spending would have a multiplier effect on the US economy, promoting economic growth. By 1935, the so-called Townsend Plan had produced seven thousand Townsend Clubs with 2.2 million members and a petition to Congress with ten million signatures. The Townsend Plan would not have worked because the tax rate was too low, the benefits were too high, and the multiplier effect did not apply as it was merely substituting retiree spending for that of the employed. However, the New Dealers were looking for a substitute for the NRA and its dismal performance. Pensions fit the bill nicely.

They even had some judicial support for the plan for what became Social Security from an unlikely source: Justice Harlan F. Stone. Frances Perkins, the secretary of labor and someone FDR had tasked with coming up with the legislation, asked the justice at a dinner party at his house whether such a plan would pass judicial review. Stone told her, according to her later memoir: "The taxing power of the federal government, my dear; the taxing power is sufficient for everything you want and need." This referred to a combination of the federal income tax from the Sixteenth Amendment and the appropriations clause of Article I. (The Appropriations Clause stated that no money was to be drawn from the Treasury except "by law.") Essentially, as long as it was a general tax on incomes, Congress could spend it how it wanted so long as it did not infringe upon life, liberty, or property—other than income.

———

A Question of Timing

Given these warnings and setbacks, the Roosevelt administration could be forgiven for wanting to go slowly on the *Schechter* case. After all, there was now political opposition, public discontent, and bad press surrounding the NRA's leadership, and some question whether Congress was going to renew the agency in the late spring of 1935. The great experiment with mobilizing an economy out of a depression with cartels had disappointed at best, and more likely failed. Why pursue a case that many New Deal attorneys were predicting would end poorly as an unconstitutional delegation of power? And yet, instead of allowing the case to wind its way through the courts, FDR and his team actually moved for an earlier argument and decision before the Court. Apparently, President Roosevelt was deeply committed to the NIRA as his signature legislation. It signified all that he stood for: the broad exercise of executive power for the public good, and modernity itself.

This should not surprise anyone. FDR was at his roots a progressive. Their and his political philosophy accepted current technology as the height of human civilization. Electrical devices for the home and office were comparatively new as were the automobile, airplanes, and radio networks. Part of the appeal of regimes like Mussolini's Fascists, Hitler's Nazis, and Stalin's Soviet utopia were their supposed embrace of the future. Hitler's autobahn could stun the world alongside the spectacle the Third Reich planned for the 1936 Olympic Games in Berlin. FDR had a natural distaste for these one-party dictatorships, but he shared their embrace of the wonders of modern life, particularly those a strong national government could sponsor. Though he had studied law at Columbia and practiced for a time after his failed 1920 vice presidential campaign, Roosevelt had no affinity for the courts and their seemingly stultified, conservative, and, thus, antiquated worldview. The 1934 by-election had proven the people were with him. So, he probably thought, should the courts.

Unfortunately for this line of thinking, this expedited review of the Schechter case placed it alongside two other cases whose decisions Chief Justice Hughes arranged to be read on the same day, Monday, May 27, 1935, in order of least important to most. All three went against the administration and, as a result, New Dealers referred to it as "Black Monday." They concerned entirely different topics, with different reasonings to support each decision, but they all centered on New Deal actions, which had, at their cores, a broad view of government authority. *Schechter* came last. Yet each, in its own way, made an important contribution to the Court's role and its assertion of such in the formulation of the US nation.

The first decision, *Humphrey's Executor v. U.S.*, dealt with FDR's dismissal of William E. Humphrey from the Federal Trade Commission. Coolidge had appointed Humphrey to a seven-year term in 1925, and Hoover reappointed him and the Senate confirmed it in 1931. In 1933, FDR fired him for not having his "confidence," in other words, for being insufficiently supportive of the New Deal. Humphrey resisted and came to work until his death in 1934, whereupon his heirs continued the lawsuit for wrongful dismissal for the benefit of his estate. They wanted his back pay, no inconsiderable matter during the Depression.

This case largely embodied Roosevelt's desire to have the sprawling executive branch drawn together under his direct control. It was an ambitious plan. Besides the departments, ranging from the military to interior, the bureaucracy included organizations like the Federal Trade Commission—independent bodies that were supposed to be bipartisan regulators of a particular area of the nation. The Federal Trade Commission had begun as the Bureau of Corporations under President Theodore Roosevelt, and he had tasked it with publicizing the activities of the trusts—the mega-companies dominating certain industries. The idea was to encourage good behavior and discourage bad behavior through publicity. Under President Woodrow Wilson, Congress transformed it into a commission with similar goals, but with a regulatory arm that enforced its mandate of fair trade and the labeling of consumer products.

These commissions had emerged at the state level during the Gilded Age (1877–1890) to oversee various industries with a light touch that was, at the same time, nonpartisan—a kind of governance by expert. The US Congress created the first federal one, the aforementioned ICC, in 1887 to regulate the interstate railroads. Since then, it had become a popular device to regulate larger and larger realms of the US economy free of the corruption and partisanship widely believed to permeate the regular bureaucracy. Yet by the 1930s many academics, writers, and activists had come to believe that these commissions, as well as other agencies, had been "captured" by the industries they were supposed to regulate, working on behalf of those businesses rather than the general public. Curiously enough, it was the same criticism that followed the NRA codes' effect on the industries they governed. Eminent legal historian Mark

Tushnet disagrees, pointing out that the NRA was not really captured so much as revising older ideas of competition.

The US Supreme Court, as noted above, had a difficult relationship with these elements of what scholars later called the administrative state, with the non-delegation doctrine at the center of the dispute. In *Humphrey's Executor v. U.S.* (1935), Roosevelt's argument that he had the right to fire commissioners without constraint contradicted the Court's distinction between independent regulatory commissions and the regular bureaucracy. Justice George Sutherland wrote for a unanimous Court that the previous decision, in *Myers v. U.S.* (1926), upholding the president's authority to dismiss a postmaster without cause or the consent of the Senate, did not apply to the "quasi-legislative," "quasi-judicial" function of the Federal Trade Commission. The legislation creating it specified not only the term of office, but that one could be dismissed only for cause. The Court argued that a "coercive influence threatens the independence of a commission."

Not so quietly, the Court had expressed another version of its skepticism of unbridled executive power. This was no mere disagreement with the executive branch. This posed a potential threat to the checks and balances of the Constitution. Again, it was significant that Sutherland did not just write for himself, the other horsemen, and a swing vote. Justices Brandeis and Cardozo joined with Chief Justice Hughes in support of Sutherland's opinion without concurrence. Sutherland's brief rejection of the president's executive authority sufficed for even the liberal, or progressive wing of the Court. There are a few possibilities to explain this result. Perhaps the president's position was poor or it was poorly argued. Or maybe the New Dealers and the Court were simply in complete disagreement about the restrictions on executive power in the US Constitution.

The second case on "Black Monday" came out of Kentucky. An owner of a farm sought relief under the Frazier-Lemke Act, the Bankruptcy Act of 1934, from foreclosure by the Louisville Joint Stock Land Bank. The Frazier-Lemke Act allowed owners of farms to retain their property and pay rent if their mortgage lender refused the act's substitute low interest rate and prolonged mortgage. It is understandable why Congress would pass and President Roosevelt would sign such a measure. Farm foreclosures were wiping out independent farmers throughout the nation, especially in the Dust Bowl region of the Great Plains. These small household farms had comprised most farming in the nation since its founding. Even though rural dwellers had become a minority since 1920, they were still numerous and politically important, especially to the Democrats, and a symbol of the nation dating back to President Thomas Jefferson's rural idyll. Electrification, crop subsidies, roads, cheap transportation, and easier lending terms were their goals and, subsequently, those of FDR's New Deal as well.

It is also comprehensible why a lender would object to replacing foreclosure with a tenancy or government-imposed loan structure that would be of no benefit or possibly a liability for the lender. The nation's financial system depended, and still does, on a set of stable rules, which serve the interests of both parties. If the rules change too frequently, investment in the form of loans becomes scarcer as fear spreads about the future. If the rules become lopsided, the disadvantaged party will be more reluctant to enter into the transaction. Both effects stifle investment and borrowing—the lifeblood of an economy. Interestingly enough, one can trace this fundamental political and economic conflict back through US history all the way to the dispute between President George Washington's secretary of the treasury, Alexander Hamilton, and his Federalist Party and Secretary of State Thomas Jefferson and the nascent Democratic-Republicans. The Federalists and Hamilton favored a hard money policy for lenders, and the Democratic-Republicans and Jefferson favored a loose money policy for debtors.

In the case of *Louisville Joint Stock Land Bank v. Radford,* Justice Brandeis wrote for a unanimous Court declaring that the Frazier-Lemke Act was an unconstitutional violation of the takings clause of the Fifth Amendment. For his home state of Kentucky, Brandeis argued the legislation extinguished the lender's property right in the collateral for the loan if they could not foreclose on at least neutral terms. Even though they had the power under Article I to make laws concerning bankruptcy, Congress had gone too far in favor of the borrower. The takings clause required "just compensation," and Congress had provided none. In Brandeis's words: "however great the nation's need, private property shall not be thus taken even for a wholly public use without just compensation." Another piece of the New Deal had received a firm rebuke from the Court.

After Much Delay

When the US government is the prosecutor, the case takes place in federal courts, as the Schechter brothers found out. If there is an adverse ruling, like any other litigant, the government lawyers—the prosecution—can appeal on the basis of law. Questions of fact are established at the trial Court level and are not reviewable unless there are extraordinary circumstances. When Hugh Johnson and Donald Richberg found out in late 1933 that public spirit would not be enough and established a compliance division in the NRA, they faced an entirely new dilemma about enforcement. In order to do so, they would have to prosecute in the courts if defendants pleaded not guilty and challenged the constitutionality of the NIRA—the enabling statute. Due to FDR's executive order and a supporting communication by his attorney general, Homer S. Cummings, all prosecutions would have to be through the Department of Justice.

Even prior to taking office, FDR had wanted to reorganize the executive branch, to streamline it, modernize it, and centralize the bureaucracy under presidential control. As a former assistant secretary of the navy, he was experienced in these matters. Even before the New Deal, the executive branch was a Byzantine labyrinth with no order. With the same attitude that led to the facts of the *Humphrey's Executor* case, Roosevelt worked with his attorney general to straighten out the mess, at least on the litigation side. Instead of every agency litigating on its own, the Justice Department would fulfill one of its original functions when it was created in 1870: concentrating the legal business of the nation under the attorney general and, more specifically, under the newly created office of Solicitor General.

Unfortunately, the first solicitor general under FDR, James Biggs, gained a horrible reputation both as an administrator and an advocate for the US government before the US Supreme Court, the other major function of his office. Quietly, Chief Justice Charles Evans Hughes, Justices Louis D. Brandeis, and Harlan Fiske Stone told the administration that Biggs was a disaster, doing material damage to the government's case in both oral arguments and its briefs. Though the justices also complained about the "sloppy" drafting of the early New Deal legislation, Biggs's lawyering had not helped. Thankfully for the administration, Attorney General Cummings fired Biggs and replaced him with the much more competent Stanley Reed, who served from March 25, 1935, until he was replaced by Robert H. Jackson on March 5th, 1938. FDR elevated both to the US Supreme Court, but not in time for the first test case of the NIRA.

That test case was not *Schechter*. It was supposed to be *U.S. v. Belcher*. William E. Belcher was another small businessman who had violated an NRA code. In his case, it was the Lumber Code, which imposed hour and wage restrictions, that Belcher continuously ignored. NRA lawyers wanted him prosecuted like the other violators. Justice Department lawyers disagreed. Belcher's business was in Alabama under a hostile Republican federal judge. In order to sustain charges, the Justice Department lawyers would have to appeal and send it to a higher court. They did not want to do so because, unlike the NRA lawyers, they did not like their chances either under the interstate commerce clause or the non-delegation doctrine.

Despite these objections, supporters of the New Deal both inside and outside the administration, including President Roosevelt, needed a test case to solidify the NIRA's standing so that enforcement could proceed in the federal courts. Avoiding the test case placed all of those criminal prosecutions in limbo while encouraging others to break the code. The uncertainty surrounding the status of the codes also prompted editorial writers like those in the *New York Times* to call for a test case to settle the matter. *Belcher* became that case. As a result, Attorney General Cummings arranged for the case to be argued before the Court. The stage was set for the showdown in late March 1935, when Cummings abruptly asked the Court to withdraw the case due to an incomplete trial record. The Court agreed and the *Belcher* test case was dead.

Behind the scenes, Solicitor General Reed in the Justice Department and Harvard Law Professor Felix Frankfurter, among others, convinced Roosevelt to abandon this case as the test of his signature New Deal program. It was a humiliating retreat, with those who supported the New Deal in the press and Congress deeply disturbed about the administration's refusal to have the NIRA get its day in court. We cannot know if one or the other side was correct. All we can derive from this episode is the role of chance in US Supreme Court decisions. The Lumber Code fell to sick chickens as the test of the NRA.

Even on that matter, it appears that the only reason Richberg, now head of the NRA, prevailed over Frankfurter and Reed was that Roosevelt was on board a ship, on a Caribbean vacation, in late March and early April, when the Department of Justice needed to decide whether to file an appeal or abandon. In the meantime, FDR had already pushed Congress to extend the NRA's life past the June expiration date. The Senate begrudgingly passed a more limited extension with intrastate businesses wholly exempt and the anti-monopoly provisions omitted. The House had yet to take up the legislation by the time the Court's expedited ruling in *Schechter* arrived. FDR maintained the same position he had in his annual message to Congress in February that the NRA was "no little Orphan Annie, but a very lively, young lady." "Little Orphan Annie" was a popular comic strip, later in the century turned into a Broadway musical, "Annie," with FDR making a guest appearance, and two movies of the same name, all with the inspirational theme song "Tomorrow." But FDR was very serious about the NRA. There would be no retreat this time.

In this fight, the administration had some unlikely allies in the press. Drew Pearson and his co-author, Robert Allen, of the syndicated *Washington Post* column Washington Merry-Go-Round, took on the task of vilifying the Schechters and defending their prosecution. They shared an antipathy for the Jewish butchers, poisoning public opinion. Compiled under the suggestive title "Joseph and His Brethren," the widely read team wrote: "where the kosher butchers of the city work in filth, blood and chicken feathers, they operated jointly a prosperous pair of smelly chicken companies." Pearson eventually gained quite a reputation for himself as an investigative reporter. Many celebrated him; an award for journalism was even named after him. Many others noted that he often wrote falsehoods and carried on personal vendettas, using a network of informants on occasion to blackmail his targets. That the columns contained more than a note of anti-Semitism was also no accident. In a time of quotas and restricted neighborhoods, anti-Semitism had not yet gained the taint of the Holocaust.

There was also a rumor that the lawyer who joined the Hellers once the case became a national one, Frederick H. Wood of the corporate New York firm of Cravath, DeGersdorff, Swaine and Wood, purposefully chose the Schechters for his big challenge to the New Deal because the defendants were Jewish. After all, two of the liberals/progressives on the Court, Louis D. Brandeis and Benjamin Cardozo, were Jewish and familiar with anti-Semitism. Not the least of the offenders was their colleague McReynolds, who persistently refused to acknowledge their existence. Brandeis was also sympathetic to a small business fighting against larger interests. He had made his name prior to his appointment to the Court on just such a position. With the Four Horsemen, that could make for a large majority against the NRA.

———

The Schechters' road to the US Supreme Court had wound its way through the thicket of national and local politics, debates over how to achieve recovery, ideological divisions running the gamut from Fascism to socialism and everything in between, and practically every significant Supreme Court case since Reconstruction. On May 29, 1935, "Black Monday" for the New Dealers, it reached an end. Yet that was not the end of the story. The case history and its context constitute only one significant part of the case. The justices, their opinions, and their immediate impact remain for us to examine in greater detail. There is also the not so small matter of how the lawyers for each side argued the case, which often turns out to be a decisive factor in the outcome before the Court.

A Unanimous Court

Before covering the two opinions in the *Schechter* case, it is necessary to take a step back and look at the lawyering that influenced the justices. According to some scholars, the solicitor generals who argued the early New Deal cases did not perform very well. The troubles in the FDR Justice Department, inexperience, and a failure to appreciate the justices' concerns led to the defeats of which *Schechter* was but the most notable. If this is true, an analysis of the pre-opinion stage might reveal these deficiencies.

Applying for Cert

To reach the US Supreme Court, there are three paths. One is original jurisdiction, specifically laid out in Article III of the Constitution. Another is to appeal from a decision of the highest court in a state. The third is the one used in the *Schechter* case, where one appeals from the lowest court in the federal system, the district court, to the appellate court, the Court of Appeals, and, finally, the US Supreme Court. However, the US Supreme Court has to review cases only if Congress has designated it a "matter of right." The rest are discretionary. The Court does not have to grant a review.

A petition to the Court for review of an appeal of an adverse lower court ruling is called a "writ of certiorari," derived from English common law pleadings. If four justices agree to review the appeal, it comes before the Court under the "rule of four." If none or fewer than four agree, the appeal does not come before the Court and the holding of the lower court stands. Usually, only one side, the appellants, will ask for Supreme Court review because they are the ones who lost. The other side, the appellees, usually do not file for "cert," because they won. *Schechter* was an exceptional case.

In addition to the Hellers asking for cert on behalf of the Schechters, Solicitor General Stanley B. Reed filed for review under the circumstances we found in the previous chapter, both asking for review in the October 1934 term. In short, the government wanted confirmation of constitutionality so that the renewal of the NIRA could move forward in Congress and other prosecutions could proceed. The Hellers renewed their arguments that, under the due process clause of the Fifth Amendment, the NIRA was unconstitutional under the non-delegation doctrine and was not interstate commerce. They repeated their claim that the punishment exceeded the Eighth Amendment's prohibition on "cruel and unusual" punishment. Finally, they included the corollary admonition that, if Congress did not have the power to regulate the poultry industry, that power was reserved to the states under the Tenth Amendment. As was customary and advisable, they submitted a brief making their case along with supporting documents including a list of cases, legislation, and constitutional clauses invoked.

Solicitor General Reed's petition for cert was a great deal briefer. After all, the government only wanted the hours and wages provisions to be affirmed. They had prevailed in the lower courts. From their perspective, it was reasonable to assume that the US Supreme Court would agree with the lower courts. Similar to the idea that a team has momentum—because they are currently doing well, they will continue to do well—relying on lower court victories is a dicey proposition. The Court had demonstrated a significant amount of skepticism with regard to early New Deal legislation, including the hot oil provision of the NIRA, which was up for review in *Schechter*. Yet it would be premature to judge the government's lawyering based on their petition for cert. The real arguments would be made in the briefs and, to a much lesser extent, in oral argument before the Court. Last, but not least, Reed's memorandum asked the Court to hear oral arguments for the *Schechter* case in late April so they could render a decision in early May 1935. The Court agreed to do so.

{ *Chapter Three* }

The Briefs

By late April 1935, prior to the Court's decision in *A.L.A Schechter Poultry Corp., et al. v. United States,* the "Sick Chicken Case," the lawyers for each side prepared briefs and presented oral arguments before the justices. Briefs are detailed written arguments submitted to the justices in advance of the oral argument, during which the attorneys have their final say on the legal issues the case presented for their clients. According to common law systems of appellate argument, like that in the United States, you may not raise legal issues in the briefs you have not raised at the lower level, nor raise a legal point in oral argument you have not raised in your briefs unless the Court expressly grants special permission. Therefore, the briefs need to be comprehensive, be well-written, and cite all relevant precedent whether it is adverse or not. Given the importance of *Schechter* to both sides, one should expect the briefs to be incredibly thorough. And they were.

As mentioned earlier, Cravath's Frederick H. Wood joined the Heller brothers in representing the Schechters at this stage. Although they submitted the brief as a group, we can be certain that Wood added his considerable expertise to the commerce and non-delegation clause sections. Wood had made it his mission to counter the New Deal in court on behalf of his large corporate clients after serving as general counsel for the Southern Pacific Railroad, nicknamed "the octopus" for its tentacles that reached everywhere. While the origins of the "test case" are murky at best, Wood was using the federal courts in that way to upend legislation that restricted his corporate clients. Wood had the reputation of being a legal conservative, one who believed that government's one and only purpose was the preservation of order, particularly the protection of private property. Franklin D. Roosevelt's supposedly modern views were abhorrent to this kind of conservative, largely because they overturned centuries of traditional values.

For the brief, the Schechters' counsel stuck with two main arguments with little fanfare: the non-delegation doctrine and the commerce clause. At the end, they spent a little effort on the defects in the criminal penalties, procedures, and judge's rulings at trial. Although earlier "writ" pleading limited the lawsuit to a single issue, modern pleading allowed litigants to offer multiple, even contradictory, pleas. As good lawyers do, counsel used this "shotgun" approach, hoping to land a hit with as many points as possible. With the non-delegation section, the Hellers and Wood took great advantage of the *Panama Refining* case's destruction of the hot oil provision of the NIRA.

Their attack centered on two late-twentieth-century legal concepts later further developed by future justice William Brennan. If legislation was either vague or overly broad, it was unconstitutional. Vagueness meant it was indeterminate. One could not tell exactly what Congress intended. Overbreadth signified it encompassed far too much. In other words, in both ways, Congress had failed to lay out specifics sufficient to meet judicial review. In the Schechters' case, Congress gave the president far too much leeway to determine the codes based on criteria that could enable pretty much everything. When the Court applied this doctrine to the poultry code's requirements, the average, rational person had no idea why "straight killing" would lead to prosperity, higher wages, more business profits, greater efficiency, or any other goal for a government seeking to end the Great Depression.

Counsel for the Schechters posited the opposite outcome concerning the interstate commerce clause. Count by count of the indictment failed to have anything to do with interstate commerce, being purely on-site, having to do with kosher laws, and being in an area covered by state law. While the US government and the lower courts sustained the proposition that the Schechters' long list of violations harmed the greater New York metropolitan area's poultry market and that market led the nation, the Schechters' attorneys emphasized the purely local nature of their clients' business. They performed their activities, housed their stock, and sold only out of one location in Brooklyn to area butchers and markets. This was not some Standard Oil, US Steel, or Sears & Roebuck type national big business. This was a neighborhood butcher of chickens.

This line of reasoning emphasized the federal or "dual" system of government the US Constitution established—as opposed to a unitary government like most other countries, including Japan, Britain, France, Italy, and China. The "states" in the United States are their own governments with almost all of the authority, tasks, and powers of government, while the national, a.k.a federal, government is one of limited powers with limited responsibilities. This reflected the United States' origins as a confederation of independent states under the Articles of Confederation, which itself was rooted in as much as two centuries of separate governments with only the English, later British, imperial authorities binding them together. They shared a language, a common law tradition, and some cultural and societal aspects but were otherwise separate.

This arrangement changed in the century and a half from the ratification of the Constitution in 1788 until 1935, most notably during Reconstruction, when three amendments vastly altered the relationship. Yet there were also amendments during the Progressive Era—including a national income tax, the direct election of senators, and the national experiment with Prohibition, as well as the Nineteenth Amendment, giving women the right to vote throughout the country. The arrival of industrialization, urbanization, and government growth at all levels, in almost all areas of life, altered what remained of the America of 1787, when the Constitution was written, and the US Supreme Court had played an important role in that transformation. The balance between the states and the federal government—federalism—existed in a state of flux by the 1930s, with FDR's New Deal threatening to undo that balance significantly. In effect, Schechters' counsel was asking the Court to repel that assault.

A brief can make the best points available, citing all available precedent and distinguishing all the adverse evidence, but still lose unless it relates its narrative of the case to something truly meaningful. In turns of phrase that likely came from Wood, the Schechters' brief stated point blank: "If the Government's view as to the scope of the commerce power be accepted, the field of individual liberty heretofore regarded as secure from governmental encroachment in certain fundamental aspects will be greatly restricted and potentially subject to complete extinction." From the Schechters' perspective, this was not merely a matter of theory, or grand policy, or a well-meaning government doing what's best in an emergency. It threatened the liberty of all against an encroaching state.

One should expect a certain amount of hyperbolic flourish in a Supreme Court brief. Yet this seems a bit overblown, unless one considers the context. Fascist Italy had established a one-party, syndicalist state and was on the march. Nazi Germany had been established only a little more than a year previously. Stalin's Soviet Union impressed many an intellectual, journalist, and observer that it was "the future." Though in the twenty-first century, accusing someone of being a Fascist, Nazi, or Communist is so commonplace it threatens to lose all meaning, these systems of dictatorial police states were not in the past or theoretical in late April 1935. They were very real. The cry of "It can never happen here" is not very convincing when the head of the NRA, Hugh Johnson, has good things to say about syndicalism, FDR has just established relations with the Soviet Union, and Hitler's Germany is working with US multinationals to create his ideal "Third Reich."

The next to last part of the Schechters' brief may have been its least noticeable, yet it represented a vital element of the overall challenge to the NIRA—the objection to the wages and hours requirements. In the present, when there is a lively debate about whether the United States should adopt a universal basic income for those who are made superfluous in our ever-automated, outsourced, and technology-driven economy, it is hard to imagine a country in which the minimum wage is not only debated but receives a hostile reception from the courts. Yet that was the environment in 1935: a government-imposed wage engendered significant pushback from those who considered it socialism, Communism, or just plain foolish.

Still, there was an argument to be made that a government making those kinds of decisions would be, in the words of the Schechters' brief: "destructive of our dual system of government and extend to the Federal Government the power to nationalize industry." Many Americans in the pre–New Deal eras would not have tolerated such a thing, but it seems that the emergency of the Great Depression provided an opportunity for substantial change. In the oft-quoted words of Rahm Emanuel, a former congressman, chief of staff for President Barack Obama, and mayor of Chicago, "never let a good crisis go to waste." Today, it has something of a quaint ring to it, but, for the people of the 1930s, the warning may well have resonated.

The final part of the Schechters' brief concerned the Hellers' consistent assertion that the trial was defective and the punishments excessive. In any trial, the judge is extremely likely to rule on a number of motions from both sides that affect the trial's outcome. For example, the rules of evidence can make or break a case. The general rule for admitting or excluding a piece of evidence is whether the prejudicial value outweighs the probative or vice versa. A chicken that was "egged"—had eggs in it—is certainly gross and an indicator of ill health, but it is not indicative of disease. Also, the Schechters and their employees could not have known the chicken was egged when they killed it and prepared it for sale. At the same time, an egged chicken did violate the poultry code as defective, a.k.a. a sick chicken. Did the judge err in allowing witness testimony as to the condition of the chicken? The Sixth Amendment guarantees a "fair trial." Counsel for the Schechters maintained that this and other rulings prevented them from receiving it.

Then, there was the topic of the punishment. Each penalty did not seem all that impressive. The fine of $350 and a month in jail were substantial, but not large. At the same time, there was no limit to the accumulation of them. For each instance, the Schechters received a fine and term in jail, and the instances piled upon one another until the fines and jail time were very significant for relatively minor infractions. The Eighth Amendment to the US Constitution prohibits "cruel and unusual" punishments. Selling an egged chicken and selective killing without NRA inspectors observing does not merit years in prison and fines that bankrupt the defendant. It was the weakest part of the brief in that all crimes possess this inherent problem. Even the theft of a pencil can add up if it is repeated several thousand times. Once again, the Schechters' attorneys were obligated to provide "zealous advocacy" on behalf of their clients according to basic professional responsibility. They had to try every argument if there was even a chance for success.

Finally, the Hellers and Wood had identified a significant number of defects in the indictment, the trial procedures, and the specific charges against their clients. Some were small. Others were more significant (something like the piling up of penalties). The overall impression is that the Hellers were concerned about all of the material the government had produced in order to secure a conviction. Prejudice, abuse of prosecutorial authority, and excessive zeal displayed by authorities in their investigation may well have occurred. After all, Walter L. Rice seemed to be doing an Eliot Ness impersonation, only the Schechter brothers were not Al Capone, the notorious Chicago gangster. The defects in the charges, trial, and evidence might also have been entirely natural occurrences, common to any human enterprise, especially one as fraught as a criminal trial for the sake of the New Deal.

The government's brief in *Schechter* was roughly one hundred and seventy-four pages, while the Schechters' was two hundred and three. Considering the government's attorneys had less to argue, thanks to their favorable outcomes at trial and on appeal, this is not surprising. In light of future events, maybe they were overconfident about their chances with the Court.

While it was shorter, the government brief had twice as many lawyers working on it. In addition to the solicitor general, Stanley Reed; the head of and former general counsel for the NRA, Donald Richberg; and Walter L. Rice from the lower courts; they had Harold M. Stephens, assistant attorney general; Charles H. Weston, Paul A. Freund, M. S. Huberman, G. Stanleigh Arnold, Golden W. Bell, and Carl McFarland, special assistants to the attorney general; Robert L. Stern and Herbert Borkland, special attorneys; and Phillip Buck, counsel for the NRA. Their biographies show that they were anything but political hacks or without merit.

Harold Stephens of Utah (though born in Nebraska) was head of the Anti-Trust Division of the Department of Justice. He was a Cornell undergrad and a Harvard Law School–trained lawyer (another of the Harvard Law School corps in DC). Shortly after Stephens worked on *Schechter*, FDR appointed him to the Court of Appeals for the District of Columbia (later renamed the DC Circuit Court of Appeals), where Truman later elevated him to chief judge. Charles Weston served in Anti-Trust starting in 1918 but resigned after Attorney General A. Mitchell Palmer launched the "Palmer Raids" against suspected anarchists in 1920. In 1928, he returned to the Anti-Trust Division, advocated for civil rights beginning in the 1940s, and headed the appellate section from 1943 until his retirement in 1961. George Stanleigh Arnold was a San Francisco–based attorney whom Attorney General Cummings appointed to be the Department of Justice's coordinator with the NRA compliance board. Robert Stern joined the Justice Department in 1934, went into private practice in Chicago twenty years later, and co-authored treatises on appellate practice for the next thirty years before writing a letter in support of William H. Rehnquist's nomination for chief justice.

Perhaps standing above everyone else, at least in jurisprudential circles, Paul Freund was a former Brandeis clerk who had worked with the Reconstruction Finance Corporation before joining the Justice Department. From 1939 to 1976, with brief interruptions to rejoin the Solicitor

General's office and lecture at Columbia Law School, he was a professor at Harvard Law School. His discussions of constitutional law, jurisprudential law, and general ideas of government became required reading, and .generations of his students went on to become Supreme Court clerks, judges, professors, and lawyers of great esteem, while speaking of their classes with Freund as a "religious experience." Consistent with his work on the *Schechter* brief, he maintained that the law should embrace contradictions as it navigates the challenges the modern world presents. At all times, it should promote order as well as diversity and chaos. Though one can disagree with shutting down a Jewish poultry processor on behalf of some wider scheme for national economic recovery, one cannot dispute the sophistication of thought behind Freund's view.

Carl McFarland was another Harvard Law graduate working in the Justice Department. Beginning in 1933, he had worked on a secret project for FDR and Attorney General Cummings on how to thwart a hostile judiciary's opposition to the New Deal. As we will see, this became the so-called Court Packing Plan of 1937. After that debacle, in 1938, McFarland joined Cummings in his DC law firm and served on the American Bar Association's Legislation and Administrative Law Committee, where he became a co-author of the Administrative Procedure Act of 1946, the foundation of much of today's administrative law. In 1951, he became president of the University of Montana, his undergraduate institution, and, in 1959, a professor at the University of Virginia School of Law. He died in 1979, four years after his retirement.

Herbert Borkland Sr., another Harvard Law graduate, worked in the Solicitor General's office until the Eisenhower administration. According to his son's blog, *Herbork*, J. Edgar Hoover's FBI raided his home after he quit. Finding nothing incriminating, even in the family safe, they had to admit he was clean. Borkland joined a law firm, where he led a successful though unpublicized life. Even his claim to fame, inventing the disclaimer on television shows for his client, ABC, and "The Untouchables," is relatively unknown.

This largely Harvard Law School team was likely the result of the Felix Frankfurter pipeline to the New Deal. With their relative youth and enthusiasm, they became known as Frankfurter's "hot dogs." By the late 1930s, they and other lawyers were the lifeblood of the larger, permanent, and pervasive bureaucracy FDR had bequeathed to the nation. Though they were joined by economists like John Kenneth Galbraith, foreign relations graduates, and other social scientists, the lawyers occupied a special place, particularly in law enforcement. Oddly enough, even J. Edgar Hoover's Bureau of Investigation became the Federal Bureau of Investigation under FDR, and many of its agents who were carrying out illegal surveillance, wiretapping, and blackmail were lawyers.

This special team of lawyers' brief for the government in *Schechter* defended its case on all fronts. As one might expect, they took the exact opposite position from the Schechters' brief. Note that, like the appellants, they used the *Nebbia* standard of review—the rational basis test—throughout. Again, the rational basis test (as it would later be known) requires a legitimate objective plus a reasonable means of achieving that objective. It is not necessarily a demanding standard, but a skeptical court can find it sufficient for its purposes.

The commerce power section attempted to prove that the Schechters' operation was not the little, local kosher business its lawyers portrayed, but in fact played a major role in an incredibly significant national market based in New York City. Their hundreds of chickens came from far afield. The industry in which they participated spread its wings far and wide. What happened in New York's metropolitan area poultry businesses reverberated around the country. Most importantly, if the national government allowed the Schechters to undercut, cheat, and otherwise defeat the recovery measures of the NIRA, the entire effort to save the national economy might fail. There could be no greater impact of interstate commerce than that. In short, the government argued for an impact theory for the interpretation of the interstate commerce clause. It did not matter that the business sold entirely to local merchants, or that it slaughtered only locally. It affected interstate commerce immensely.

In the same way, the government lawyers also took on the Second Circuit's voiding of the wages and hours restrictions. In addition to the decision in *Lochner*, which concerned a state's ability to limit hours and regulate working conditions, they had to contend with *Hammer v. Dagenhart*, a 1918 case in which the Supreme Court, through an opinion by Justice William R. Day, voided the Keating-Owen Act. The act had prohibited the sale, via interstate commerce, of any goods manufactured using child labor. Day and seven other justices declared that manufacturing of cloth, the item in this case, was not "commerce" and, therefore, only the states could regulate it under the requirements of the Tenth Amendment. The Justice Department contended that, unlike the Keating-Owen Act in *Hammer*, the NIRA overtly targeted activities that "burdened, obstructed, or diminished the flow of interstate commerce" as opposed to child labor states harming non–child labor states.

The non-delegation section of the government's brief took its cues from the failed position and the Court's instructions in the *Panama Refining* case. Instead of some vague standard stating one should do what was right and good, the brief emphasized the clauses of the NIRA that held the president to specific goals, measures, and processes. The government lawyers detailed the origins of the poultry code, the Department of Agriculture's review, the NRA's evaluation, and, finally, the president's certification of the code. Everyone's signature, attestation, and assurance that they had performed their duties conscientiously reinforced the impression of a thorough, rigorous, and determinative system for achieving Congress's purpose. What more could any court want than a great many signed and stamped documents asserting that the machinery had produced its best product?

The final section of the government's brief refuted the appellants' contention that the indictments, charges, and trial rulings violated due process. They devoted very little space to these points, relatively speaking; however, it was important to do so. Topics left out of the brief are almost always conceded to the other side. It is a fundamental rule of lawyering. If you do not object, you cannot complain about it later. Only in extremely rare circumstances will a court rule in your favor on a point you did not raise. The later Warren Court, from 1953 until 1969, gained that reputation, and commentators later accused them of judicial activism—an improper use of judicial power to achieve objectives assigned to the political branches (the executive and legislature). On any one of the appellants' contentions, the Court might well declare the trial void, especially based on the idea that the judge erred in his instructions to the jury, which is a vital part of any trial by jury. The government's attorneys wisely did not take any chances.

One additional characteristic of the government brief deserves mentioning. In addition to a very long list of cases cited, the government's brief used quite a few Department of Labor and other reports relevant to the overall purpose of the NIRA and the poultry industry in the New York metropolitan area. It was not as many as the social science briefs in other cases, which Justice Louis D. Brandeis had pioneered as a lawyer in the *Muller v. Oregon* (1908) case. Brandeis had used a tremendous amount of data to show the unique vulnerability of women workers in industry. In *Muller* he used that data to argue for protecting women by limiting their working hours and regulating the conditions under which they worked. This was in direct contravention of the Court's decision in *Lochner*. Yet, the government brief's use of these reports helped their position immensely.

A disputatious person might object to the government introducing factual evidence in their appellate brief given that the time to introduce facts is in trial court and before a jury or, in the case of legislation, for legislatures to decide. But, as Brandeis had shown in *Muller*, parties could produce factual evidence related to their legal arguments that were not at issue at trial, but were preserved when the Hellers had objected to the NIRA on constitutional grounds and the prosecutors had maintained its legitimacy. The bar on additional evidence does not apply to the appellate stage's consideration of the legal issues, items that a jury may not determine.

The Justices of the *Schechter* Court

There is a common teaching in law schools, to this day, which was prevalent in law schools, the bar, and the bench during the time of *Schechter*, that Supreme Court justices' personal histories are not very relevant to the decisions they make. Judges rule based on the requirements of law, whatever their preferences, politics, or life experiences. While this may seem bizarre to people today, who contest the nomination of certain justices by pounding on the walls of the Court or confronting US senators outside their offices or in corridors or restaurants, the belief system behind judges' neutrality was of long standing, dating back to the common law roots of American law in England. Historians of the Supreme Court long ago came to a general consensus that this is an exaggeration if not false. The justices' politics, backgrounds, and circumstances are likely very important to how they approach, examine, and decide cases as well as how they interact with each other in conference and outside of the conference where they discuss, then vote on cases.

We have already met Justice Cardozo. He was appointed to the Court in 1932 by President Hoover. The other justices and brief biographies follow in order of their appointment to the Court. President William Howard Taft nominated Willis Van Devanter from Wyoming in 1911, and he served until 1937. Although a lawyer for railroads, he defied easy characterization as a tool of establishment interests. While on the Court, his voting record veered from anti-regulation to pro-regulation, a supporter of civil rights to one skeptical of civil rights legislation, and a conservative to a liberal. His only definable characteristic was his comparative lack of authorship of opinions, either for the majority, or, in rare cases, in dissent. Brandeis commented that he contributed substantially behind the scenes, but that is hard to discern by its very nature.

Justice McReynolds was less of an enigma, but his notorious anti-Semitism; "boorish" behavior, according to Chief Justice William Howard Taft; and general unlikability do not commend him to posterity. (No justices or former justices of the Court attended his funeral in a tremendous break from tradition.) President Woodrow Wilson nominated him to the Court in 1914 on the basis of his service as attorney general, although some believed it was to promote him out of the cabinet. Given McReynolds's later record as a staunch conservative, commentators often wonder whether Wilson blundered. Though this might be true, one should also remember that Wilson's "progressivism" often took the form of a states' rights Democratic conservativism. After all, it was Wilson who segregated the executive branch and reportedly described the movie *The Birth of a Nation*, a demonstrably false retelling of Reconstruction, which glorified the Klan, as "history writ with lightning." Justice McReynolds held to this end of Wilsonian "progressivism" with two notable exceptions: his majority opinions in *Meyer v. Nebraska* (1923) and *Pierce v. Society of Sisters* (1925). Both upheld minority rights against legislative majorities, though he heavily relied on economic rights for his views. Otherwise, he was a reliably conservative, if not reactionary, vote against civil, individual, or public rights.

Wilson's next pick for the Court, in 1916, garnered long-term acclaim but short-term controversy: his Jewish adviser for the "New Freedom" campaign in 1912, Louis D. Brandeis. Those senators, and the American Bar Association, who opposed the nomination, criticized Brandeis's supposed radicalism, lack of judicial experience, and lack of a "judicial temperament" as a prominent litigator for progressive causes. What they may have meant was that he was Jewish. Eventually, sanity prevailed (Wilson provided strong support), and progressive Democrats and moderate Republicans confirmed the first Jewish justice. Brandeis's stunning achievements as a student at Harvard Law School and his New Freedom accomplishments at the bar foretold his massive contributions to American law.

In his early years on the Court, sometimes with the aid of Justice Oliver Wendell Holmes Jr., Brandeis championed privacy rights, political liberties, and protections for minorities. Quietly, he aided the Civil Rights Movement, advanced progressive causes, and, through his clerks, created a coterie of successors great and small, mostly from Harvard Law School, including Professor Felix Frankfurter. Importantly, though, his progressivism centered around the states as "laboratories of democracy," leading him to be skeptical of the hastily constructed New Deal, especially the NIRA, while his jurisprudence emphasized judicial restraint rather than activism. Frankfurter reported that in the summer of 1933 Brandeis had said to him: "Our Court will apparently be confronted, in a time of greatest need of help, with a Department of Justice as incompetent as was that of Mitchell Palmer." (A reminder: A. Mitchell Palmer was attorney general toward the end of Woodrow Wilson's presidency and became infamous for his "Palmer Raids" during the first Red Scare—prosecution and persecution of the far left at the close of World War I and just afterward.)

The next justice appointed to the Court, George Sutherland, came from the frontier politics of Utah. His law career, as it did for many, led to politics, first as a member of the inaugural state legislature, then the House of Representatives, then the Senate. All the while he established a record as a progressive Republican. After the Seventeenth Amendment commanded the direct election of senators, he returned to private practice, with a stint as president of the American Bar Association and adviser to the State Department for the International Conference on the Limitation of Naval Armaments in the Harding administration. His

{ *Chapter Three* }

former colleague, Warren G. Harding, nominated him to the Court in 1922. Though grouped with the conservative bloc, he voted with them less consistently than others in that group. On occasion he supported progressive legislation, restraints on government power, and basic civil rights.

Harding also nominated, and the Senate overwhelmingly confirmed, Pierce Butler, a devout Roman Catholic from Minnesota, whose parents were Irish immigrants. He had spent most of his legal career in private practice, representing railroads, with a time as a county prosecutor. Chief Justice Taft and Justice Van Devanter practically recruited him for the Court. With a solid reputation as a former president of the Minnesota State Bar and member of the Board of Regents of the University of Minnesota who campaigned against what he called their "radical" faculty members, he became a solid conservative with several notable exceptions. He dissented in *Buck v. Bell*, *Palko v. Connecticut* (1937), and *Olmstead v. United States* (1928). Justice Holmes suspected his dissent without opinion in *Buck v. Bell* (1927) was due to his religion, while in *Palko* (double jeopardy) and *Olmstead* (federal wiretapping) Butler supported civil rights through the due process clause, although he supported Jim Crow laws. Economic rights were his signature issue, steadfastly defending businesses and businessmen against regulation from either the states or national government. He believed until his death in 1937 that the Constitution enshrined laissez-faire economics.

Harlan Fiske Stone's rise to the Court, then chief justice in 1941, was fairly circuitous. Originally from New Hampshire, he practiced law with the prestigious firm of Sullivan and Cromwell in New York City. He migrated onto the law faculty of Columbia, eventually becoming its dean. President Calvin Coolidge appointed his former Amherst classmate to be attorney general in 1924 in order to clean up the department after the previous Harding appointee. Among Stone's notable reforms was his tapping of a young lawyer by the name of J. Edgar Hoover to head the Bureau of Investigation. After joining the Court in 1925, he disappointed the conservative Coolidge by joining the progressive wing. Apparently, Coolidge had been unaware of Stone's support for legal realism at Columbia and his sharp criticism of Attorney General A. Mitchell Palmer's raids on suspected anarchists during the late Wilson administration.

(Legal realism is a school of jurisprudence that calls for investigations into the human condition using the social sciences as opposed to looking to a traditional, classical jurisprudence.)

In early 1930, President Hoover reappointed Charles Evans Hughes to the Supreme Court, but this time as chief justice. Hughes's first stint on the Court lasted from 1910 to 1916, when he resigned to run for President. He succeeded in gaining the Republican nomination but failed to overcome a late western surge for Wilson's second term. This graduate of Brown University and Columbia Law School and former progressive reform governor of New York returned to private practice in New York City until President Harding appointed him secretary of state. He stayed in that post under Coolidge until 1925, when he retired after successfully negotiating the Naval Arms Limitation Treaty of 1925.

Both as an associate justice and chief justice, Hughes generally joined the progressive wing of the Court. As chief justice, he managed the conference quite well, according to his fellow justices, with the exception of the crisis years, between 1935 and 1937, when the Court splintered into the Four Horsemen of Van Devanter, McReynolds, Sutherland, and Butler against the Three Musketeers of Brandeis, Cardozo, and Stone with the next justice, Owen Roberts, left out. Of the early New Deal, according to Senator Burton K. Wheeler, Hughes remarked: "The laws have been poorly drafted, the briefs have been badly drawn and the arguments have been poorly presented." He went on to declare: "We've had to be not only the Court but we've had to do the work that should have been done by the Attorney General."

Owen Roberts, a graduate of both the University of Pennsylvania and its law school, was Herbert Hoover's second choice for the seat vacated in early March by Justice Edward Terry Stanford. The Senate had voted by a slim majority to reject the first choice, Judge John J. Parker of North Carolina. Parker had disparaged African Americans while campaigning for governor of his home state in 1920 when he called their political participation "a source of evil and danger to both races." The American Federation of Labor had also opposed his nomination for a decision Parker made, while on the Fourth Circuit, against the United Mine Workers. Roberts, who had an unblemished record in private practice, as a district attorney, and as special prosecutor for the Harding administration's

Teapot Dome scandal, was comparatively an easy vote. For those who wanted a consistent jurist for either side of the liberal-conservative divide, Roberts perpetually disappointed. Sometimes he voted in favor of government action, sometimes against.

Hoover's last appointment to the Court filled out its roster for the *Schechter* case with one of the most distinguished jurists of the early twentieth century. Benjamin Cardozo, a descendant of Portuguese Sephardic Jews, had gained his reputation almost entirely during his service on the New York Court of Appeals, the highest court in the New York judicial system. His majority opinion in *Palsgraf v. Long Island Railroad Co.* (1928) is required reading in first-year torts classes for establishing the doctrine of "proximate cause" and "breach of duty" in American negligence law. His outside writings on the law also garnered high acclaim. He cofounded the American Law Institute, an organization responsible for law reform throughout the United States. When Justice Oliver Wendell Holmes Jr. acceded to pressures from his fellow justices to retire at ninety years old, in January of 1932, deans of law schools and much of the American bar called for Hoover to nominate Cardozo to succeed him, even though Cardozo was a Democrat. Hoover did so, and Cardozo joined the liberals after his confirmation in February.

Cardozo's jurisprudence does not adhere to the current divide between liberals and conservatives, which is appropriate given his leanings toward finding a path between political thickets. His concept that the Court's interpretation of the Constitution should go "beyond the experience or the thought of a century ago," in *Home Building & Loan Ass'n v. Blaisdell* (1934), certainly sounds liberal, but his lack of concern for the specifics of Palsgraf's case against the railroad resonates with the conservatives. In other words, Cardozo accepted much of the New Deal's progressivism, but even he believed that there were limits to judicial restraint in the face of a government's infringement of individual rights.

This was the bench that confronted the lawyers in the *Schechter* case. All were born in the preceding century and had come of age before the widespread use of the automobile, electricity, airplanes, and radio. Legal orthodoxy held sway during their youth while the casebook method for law schools that Christopher Columbus Langdell introduced at Harvard Law School had just begun to transform legal education. They were also from an era that did not require law degrees, and three of them (Butler, Cardozo, and Sutherland) did not have them. Governments had only recently undertaken the task of regulating the marketplace with bureaucracies, instituting public utilities, and creating mandatory high school education systems. They now confronted all of these changes, along with a Constitution whose foray into Prohibition had recently ended poorly. For the record, at the time of oral arguments in *Schechter*, Brandeis was seventy-eight years old, McReynolds seventy-three, Butler sixty-nine, Sutherland and Hughes seventy-three, Roberts sixty, Cardozo sixty-four, Stone sixty-two, and Van Devanter seventy-six, for an average age of over sixty-nine and two-thirds years.

Oral Arguments

Oral arguments in *Schechter* began on Thursday, May 2, 1935, at 3:47 p.m. Because the new Supreme Court building was still under construction, they took place where they had since the second half of the nineteenth century, on the floor of the old Senate chamber. With the chief justice in the center chair and the justices alternating on either side based on seniority, they sat on an elevated platform, where they would shake hands with one another before proceeding, with one notable exception. Justice McReynolds refused to shake the hands of or even acknowledge Justices Brandeis and Cardozo. The attorneys addressed the justices at a lectern. A clerk kept the transcript of what was said, and their appearances were timed.

Solicitor General Reed opened for the government. Each side received two hours to present its case, with the government given an additional slot at the end for rebuttal. It took into the next day to finish. Each attorney, Reed followed by Donald Richberg (head of the NRA and former counsel) then Joseph Heller and Frederick Wood, had time to present their key arguments before the justices peppered them with questions. Chief Justice Hughes kept the time and let the lawyers know how much time they had left if they asked. The initial presentation of each did not vary from the briefs. It became very clear from the justices' questions what the key issues were.

Reed attempted to forestall any concerns about whether Schechter

Poultry engaged in interstate commerce and the lack of requirements in the NIRA for the codes with a detailed recitation about the importance of the New York poultry market. It set the standard for the country, and the Schechters' code violations undermined the "fair competition" goal of the act. The justices, starting with Brandeis, began and ended their questions on those two topics. In summary, they attempted to get Reed to explain how the process for creating the codes had any due process. Could the Schechters object? Did the poultry association who wrote the code have anything resembling representation? Did the code provisions themselves detail how they were related to interstate commerce? Did the Schechters engage in any interstate commerce transactions? Last, and certainly not least, did anything in the NIRA bind the president in the promulgation of these codes?

Reed withstood the questioning, which lasted throughout the day and into the next fairly well, though he admitted afterward the justices had grilled him without mercy. The only justice not to ask any pointed questions was Chief Justice Hughes, who merely asked for clarification on certain sections of the NIRA in order to help Sutherland, who struggled to find the enforcement section. Reed, and the government brief he was responsible for presenting, wanted to analogize the NIRA's regulatory apparatus to either the Sherman Anti-Trust Act or the Federal Trade Commission. There were several Supreme Court cases, including *Local 187* for the New York poultry market, that upheld those laws, thus offering safe harbor for the NIRA. Unfortunately, the justices very quickly made him admit the NIRA lacked the part of the anti-trust laws that restricted interstate conspiracy, and the Federal Trade Commission had an apparatus to make determinations under the standard explicitly set by Congress in the enabling statute. After all, "fair trade" had no definition in law, unlike "unfair trade."

Richberg's presentation did not fare any better. Strangely enough, he decided to stick with his and Johnson's idea that the US economy needed sorting in order to emerge from the Great Depression. Trade associations, a.k.a. syndicates, had to replace the chaos of the market with standards the government enforced so that individual businesses could not undercut the syndicates with lower prices, lower wages, longer hours, or, in the case of poultry, practices like non-straight killing. Diseased poultry, especially, harmed the entire industry. Businesses like the Schechters' needed to adapt or, if they could not, die. After his effort to make syndicalism sound consistent with precedent, the justices tried to pin him down on whether anything in the NIRA bound the president.

Richberg had to walk a fine line with this presentation. After all, it was his agency, the NRA, that had produced these codes while he was counsel. On facts and figures, he, like Reed, had become a master. Unfortunately, that had very little to do with either how the poultry association had written the code or whether anyone else had evaluated its compliance with any kind of standard. Was there anything beyond assertion that the poultry code did what it was supposed to do? Was there any real check on the president's authority? Was there anything beyond the president's word: a hearing, a finding, or an investigation? Could the president create a code on his own or not approve an association's code regardless of the results of the fact-finding? Richberg tried to argue that "may" was "must," but he could not pull off that piece of legal legerdemain.

With that strange exchange complete, Heller presented his section of the oral argument, focusing on the defects at trial, the overreach of the code, and the lack of accountability in the overall process. This was the part of the oral argument in which the appellants tried to deploy decisive details to undermine the government's case. As Heller described it, the NRA agents' undercover operation to reveal sick chickens resulted in three autopsies with only one bird being "egged." Although he used a flurry of Supreme Court and lower court precedents during his presentation, the justices simply could not get over the nitty gritty details of the code's effects on his clients' business.

Straight killing proved to be an especially difficult topic. Justice McReynolds attempted to delve into how exactly one was to "straight kill." Heller did his best to explain how live chickens were transported in wooden coops, that half a coop (roughly twenty to thirty chickens) was the smallest division, and how the chickens were straight killed. Ultimately, Justices Stone and Sutherland intervened to try to understand the standard or make fun of it. One cannot tell from the transcript. There was occasional laughter during this line of questioning, particularly when Sutherland asked: "Well suppose, however, that all the chickens have gone over to one side of the coop?" Behind the joking, McReynolds did get Heller to relate that his clients had received a hefty fine and been sentenced to jail for selling chickens in violation of the code in a sting operation.

Without any joviality at all, Wood's presentation hammered down that this was neither interstate commerce nor a proper delegation of congressional authority. He concentrated on the wages and hours provision, but the argument encompassed wider issues. Taking the exact same cases Reed and Richberg had used to buttress their positions, Wood distinguished and analogized to fit his narrative of a piece of legislation out of control. Moreover, he noted that, contrary to Richberg's presentation, the NIRA was far from a necessary exertion of federal authority. Like the government's attorneys, he cited James Madison's *Federalist Papers*. Why they belonged in the argument is not clear. They were not law themselves, only federalist advocacy intended to convince members of the New York ratification convention to vote for the new Constitution.

The supposed limited nature of the national government and its reliance on the states to do much of the work of government, on which Wood relied, was close to orthodoxy in the pre–Civil War years. Both Lincoln and the secessionists believed in a limited federal government under the Constitution. (The difference was whether states could secede from the Union.) Nationalists like Alexander Hamilton had in mind something very different, of course, as did Chief Justice John Marshall (1801–1835). After the Civil War, the old Constitution's ideal lingered on in the Gilded Age and Progressive Era, in what eminent legal historian William Wiecek called "legal orthodoxy" or "classical legal thought." It upheld laissez-faire doctrines, which hobbled legislatures in their quest to closely regulate the marketplace. FDR's New Deal was the latest threat to this old world of jurisprudence. Wood's fervent advocacy went beyond those doctrines, however, as he summarized: "If, as many believe, the Federal Government should be converted into some form of National Socialism—whether Soviet, Fascist, or Nazi—it may be accomplished only by the submission of a constitutional amendment.... It may not be made by an act of Congress."

Oral argument concluded with Solicitor General Reed's rebuttal. He used it in order to clarify the code approval process. It went as well as it had before. Justice Butler interrogated Reed mercilessly on the NIRA's standards, or lack thereof, for the approval of a code. Reed did his best to cite the clauses governing the creation of a code, but he ultimately fell back on his earlier position, and Richberg's presentation, that somehow having a process without any restrictions constituted sufficient process for a federal law. At the end, Justice McReynolds finished the question by having Reed assert that the president "may" act was actually "must." It was a sour note to end his defense of the NIRA, but he had run out of time. It was 4:10 p.m. on Friday, May 3, 1935.

The Opinions

Chief Justice Hughes read the opinion for the unanimous Court in *A.L.A. Schechter Poultry Corp. v. U.S.* on May 27, 1935, after the other two cases, on what the FDR administration called "Black Monday." There is some suggestion that Hughes was offering the parties a lesson in how to draft legislation. Historian Barry Cushman suggests this possibility in his study of the case. In this case, as in *Panama*, "the problem was not irredeemable." When serving as governor of New York, Hughes had a hand in crafting some of its progressive legislation. In any case, he began with a recitation of facts taken almost entirely from the government's brief. It contained one statement of fact that proved deadly to the government's case: "Defendants do not sell poultry in interstate commerce." He also laid out, with appropriate quotations, the provisions of the NIRA involved, the nature of the poultry business in the New York metro area, the Schechters' operations, and the charges they faced. Although one would think the fact pattern of the case is the least important part of the Court's decision, it can be the only important part. On occasion, one factual determination can determine the case's outcome.

His opinion's first major finding ended the FDR administration's hopes that the national emergency would give them leeway. "Extraordinary conditions do not create or enlarge constitutional power," Hughes stated. Moreover, "Such assertions of extra-constitutional authority were anticipated and precluded by the explicit terms of the Tenth Amendment." What he meant was that federalism, the balance between the states and the national government, mattered. Hughes did not cite any authority for this reading of the original intent of the Tenth Amendment. One can surmise he believed the language of the amendment signified its intent sufficiently. Given that the NIRA and the FDR administration's entire approach to the Great Depression required extraordinary powers, this blew up a large part of their case. And Hughes had only begun.

The chief justice also stipulated that the codes the NRA adopted were "codes of law." They were not voluntary. They were coercive, with fines and punishments for noncompliance. They were "punishable as crimes." The violations were in fact crimes per the statute itself. The other curious matter that springs to mind is what would have happened if the statute had stated that the would-be "codes" were "regulations." Did Congress undermine its case before the Court by using the wrong verbiage? In William Shakespeare's *Romeo and Juliet*, we get the question of whether "a rose by any other name would smell just as sweet." In *Schechter*, we get the question of whether a code is a code by any other name. However, the Court did not explain its answer further.

The opinion next turned to the non-delegation doctrine, with *Panama Refining* as its most recent benchmark. The test it cited was Congress "laying down policies and establishing standards, while leaving to selected instrumentalities the making of subordinate rules within prescribed limits and the determination of facts to which the policy as declared by the legislature is to apply." In other words, Congress needed to specify its objectives, the means to achieve them, and the scope of the law. It could not be vague or overly broad. While Hughes and the Court may have thought this circumscribed congressional authority, it left a lot vague and indeterminate. How much of a standard? What level of review? How much detail did Congress need to give? In the end, the only safe conclusion was that the NIRA did not pass the test.

Hughes then dispensed with the government's analogy to the Federal Trade Commission Act's outlawing of "unfair trade practices." The FTC carried out the investigation and determination as a "quasi-judicial" body. The NRA had no such procedures. Yet, even if Congress had given it such a procedure, the Hughes Court found that the very idea of giving trade associations code-making authority contravened the Constitution's division of labor into separate executive and legislative areas. "Such a delegation of legislative power is unknown to our law and is utterly inconsistent with the constitutional prerogatives and duties of Congress." The government had failed to convince the Court of the procedural and substantive safeguards of the NIRA.

The next target for the opinion was the unfettered discretion the

NIRA gave the president. First, it took issue with "the finding" the president was to make: "While this is called a finding, it is really but a statement of an opinion as to the general effect upon the promotion of trade or industry of a scheme of laws." It then noted that the president could make codes with or without a trade association, did not need administrative agency support, and was free to not have a code at all. In conclusion, "Such a sweeping delegation of legislative power finds no support in the decisions upon which the Government especially relies." Neither the Interstate Commerce Commission, the Tariff Act of 1927, or any other case gave such discretion. "Section 3 of the Recovery Act is without precedent." Without restrictions other than a general exhortation to help the economy, the executive branch could do whatever it wanted. In conclusion, "We think that the code-making authority thus conferred is an unconstitutional delegation of legislative power." Under the non-delegation doctrine, which separated the judicial, legislative, and executive functions among the three branches, the unanimous Court ruled the NIRA, section 3, unconstitutional, thus null and void. Even though they could have stopped there, the Court was still not done.

Hughes's opinion proceeded to dismantle the government's interstate commerce contentions. Disregarding the flow of poultry into the New York metro area and its influence on the nationwide poultry market, the Court concluded: "The undisputed facts thus afford no warrant for the argument that the poultry handled by defendants at their slaughterhouse markets was in 'current' or 'flow' of interstate commerce and was thus subject to congressional regulation." Apparently, wages and hours restrictions for a slaughterhouse that deals in poultry shipped from the rest of the country was too local for the Court. Inflow was not enough. There had to be outflow as well: "the flow in interstate commerce had ceased. The poultry had come to a permanent rest within the State." They made a distinction from the prior rulings. There had to be both inflow and outflow for the activity at issue.

In addition, the Hughes Court ruled that the "effect" on interstate commerce or "affected interstate commerce" was insufficient to warrant the hours and wages restrictions. To do this, the opinion referenced the distinction prior courts had made between "direct" and "indirect" effects. They did so ostensibly to preserve the balance between the states and the national government. "Otherwise, as we have said, there would be virtually no limit to the federal completely centralized government." Under the present Court's analysis, "Their [the Schechters'] hours and wages have no direct relation to interstate commerce." In their view, the government's arguments would lead to discretionary control over the entire economy, both national and intrastate. "It is not the province of the Court to consider the economic advantages or disadvantages of such a centralized system. It is sufficient to say that the Federal Constitution does not provide for it." The Hughes Court stated its intention to hold the line on expansive national power. Therefore, they found the hours and wages provision unconstitutional. Wood's contribution to the Schechters' case had done its job.

Finally, the rest of the violations collided with the interstate commerce clause's limitations. They were "intrastate transactions." The Court voided them all as unconstitutional. At one swoop, the Court dismantled the NRA, a key pillar of the First New Deal. Once again, it was a unanimous Court with an opinion by the chief justice of the United States. They had reinforced traditional doctrines against the New Dealers' experimentation. They would hold the line against the president and Congress. Alone, this blow to the FDR administration constituted an enormous defeat, but it had come with two other cases that ruled FDR and Congress had violated the Constitution. This was an incredibly risky play if they intended to eliminate all innovations rather than just hastily drafted ones.

In addition to the opinion of the Court, which Hughes authored, Justice Cardozo wrote a concurring opinion with Justice Stone joining, which elaborated on certain points not in disagreement with the rest of the Court in terms of the outcome but clarifying his and Stone's distinct views of the law. While the concurring opinion would not have the force of law like the majority opinion, Cardozo did have a chance in his concurrence to make an official contribution for future Courts to consider. In this instance, he and Stone wanted to repeat their disagreement with the Hughes Court's decision in *Panama Refining*, the "hot oil case" involving section 7 of the NIRA. Precisely, "I thought that ruling went too far."

Cardozo agreed with the rest of the Court that section 3 violated the non-delegation doctrine. Using a metaphor, which he frequently and notably did, he wrote: "The delegated power of legislation which has found expression in this code is not canalized within banks that keep it from overflowing." However, rather than give a "standard, definite or even approximate," he preferred to prescribe a process, like a commission ascertaining the facts then judging them against the requirements of the law. The key flaw for Cardozo was that acts like that establishing the Federal Trade Commission banned specific practices as "unfair trade" instead of asking the executive branch to determine what constituted "fair trade." "The extension becomes as wide as the field of industrial regulation." In other words, "This is delegation running riot." Thus, we have what is permissible, banning a practice and allowing a commission to determine what specifically constitutes the banned practice, and what is not, giving the executive branch blanket authority to determine how all businesses are to be run in the United States.

Cardozo offered a distinction between the harsher standard of the Hughes Court and his more tolerant, flexible one. The poultry code's "comprehensive body of rules" had within it the straight killing command, which was "not unethical or oppressive." And this was only one example. The inescapable conclusion was: "What is excessive is not sporadic or superficial. It is deep-seated and pervasive." Like Hughes's opinion, Cardozo did not stop there.

He also found the NIRA's wages and hours provision exceeded Congress's power to regulate interstate commerce under Article I, Section 8. He found the government's expansive view unsustainable. "Activities local in their immediacy do not become interstate and national because of distant repercussions." Apparently, the government's detailing of the New York metropolitan area's importance to the nationwide industry did not convince Cardozo and Stone when it came to the Schechters' local sales operation. Cardozo used the phrase "penumbra of uncertainty obscuring judgment" to describe a situation when an expansive reading would be permissible. ("Penumbra" would later play an important role in *Griswold v. Connecticut* [1965] in defining privacy rights like access to contraception and, later, abortion rights in *Roe v. Wade* [1973]).

Cardozo proceeded to determine whether the wages and hours provision was severable from the rest of the legislation. According to the rules of statutory interpretation, courts should not only defer to legislatures' intent but should try to preserve the legislation as much as possible. They should void only the offending clause rather than the whole legislation unless the clause's removal destroys the legislation. Cardozo with

Stone argued that: "Wages and the hours of labor are essential features of the plan, its very bone and sinew." Therefore, "There is no opportunity in such circumstances for the severance of the infected parts in the hope of saving the remainder. A code collapses utterly with bone and sinew gone." With the gruesome metaphor completed, he could void the entirety of section 3, effectively the entire NIRA. Though differing in certain specifics, Cardozo and Stone joined the rest of the Court in eliminating the signature legislation of the First New Deal.

Aftermath

A.L.A. Schechter Poultry Corp. et al. v. United States' implications could not have been clearer. With section 3 null and void as unconstitutional, the codes disappeared. Without any codes to enforce, the NRA also had to disappear. The prosecutions of violators ceased. The Schechters no longer faced fines and imprisonment. Congress had to abandon the renewal of the NIRA and start over from the beginning, if it wanted to do so. The FDR administration had to accept a total defeat in addition to the NIRA's failure to end the Great Depression.

The NIRA's supporters decried the decision while their opponents celebrated. Richberg and Johnson called for a new and improved law. Industries like the poultry association in New York City overwhelmingly supported some kind of replacement. Organized labor wanted the wages and hours restrictions to be enacted in a fashion that would avoid a successful constitutional challenge. There was still a reservoir of support for New Deal solutions, especially the Public Works Administration (PWA) part of the NIRA, that the Court now might seem to threaten. For the New Dealers, the war continued in spite of the battle lost.

As for the defendants and litigants who gave their names to the case, they faded into obscurity. The *New York Times* reprinted the brothers' statement through their lawyer, Joseph Heller: "We feel most happy to be able to say that the highest court of this land has definitely stated that we are not guilty of any misconduct in business." Further, "We always claimed that the Code Authority attempted to make us the 'goat.'" They closed on a high note. "Our victory indicates that American justice does not permit persecution." However, Joseph Schechter, according to the

Times, was not celebrating. They owed $60,000 in legal fees and could only pay $22,000. Their business had suffered terribly. Very soon afterward, their business disappeared. The brothers went their separate ways after having declared bankruptcy. Though supporters of FDR and the Democrats, it did not save them from the destruction of the Great Depression.

What remained to be seen was the Court's response to the rest of the New Deal and the additional enactments that came to be known as the Second New Deal. Would they handle those as roughly as they did the NIRA? As yet, FDR had had no appointments to the Supreme Court. Maybe there was something he could do about that. He denounced the decisions of "Black Monday" as antiquated jurisprudence, inadequate to the task, and inappropriate for the present times. In a widely quoted press conference on May 31, 1935, FDR addressed the *Schechter* decision. He completely ignored the non-delegation aspect of the case in favor of painting the interpretation of the interstate commerce clause in stark terms. "We have been relegated to the horse-and-buggy definition of interstate commerce." Roosevelt's worries were well grounded. In case after case, although not in every case, a majority of the Court found fault with more of the First New Deal enactments.

Coal

On May 18, 1935, the Supreme Court voided another New Deal law. The US Congress passed and President Roosevelt signed into law the Guffey-Snyder Bituminous Coal Conservation Act of 1935, on August 30, 1935, to replace the coal code the Court had eliminated with its destruction of section 3 of the NIRA in *Schechter*. As with all the other codes, the Guffey-Snyder Act attempted to rescue the coal industry with uniform practices, price controls, and wages and hours requirements. Unlike the poultry code in *Schechter*, though, the Guffey-Snyder Act had a commission, a process for unionization, and a tax to be assessed by the Internal Revenue Service to encourage participation and fund the subsidy. In theory, these provisions addressed the defects in the NIRA.

The reasons for the act are readily apparent. At this time, coal was an essential fuel for industry, generating electricity and heating a large number of homes and public buildings. Its use had led the Industrial Revolution in the United States as well as the rest of the world. Several US states had substantial coal mines, and the United Mine Workers was the most powerful union in one of the most fractious, occasionally violent labor sectors in the US economy. On both sides of the political aisle, coal had powerful political sponsors. As much as oil, the US ran on coal. If any industry could be considered a national one with an underlying national interest in its well-being, it was coal. In a 5–4 decision, the US Supreme Court disagreed.

Writing for the Court, Justice Sutherland voided the entire act. After disposing of the objection to a stockholder bringing a lawsuit before the legislation had fully taken effect, Sutherland declared that the tax "is clearly not a tax, but a penalty." Therefore, it was not intended to raise revenue, only to compel compliance with the code. Then he affirmed a test for whether the means to achieve the legitimate objective was constitutional: "They must be appropriate plainly adapted to the end, and not prohibited by, but consistent with, the letter and spirit of the Constitution." In other words, "Thus, it may be said that, to a constitutional end, many ways are open, but to an end not within the terms of the Constitution, all ways are closed." Knowing Sutherland's conservative views, the act was unlikely to meet this test.

Sutherland cited a wealth of precedents from the nineteenth century as well as "the Framers' Convention" for the sharply circumscribed national government on which he based the opinion. The states were supreme in their realm; the national government was limited to its specified list. Federalism ruled the day. The government's argument in favor of the act, if taken to its natural endpoint, would "reduce them [the states] to little more than geographical subdivisions of the national domain." Importantly, the Supreme Court had the duty to nullify any law that violated the Constitution. He had finally arrived at the interstate commerce clause—the object of his reasoning and, because of that reasoning, the only source of legitimacy for the legislation.

Through Sutherland's opinion, the Court limited commerce to "intercourse for the purpose of trade." It revived the case law that had reached its apogee in *E. C. Knight* in which the late-nineteenth-century Court had exempted manufacturing from the Sherman Anti-Trust Act of 1890 because it was not "commerce." Although they recognized that almost every activity in the modern economy involved interstate commerce, the Fuller Court concluded: "Nevertheless, the local character of mining, of manufacturing and of crop growing is a fact, and remains a fact, whatever may be done with the products." This was what FDR had called "horse and buggy" jurisprudence.

To deal with the government's argument that the coal industry was vital to the nation and, therefore, labor peace within it was a legitimate object of interstate commerce, Sutherland's opinion revived the "indirect" versus "direct" distinction. If the effects were the direct result of the industry's activity, then it would count as interstate commerce. If the effects were secondary or incidental, they were indirect and not interstate commerce. "An increase in the greatness of the effect adds to its importance. It does not alter its character." In a 5–4 decision, the Court found coal mining to be local and not subject to the interstate commerce clause.

Citing the *Schechter* case, the majority voided the wages and hours provision along with the entire act because they also found compulsory enforcement, only this time it was part of a subsidy program. "To 'accept,' in these circumstances, is not to exercise a choice, but to surrender to force." Further, "the power conferred upon the majority is, in effect, the power to regulate the affairs of an unwilling minority." The opinion concluded: "This is legislative delegation in its most obnoxious form, for it is not even delegation to an official or an official body, presumptively disinterested, but to private persons whose interests may be and often are adverse to the interests of others in the same business." The Court had taken a stand against cartels on the basis of individual liberty. This is known as economic rights, though the distinction between this and civil rights is often debated. In the former, the power to destroy one's livelihood, the wherewithal for living, is very much a deprivation of liberty.

Sutherland's opinion completed its review of the coal act with an examination of the wage and hours provisions' severability from the rest of the law's regulation of pricing. To no one's surprise, he found an inextricable link in both the congressional intent and the nature of the act's goal of "stabilizing" the industry. "The interdependence of wages and prices is manifest." They were not like "bricks" that could be taken out without damaging the wall. They were "like the interwoven threads constituting the warp and woof of a fabric." We can guess from context that the metaphors have something to do with the integrity of the material. Thus, the Four Horsemen plus Justice Roberts voided the Guffey-Snyder Act as unconstitutional.

Chief Justice Hughes voted with the majority, though he submitted a separate opinion. Apparently, he did so because he agreed with the Sutherland opinion except in one area: Congress's ability to set prices for bituminous coal. In Hughes's view, that aspect of the law should have survived judicial review. Therefore, the majority went too far in invalidating the entire legislation. If that were not enough, he relied on Congress's own declaration that the law was separable if any part of it were held "invalid." This reader is not sure whether Hughes was serious about this. What if Congress had stated that the legislation was completely consistent with interstate commerce jurisprudence? That it was not intended to overrule the Court's previous decisions? Since when did Congress's statement of its intent bind the Court in its opinion of what they had actually done?

Nevertheless, Hughes found that the very structure of the act supported the severability of the odious wage and hours measure from the other elements. After all, Congress had put them in different sections. They had different topics. They existed independently of one another. He rejected the Sutherland opinion's notion that all provisions were interwoven. They were part of the same industry and, even though the act stated it needed all of its provisions to accomplish its objective, they were not mutually dependent in Hughes's view.

Cardozo wrote a dissent for himself, Brandeis, and Stone on behalf of a much broader construction of the interstate commerce power. He disagreed with the majority on all counts. The suit was premature because there had been no penalty yet. The coal industry was well within the interstate commerce clause's authority to regulate. Price fixing was a legitimate use of congressional authority. The provisions of the act were severable. The majority had overreached and should have deferred to the political branches. Cardozo cited *Schechter* for the concept that non-commercial activities could be classified as interstate commerce if their "relation to that commerce may be such that, for the protection of the one, there is need to regulate the other." This more expansive reading of government power constituted the key difference between the two wings of the Court.

Cardozo's next task was to make the conditions in the coal industry of national importance. To do this, he described it in the following terms: "Overproduction was at a point where free competition had been degraded into anarchy." Prices had fallen too low. Wages fell as a result. Strikes swept the coal regions. "The hope of betterment was faint unless the industry could be subjected to the compulsion of a code." This was an interesting description of what had happened. The account did not deeply analyze the sequence of events. It did not cite any data. It lacked scientific analysis. It took Congress at its word for what had happened. If Cardozo had used any of the economic theories available at the time, he would have rejected this tale of overproduction. The Depression had happened first. Overproduction resulted from the lack of demand.

As for a code being the only solution, Cardozo and the dissenters distinguished between the present situation and the previous history of the bituminous coal industry. Like any other industry, it had a cycle of boom and bust punctuated by the introduction of new technologies that altered the economics of the industry. There had been times in the past, such as during World War I, when there had been calls for a government-enforced cartel. Though experiments abroad had recently popularized the idea, nothing mandated its use. In the view of Cardozo and the dissenters, this was "necessity," not congressional expediency. Once again, present-day considerations prevailed over prior precedents' concern with a more traditional view of the spirit of the Constitution. They cited *Nebbia* to support a price fixing regime but purposefully avoided the fact that *Nebbia* concerned a state government, not the national government. It was an important distinction in a federal system, yet one they wanted to avoid for the sake of judicial restraint.

Cardozo and the dissenters also held the provisions of the act to be entirely voluntary. The boards were independent decision-makers like the FCC. Everyone was free to assemble and speak their mind. They could freely participate or not. "No threat has been made by anyone to do violence to the enjoyment of these immunities and privileges." Being excluded from the code's cartel and, thus, at a debilitating disadvantage leading to sure ruin did not constitute a threat, according to the dissenters. Furthermore, the penalties for not complying with the act's collective bargaining requirements were completely appropriate given that violations would be violations of the statute. Because bituminous coal mining was subject to Congress's authority to regulate interstate commerce, Congress could impose collective bargaining on the industry.

Cardozo closed his opinion with the same plain language that he used to dismiss Palsgraf's claims for damages against the railroad whose scale's collapse had left her with permanent damage (*Palsgraf v. Long Island RR* [1928]). "To adopt a homely form of words, the complainants have been crying before they are really hurt." In Justice Cardozo's world, like the Schechters, they should have waited for a more imminent danger and the threat of imprisonment before challenging the national government's plan to rescue the coal industry. It placed a tremendous amount of trust in Congress and the president to experiment before the Court could intervene.

The stage was set for a constitutional crisis. The US Supreme Court confronted the still-popular president and his party's overwhelming majorities in Congress. At least that is the way some observers portrayed it. Political actors tend to paint a picture of a situation with bright colors, vivid contrasts, and simple moral principles. Their side is good, and it is fighting a war with evil. Yet, reality very rarely conforms to those Manichaean dichotomies. Extremism gets people to be passionate, but it seldom proffers reasonable solutions to actual problems. When, in that same press conference of May 31st, FDR compared *Schechter* to the *Dred Scott* decision, a case commonly understood to have led to the US Civil War, the lawyer president probably knew the causes of the Civil War were far more complicated than Chief Justice Roger B. Taney's opinion on whether Dred Scott was still a slave. Yet FDR made the analogy anyway. Sometimes, constitutional crises come to the president. At other times, the constitutional crises are of their own making.

A Kritocracy

On the one hand, the Court's decision in *Schechter* did not deter Congress and the president from their program, striving to use federal legislative and executive power to restructure American life. Indeed, a wave of acts comprising part of the "Second New Deal" appeared even as the Court was striking down the NRA, and it was even more substantive than the first. One might have thought that "Black Monday" meant the end of the US Supreme Court's confrontation with the New Deal. After all, a unanimous Court in *Schechter* had dealt a solid blow to the experiment on the grounds of interstate commerce, the non-delegation doctrine, and a singular commitment to a version of federalism based on states' rights. Decisions in cases that followed showed that *Schechter* was not an anomaly.

According to two New Deal lawyers, Tommy Corcoran and Ben Cohen, Justice Louis D. Brandeis had been even more blunt with them in the robing room after Hughes had read the decision. "This is the end of this business of centralization, and I want you to go back and tell the president that we're not going to let this government centralize everything. It's come to an end." He advised all of the New Deal lawyers to go back to the states. "That is where they must do their work." Brandeis, whose firm belief in each state as a "laboratory" of democracy, as per his dissent in *New State Ice Co. v. Liebmann* (1932), had advanced a progressive agenda, could not have been clearer. Yet this was not the end of the conflict between the Court and the New Deal.

The disagreement over the meaning of the US Constitution during this period was certainly not unique. Yet it did turn out to be one of the most contentious periods—if not the most contentious period. On one side were the Three Musketeers of Brandeis, Cardozo, and Stone, who argued for judicial restraint and a standard of review that gave due deference to the political branches. On the other side were the Four

Horsemen, who insisted on what later scholars termed "economic rights," but what the Four Horsemen understood as basic private rights, as opposed to public rights like free speech. Once the division became extreme, the Three Musketeers and the New Dealers insisted they were on the side of democracy and progress. The Four Horsemen declared themselves the protectors of the Constitution. Their opponents increasingly labeled them reactionary, supporters of rule by judges, in other words "kritocracy" or "kritarchy."

Agriculture

The First New Deal included the Agricultural Adjustment Act of 1933. Similar to the NIRA, the legislation sought to end the Great Depression in agriculture by addressing overproduction. Though hundreds of thousands of Americans were malnourished, and struggled to feed themselves and their families, the New Dealers fervently believed that restricting production was the appropriate solution to the agricultural crisis. In their view, there was too much farmland under cultivation, prices were far too low, and this was causing the downturn. Even though farmland was literally blowing away in the Dust Bowl and the boll weevil was destroying the cotton crop, this remained their plan.

At the same time, FDR and the Democrats were still committed to balancing the budget. They needed a way to finance the payments to farmers to take land out of cultivation and buy any surpluses so they could keep surpluses off the market. The answer came in the form of a tax on the processors of farm produce. Raw grain, cotton, sugar, fruits, and vegetables do not go straight to grocery stores. The vast bulk of it needs to be stored prior to being sorted, treated, and packaged for sale. The middlemen, or businesses that perform this task, are called processors. For example, if the crop was cotton, the mill or the cotton gin owner that turned the raw fiber into usable material would pay the tax. Under the AAA, the Department of Agriculture assessed this tax and used the money to pay farmers for their excess production and/or to leave their land idle, which would raise the price at the ultimate expense of consumers. Unlike the NIRA, the contracts with the farmers were not mandatory, only voluntary.

This crop subsidy plan could help ease the effects of the Great Depression on agriculture, particularly because the AAA had in mind the extremely prosperous years of 1909 to 1914 as the benchmark for the subsidies. Farmers gained their best prices, regardless of market demand, so long as they obeyed the restrictions the Department of Agriculture set up through the AAA. With this additional income for doing less, farmers realized a profit instead of suffering a loss. Their incomes increased. They could use that additional profit either to spend on luxuries or reinvest in their farms with new equipment or better facilities. Unfortunately, the general consumer of agricultural products would pay more, because the processors would pass the tax on to them. This is why the AAA was supposed to work in tandem with the NIRA. With agriculture, commerce, and industry all restricting their production, prices would rise, profits would increase, businesses would hire more, and the economy would recover. It did not work, but it was not for a lack of trying.

On January 6, 1936, in a case argued on the 9th and 10th the preceding December, the US Supreme Court, in an opinion by Justice Owen Roberts, had declared the Agricultural Adjustment Act of 1933 unconstitutional, thus null and void. In his opinion for the Court in *U.S. v. Butler*, Roberts found that the tax was both inseparable from the rest of the law and an "exaction" (tax) for a particular purpose. "The exaction cannot be wrested out of its setting, denominated an excise for raising revenue, and legalized by ignoring its purpose as a mere instrumentality for bringing about a desired end." A second issue was whether Butler had standing to bring the appeal, that is, was he allowed to bring suit as well as showing he had been harmed? Appellee Butler was a cotton processor. The tax harmed his business, according to his lawyers. Therefore, he had standing to sue despite the prohibition on lawsuits concerning general appropriations.

Moreover, Roberts attempted to insulate the Court from the charge that it was assuming the "power to overrule or control the action of the people's representatives." The judiciary was merely rendering "its considered judgment upon the question." It had a duty to interpret the Constitution. As it thwarted the president and Congress, the Court simply compared the law with the Constitution. The Constitution had set up a national government of limited powers. The ability to set up a system of crop subsidies had to come from some clause of the Constitution. On behalf of the Court, Roberts rejected the government's assertion that the Preamble's ability to "provide for the common defense and general welfare" sustained the legislation.

Going further, his opinion for the Court stated that the object—subsidies to farmers—was a local matter. General taxation could not be used to invade a purely intrastate matter. The Tenth Amendment forbade this purpose. One could be legitimately confused as to Roberts's reasoning, but one should note that, because it was solely a tax on processors and not an income tax under the Sixteenth Amendment, the AAA of 1933 had to rely on the Article I taxing power. This, according to Roberts's opinion, corrupted the entire project. Even the voluntary nature of the contracts violated federalism. "The power to confer or withhold unlimited benefits is the power to coerce or destroy," he reasoned.

Roberts did not stop there. The opinion went on to declare that the appropriations power of Congress was limited to constitutional objects. "An affirmance of the authority of Congress so to condition the expenditure of an appropriation would tend to nullify all constitutional limitations upon legislative power." In other words, Congress could not spend on whatever it liked. The purpose had to be constitutional. Even Roberts had to admit that showing standing, the court-granted ability to challenge such an appropriation, would be difficult. Still, the Court, seemingly, had taken a strong stand against what the opinion termed "a central government exercising uncontrolled police power in every state of the Union, superseding all local control or regulation of the affairs or concerns of the states." As for the fact that the US government presently does just that almost entirely through the appropriations power, we will address that later.

Justice Stone, writing for himself, Brandeis, and Cardozo, dissented. As one might have expected, he reversed Roberts's points. The tax served a legitimate purpose. The tax itself was legitimate. Federalism's constraints did not apply. The scheme under the AAA of 1933 was not coercive. The present case was different from the previous cases because it was the spending that affected local affairs, not the tax. Despite the figures showing the incorporation of almost all of the agricultural land, Stone wrote that it was "groundless speculation" to assume coercion. Yet behind the individual points lay a different jurisprudence, one of judicial restraint. "For the removal of unwise laws from the statute books appeal lies not to the courts, but to the ballot and to the processes of democratic government." Justices Stone, Brandeis, and Cardozo urged the Court to defer to Congress and the president but did not specify when that deference would end, yet.

Stone's dissent embraced a flexible reading of the appropriations power on behalf of "the general welfare." "The spending power of Congress is in addition to the legislative power, and not subordinate to it," he reasoned. Rather than limit congressional outlays to specified, a.k.a. enumerated, powers, he made spending the people's money its own activity. As such, it was potentially boundless. As a fan of the cartoon show *The Simpsons*, I am compelled to reference the government-built skyscraper made of popsicle sticks in "Marge v. The Monorail" (Season 4, Episode 12). The giant magnifying glass puts it on fire, and it has an escalator that goes nowhere. In the show's setting, Springfield, USA, these were determined to be legitimate projects. While Roberts recognized only the inability to sue for lack of standing, Stone and the dissenters refused to grant the wrongness of the activity.

Stone's examples attempted to show that the absurdity of the Court majority's limitations ranged widely. For instance, "It [the federal government] may spend its money for the suppression of the boll weevil, but may not compensate the farmers for suspending the growth of cotton in the infected areas." It is difficult to understand why Stone thought a casual observer would find this difference absurd. A government of limited, enumerated powers may not go beyond them even in its appropriations because of the danger of it infringing on the states in a federal system. Not being able to create a nationwide program of removing land from cultivation and, instead, being limited to boll weevil eradication is not a severe constriction on the national government. There had to be something else underlying Stone and the dissenters' desire to thwart the majority in *Butler*.

Stone's opinion centers on judicial restraint far too much for it to be incidental. Rather, judicial restraint appears to be the entirety of the reason for the dissent. Referring to the majority's scenarios of malfeasance, Stone wrote: "Such suppositions are addressed to the mind accustomed to believe that it is the business of courts to sit in judgment on the wisdom of legislative action." The dissenters did not like the so-called *Lochner* Era of the US Supreme Court, in which the Court closely scrutinized legislation and frequently invalidated it as unconstitutional. For them, this was the true threat to the constitutional order. Again, they had not yet formulated when the Court should exercise that authority, but they had begun laying the foundation for a different jurisprudence.

The TVA

What was almost entirely absent from the New Dealers' thinking was the possibility that the Court was not uniformly hostile to the New Deal, nor did the Court's adverse majorities confine themselves to a laissez-faire reading of the interstate commerce clause. *Schechter*, after all, had been unanimous and based substantially on the non-delegation as well as interstate commerce clause. As if to remind everyone of their restraint, the Court issued an 8–1 verdict in favor of the TVA in *Ashwander v. TVA* on February 17, 1936. Chief Justice Hughes wrote an opinion for himself, Sutherland, and Butler, which became the official opinion of the Court. It decided the case on narrow grounds—upholding a contract with the TVA on the basis that the legislation from 1916 and the later law creating the TVA successfully authorized the creation of a government utility company with a reach across much of the southeastern United States. In effect, Congress could do this because it affected navigable interstate waters, an area courts recognized as constitutional.

Unfortunately, Hughes was unable to get the Three Musketeers to join his opinion. Justice Brandeis wrote a concurrence in which Stone, Roberts, and Cardozo joined. They affirmed the decision but denied Hughes a majority of the Court. We do not know their reasons other than what Brandeis wrote. Apparently, Brandeis's opinion announced doctrine so important it overruled the need to give the law a clear reading. The concurrence stated outright that it agreed with Hughes's opinion on every issue except one—Brandeis stated that the Court should not have commented on the constitutional issues at all. Later scholars would refer to Brandeis's extensive argument for deciding the case on procedural grounds rather than constitutional grounds as the "avoidance doctrine." Brandeis and his fellow justices wanted the Court to use the power of judicial review only as a last resort. The presumption, beyond a reasonable doubt, should be that Congress's enactment was constitutional. He warned, "One branch of the government cannot encroach upon the domain of another, without danger. The safety of our institutions depends in no small degree on a strict observance of this salutary rule."

It is a reasonable conclusion that Brandeis and three other justices now argued for judicial restraint in the face of the New Deal's experiment. This was not a new position. Justice Holmes had announced it most infamously in *Buck v. Bell.* Whether it concerned a state government's ability to forcibly sterilize people or the national government's authority to create public utility companies, the US Supreme Court should defer to the legislative branches and the popular will unless it was absolutely necessary to contravene them. Once again, while Brandeis was very clear on his seven rules for "avoidance," he did not specify when the Court would find that government had overstepped the constraints of either its limited powers, in the case of the national government, or basic civil rights, including property rights, in the case of both the national and state governments.

<hr/>

The SEC

On April 6, 1936, a majority of the US Supreme Court again struck down a New Deal act, in *Jones v. SEC.* Justice Sutherland wrote the opinion for himself and the rest of the Court minus the dissenting Three Musketeers. Comparing the action of the SEC in prosecuting Jones, in violation of SEC regulations, to the "star chamber" of England, he maintained that the SEC had exceeded its authority because the statute did not give it that ability. Sutherland's opinion did not touch on the constitutionality of the Securities and Exchange Act of 1934, the agency, or any of its regulations. Though blistering in its denunciation of the SEC's actions, Sutherland's opinion did not threaten this key reform of the public disclosure rules that governed publicly traded corporations.

But the opinion did liken the SEC's actions to that of an "autocracy" and alleged it threatened the rule of law. Sutherland's opinion pointed out that allowing an agency of the government to institute inquiries after the defendant had withdrawn the official filing with the SEC would lead to abuse of authority. The "private affairs" of the citizen would become targets for law enforcement without any recourse. At the time, it may have seemed like a nightmare scenario. However, Nazi Germany and fascist Italy were very real in 1936. Maybe the majority was reading the headlines from abroad, not domestic news. It was this language, perhaps, that elicited a strenuous dissent from Justice Cardozo.

Fundamentally, Cardozo objected to the very idea that a criminal filing could be undone by withdrawing it after an investigation indicated its criminality. "Recklessness and deceit do not automatically excuse themselves by notice of repentance," he aphorized. The filing violated the law. The SEC was performing its function of ridding the financial markets of falsehoods. Prosecution should follow. It was not an abuse of authority, nor unauthorized by Congress. To the contrary, Congress intended exactly this. Withdrawal was irrelevant. "When wrongs such as these have been committed or attempted, they must be dragged to light and pilloried." To do otherwise would "invite the cunning and unscrupulous to gamble with detection." A classic debate had emerged between Sutherland's call for protection of the accused versus Cardozo's call for the prosecution of the guilty.

Cardozo concluded that there was nothing private about a public filing with the SEC. The defendant had opened the door to investigation with an attempt to deceive. The SEC had to be allowed to investigate, pursue, and prosecute the offender. He did not at any time wonder about the guilt of the SEC's target. Cardozo's principles were above that. He dismissed the "star chamber" analogy. "Historians may find hyperbole in the sanguinary simile." For Cardozo, the "knaves" deserved all that they got regardless of whether the filing had an impact on the public. Congress's goal to avoid adverse impacts on the public appears to have disappeared in Cardozo's sophisticated reasoning.

Bankruptcy

On May 24, 1934, the US Congress amended the Bankruptcy Act to allow state-created entities to file for bankruptcy protection in federal court. If they met the criteria, these state corporations could renegotiate their bonds, their debt, such that they could pay a lower interest rate and much less than they owed on the original issuance. This made a great deal of sense for states whose primary means of providing certain services came not from their general budget, but from their ability to create these public-private corporations. Many of the public utilities, roads, bridges, and other infrastructure projects would not exist otherwise. Though it was effectively a means of spending off-budget through borrowing backed by state governments' superior credit rating, it had existed in one form or another since the colonial period. With the effects of the Great Depression on these corporations' revenues, many of them faced collapse.

Most likely attempting to avoid the US Supreme Court declaring this legislation unconstitutional, Congress declared outright that this would not violate or impair states' obligations under the contracts clause, Article I, Section 10. What they did not anticipate was the Court's renewed concern with federalism. On May 25, 1936, in an opinion by Justice McReynolds, the Court struck down the 1934 addition to the Bankruptcy Act in *Ashton v. Cameron County Water Improvement District No. 1.* McReynolds maintained that, even though the federal government had the specific power to write bankruptcy law under Article I, Section 8, that power had to be exercised in such a way that it did not impinge on the states.

McReynolds arrived at this contradictory notion by placing the "lay and collect taxes" power alongside the bankruptcy laws' authority because they were in the same section. "Both are granted by the same section of the Constitution, and we find no reason for saying that one is impliedly limited by the necessity of preserving independence of the states while the other is not." Thus, they were both limited by the federal nature of the Union. He saw that behind the well-meaning intentions of Congress lay the encroachment of the national government on the independence of the states. "If obligations of states or their political subdivisions may be subjected to the interference here attempted, they are no longer free to manage their own affairs; the will of Congress prevails over them." But what of the Fourteenth Amendment's effect on that relationship? McReynolds did not address it.

To drive the point home, McReynolds linked the bankruptcy provisions to the long-rejected notion that Congress could levy taxes on the states or their units. He cited a revered opinion, author, and case: Chief Justice John Marshall's opinion for a unanimous Court in *McCulloch v. Maryland* (1819) had established both that precedent and the famous statement "the ability to tax is the ability to destroy." (What McReynolds probably did not know was that the maxim came from Senator Daniel Webster's brief.) Again, McReynolds harkened back to an earlier period's jurisprudence, something that lawyers appreciated, but did not play well in the political arena.

Cardozo again wrote for the dissenters, but this time Chief Justice Hughes joined them, leaving Justice Roberts as the deciding vote for the majority. Cardozo began with a detailed recitation of the facts, including the congressional hearings leading to the adoption of the legislation. He outlined Congress's motivation in stark terms. The toll of the Great Depression on state corporations was staggering. The safeguards Congress enacted were rigorous. The law on bankruptcy was that of "an expanding power." The entity in question had no viable assets for its creditors to seize in compensation.

In contrast the Court's burden was strenuous. "Invalidity must be proved beyond a reasonable doubt." Cardozo seems to be importing a criminal law doctrine into constitutional interpretation. It is not hard to understand why. Judicial restraint meant a deference to the legislature. Only if there was an overwhelming threat to a basic right not available through any other means should the courts intervene. In this particular instance, the states themselves had agreed to the measure, but their obligation to uphold contracts was furthered under the legislation, not impaired. "To hold that this purpose must be thwarted by the courts because of a supposed affront to the dignity of a state, though the state disclaims the affront and is doing all it can to keep the law alive, is to make dignity a doubtful blessing." It is unclear how federalism's command is the equivalent of a state's "dignity," a much lesser quality, but Cardozo's felicity of phrasing did not admit of such distinctions.

By the time of *Ashton*, a clear division of the Court had emerged, not between elderly justices and younger ones, but between two rival schools of thought. The so-called Four Horsemen (Butler, McReynolds, Sutherland, and Van Devanter) were conservatives in all senses of that word. They were skeptical of broad readings of the Constitution in order to address the supposed national emergency. They wanted to preserve the balance between the national government and the states under federalism, the balance between the government and business under contract theory, and the limitations on government under laissez-faire sentiments.

The so-called Three Musketeers (Brandeis, Cardozo, and Stone, sometimes Hughes) governed themselves by the jurisprudence of judicial restraint. First and most prominently given voice in the twentieth century by Justice Oliver Wendell Holmes Jr., this set of ideas sought to conserve judicial power and defer to the legislative and executive branches whenever possible. These branches were political, while the judicial branch was legal. "Legal" meant apart from current political debates, above them in that judges were to refrain from policy debates. Those were for the people's representatives to decide. The courts held themselves aloft, aloof, and circumspect. Though one could plausibly argue that the justices on both sides appeared to be immersed in politics regardless of their jurisprudence, impartial observers had trouble doubting the Court was deeply divided in late 1936 on the New Deal.

Tipaldo

When New York State decided to impose a minimum wage law on its businesses, the legislature knew they faced an uphill battle. The US Supreme Court had already ruled a similar law in Washington, DC, unconstitutional in *Adkins v. Children's Hospital* (1923). Congress had imposed the minimum wage solely for women and children. In theory, under the precedent of *Muller v. Oregon* (1908), in which the Court upheld maximum working hours for women, this should have passed constitutional muster, but, over Justice Brandeis's objections, the Court thought otherwise. The *Lochner* case still governed the employer-employee relationship with its enshrining of "liberty of contract" as a barrier to even state government's ability to regulate private businesses. Under these circumstances, it made sense for New York to consult with Professor Felix Frankfurter on how to write their minimum wage law in order to survive US Supreme Court scrutiny. After all, *Nebbia*'s rational basis test was based on a New York case, and the emerging swing vote, Justice Roberts, had written that opinion.

On June 1, 1936, Justice Sutherland issued the majority opinion in *Morehead v. New York ex rel. Tipaldo* declaring that the minimum wage law was unconstitutional entirely on the basis of the Court's previous decision in *Adkins*. Roberts was the deciding vote. Apparently, the state of New York had not bothered to argue against *Adkins*. "No application has been made for reconsideration of the constitutional question there decided. The validity of the principles upon which that decision rests is not challenged." Tipaldo had not only refused to pay the set minimum wage for the female workers in his laundry; he had not properly reported it. In prison, he appealed on the grounds that the law violated his due process rights under the Fourteenth Amendment using the writ of habeas corpus, hence the "ex rel." in the case title. It was a curious victory for the Four Horsemen, but an extremely tenuous one.

With that aspect of the case settled, Sutherland's opinion repeated the Court's commitment to liberty of contract. The *Lochner* precedent still held. Only in exceptional circumstances could the states act otherwise. He then dispensed with all of the distinguishing features from *Adkins* the attorneys for the state of New York had asserted. By a 5–4 majority, the Court reasserted the limits on state government power it had upheld in 1905 with *Lochner*.

The dissenters lodged two different opinions: one by Chief Justice Hughes, in which the Three Musketeers concurred, and another by Justice Stone, for himself, Brandeis, and Cardozo. The reason for this odd bifurcation lay in Hughes's refusal to overrule *Adkins*, at least for the present. He spent the bulk of his dissent differentiating between *Tipaldo*'s fact pattern and that of *Adkins*. For him, *Muller* was controlling. After all, New York State needed to protect women the same as underage males. In an era long before modern feminism had taken hold, rampant sexism still held sway. By their nature, women were vulnerable, in need of safeguarding, and not in a position to negotiate reasonable wages for themselves. One could argue this is an origin of the so-called nanny state, in which government treats everyone like children, not capable adults able to decide their own best interests.

Hughes dismissed the Court of Appeals (the highest appeals court in New York) majority that had declared the law unconstitutional because of state and federal concerns. The *Adkins* case had exercised an undue influence on their decision. He maintained that the US Supreme Court should clarify the matter. The new minimum wage laws, in light of *Adkins*, met that standard when they required "a fair equivalence of wage and service" and provided a rigorous procedure for determining what was "fair."

Furthermore, Hughes declared that the closeness of the 5–4 decision in *Adkins* qualified it to the point where a change of conditions should overturn the finding. New York State had proven those conditions. "We are not at liberty to disregard these facts. We must assume that they exist and examine respondent's argument from that standpoint," he pro- claimed. Citing *Nebbia*, Hughes stated the standard of review: "The test of validity is not artificial. It is whether the limitation upon the freedom of contract is arbitrary and capricious, or one reasonably required in order appropriately to serve the public interest in the light of the particular conditions to which the power is addressed." In other words, he wanted the lowest level of scrutiny: the rational basis test. He concluded: "The end is legitimate and the means appropriate." Without explicitly overruling *Adkins*, Hughes had limited it to its set of facts.

Justice Stone took a different view in his dissent for the Three Musketeers. Although he stated, "I agree with all that the Chief Justice has said," he clearly disagreed with the substance of Hughes's opinion. In brief, the three had a very different view of what the Fourteenth Amendment's due process clause meant. Stone began by making the clause fluid. "The vague and general pronouncement of the Fourteenth Amendment against deprivation of liberty without due process of law is a limitation of legislative power, not a formula for its exercise." In addition, "It does not purport to say in what particular manner that power shall be exerted." This was a very dangerous road he was paving for the Court. If states and their entities could act against a person's liberty—put them in prison or threaten to do so—without restraint, they could reinstall Jim Crow unchecked. Of course, in 1936, Jim Crow was in full force and the horrors of lynching and the Ku Klux Klan were still part of American life.

Having made the Fourteenth Amendment less restrictive, Justice Stone proceeded to place New York State's mandate of a minimum wage for women and boys within the scope of the *Nebbia* rational basis test. If it was a reasonable means to achieve a legitimate goal, it passed constitutional muster. Moreover, if that overruled *Adkins*, that would be fine. "They are irreconcilable with the decision and most that was said in the *Adkins* case." The Court was in a new era, and that thirteen-year-old precedent no longer applied. "A generation ago, they [the wage problems] were for the individual to solve; today they are the burden of the nation."

Justice Stone concluded with a decisive statement for judicial restraint. "We should follow our decision in the *Nebbia* case and leave the selection and the method of the solution of the problems to which statute is addressed where it seems to me the Constitution has left them, to the legislative branch of the government." However, the Constitution had made no such determination with regard to the state governments. The non-delegation and separation of powers requirement on which Stone relied was for the national government. The Fourteenth Amendment, the provision of the Constitution at issue in *Tipaldo*, applied to the states and had no separation of powers dictate. Stone seems to have been arguing that New York State's highest court should have deferred to the legislature, and the US Supreme Court should have left it there. Or that is the more charitable interpretation of this problem with Stone's dissent.

A Second New Deal

After President Roosevelt's "horse and buggy" conference, he faced a flurry of criticism, largely because the hostile press jumped on the criticism of the Court's interpretation of the interstate commerce clause to turn it into an attack on the Court. Privately, Attorney General Homer Cummings, Professor Felix Frankfurter, and Roosevelt himself may have been thinking that way, but the ninety-minute press conference did not contain any such attack. The public relations disaster did seem to convince FDR that he and Congress had work to do in light of recent Court decisions, especially *Schechter*. He and the leaders of Congress canceled their summer break and passed a flurry of legislation. Though some of it filled gaps left by the now dead codes of the NRA, others were more significant. These permanent changes to the national government are known to many scholars as the Second New Deal.

Although Roosevelt proposed it in January and Congress enacted it on April 6, 1935, the Emergency Relief Appropriation Act does establish the spirit of the Second New Deal. In addition to setting up Harold

Ickes's Public Works Administration independently of the NIRA, the act established the National Youth Administration, the Resettlement Administration, the Rural Electrification Administration, and the Works Progress Administration under Harry Hopkins, Ickes's great rival. While Ickes continued to fund large dam projects and bridges, the rest of the agencies were meant to fulfill FDR's commitment to work, not "the dole." As noted in chapter one, these temporary agencies very much altered the political, social, and physical landscape of the United States.

While the work of these entities is extremely important, it is their overall thrust that matters to our topic. In almost every respect, they signify a swing to the moderate left of American politics. The Works Progress Administration (WPA) in particular employed socialists, some communists, and other similarly inclined historians, artists, journalists, and playwrights to create an overall narrative for the New Deal program. The construction projects, the plays, the historical records accumulation and preservation, and the tourism promotion guides represented an inclusive, diverse, and community-based America. Diego Rivera's artwork in post offices and outdoor murals exemplified this messaging. The National Youth Administration, the Rural Electrification Administration, and the Resettlement Administration's commitment to outdoor living, the countryside, and roads and airports cemented government efforts for rural life and what later Americans would call ecotourism, such as public parks, hiking trails, and camping, all centered around the automobile. While all of these agencies disappeared either immediately before or during World War II, their impact on the fabric of American life and politics was permanent.

On July 6, 1935, President Roosevelt signed into law the National Labor Relations Act of 1935, also known as the Wagner Act after its chief sponsor, Senator Robert Wagner of New York. The negotiations were long and difficult yet necessary after the US Supreme Court in *Schechter* voided the codes, including the wages and hours provisions, in the NIRA. Prior to those codes, American labor had been divided into two large groups: the skilled workers, many of whom found a home in the more conservative American Federation of Labor (AFL), and the unskilled and semi-skilled workers, such as auto and steel workers and miners, the last of whom found representation in the United Mine Workers, led by John L. Lewis. The latter group pushed hard for the "closed shop" to be enshrined in federal law so that, once they had formed a union at a particular company, that union would have exclusive authority to negotiate on behalf of the membership and every position covered would require union membership. Wagner and the New Dealers were happy to oblige, but their support came at a price.

The Wagner Act created the National Labor Relations Board (NLRB), a commission that, in effect, administered the regulations, which in turn governed the process for employees to certify a collective bargaining unit—a union—and how that union would operate. There was precedent, of course, for in law one can always find precedent. The Railway Labor Act of 1926 guaranteed the right of workers to organize. For obvious reasons, manufacturers, individually and through their lobbying arm, the National Association of Manufacturers (the NAM), fought the measure, and then its implementation. However, the NLRB proved a powerful ally of organized labor, though it also asserted national government control over those unions in exchange.

Despite the hopes of its sponsors, the Wagner Act did not prevent strikes, even violent ones, but it did promote unionization, especially in the Northeast, Midwest, and West, where most industry existed at the time. It also did not alleviate either unemployment or the poor wages of the Great Depression. Like almost all of the New Deal, either First or Second, it did not have its full effect until after World War II. The workers who benefited from the Wagner Act, and there were many, moved into the middle class of the 1950s and 1960s. Notably, small businesses and agriculture were exempt from the Wagner Act as were so-called service jobs. Nevertheless, organized labor became a key constituency of FDR's Democratic New Deal coalition.

On August 14, 1935, the Social Security Act became law after a prolonged period of negotiations. The law itself stemmed from the work of the Committee on Economic Security Roosevelt created on June 29th, 1934. Arguably, the system's legitimacy stemmed from Justice Stone's answer to a question from the chair of the committee, Secretary of Labor Frances Perkins, at a dinner party. She had asked how to survive judicial review. His answer was to base it on "the taxing power." Regardless, FDR considered Social Security one of the pillars of the new order he and his New Dealers were creating. Although it did not alleviate the ills of the Great Depression much, eventually Social Security did significantly reduce poverty among the elderly and fundamentally alter Americans' relationship with the national government. It also provided disability insurance to a large portion of American workers, a plan that had begun as a state-based system in Progressive Wisconsin under Republican governor "Battlin' Bob" LaFollette. Finally, unemployment insurance provided assistance if the former employee met the requirements. Supposedly, both employers and employees made payments to the system, though it was highly likely employers simply regarded their Social Security contributions as salary in another form.

An important corollary of the system, which applied only to wages and employers above a certain size, was the immense amount of information the national government collected every time employees were paid or people filed for unemployment compensation. The national government could now monitor large portions of the economy, including monthly employment rates, wage incomes, and who occupied what types of jobs at any given time. To receive Social Security or be eligible for disability or unemployment benefits, one had to have a Social Security number, a form of national identity. Based on this information, the national government gained the ability to manage the economy whereas, prior to this, it was dependent on state figures, if there were any, and indicators like the stock market.

There were some potential drawbacks to Social Security. The tax and employer contribution were relatively flat, and the taxable wages had a cap. This meant that it was a largely regressive tax—it did not tax according to ability to pay. It also probably had a negative impact on economic growth, as any tax would. There is some evidence that anticipation of Social Security benefits has diminished savings rates as well as removing capital from private investment and placing it into the national government's hands instead, distorting capital markets. Finally, Social Security would eventually grow into the national government's single largest expenditure, recently leading one economist, Paul Krugman, to comment that the US government is "an insurance company with an army." While this may be an exaggeration, there is little doubt that Social Security is extremely important, with a built-in constituency—retirees and those who expect to retire—who form a substantial political bloc, the ideological heirs of FDR's New Deal Democrats

The Banking Act of 1935, which Congress enacted after substantial debate on August 23, 1935, formalized the reforms of 1933, including the Federal Deposit Insurance Corporation and centralized control over monetary policy by a Board of Governors and an Open Market Committee under the directorship of a chair. Marriner Eccles, a New Dealer and banker from Utah, helped write the legislation for the administration and became the first chair of the Federal Reserve Board. The ever-present Senator Carter Glass, a Democrat from Virginia, had sponsored the original Federal Reserve law as well as the Glass-Steagall law, which separated investment banks from commercial banks. He objected to the partisan nature of and lack of restraint on Fed purchases and successfully fought for amendments. The Federal Reserve Board that emerged from the Banking Act of 1935 had members with seven-year terms and a substantial degree of independence from the executive branch. It even moved out of the Treasury building to a new, grand building of its own.

Whether conservatives like Senator Glass realized it or not, the resulting Federal Reserve Board was arguably the most powerful institution in Washington, DC. With almost unchecked authority over the nation's currency and financial services sector, they could either spur or stifle the American economy at will. Because the United States had come out of World War I as the financial and economic center of the world economy, this meant the Fed's almost complete control of US monetary policy also had a massive global impact.

Yet, to this day, monetary policy is not very well understood. Beyond the inaccuracies of laissez-faire economics, which contributed to the Great Depression, even the Keynesian economics that took hold after John Maynard Keynes published his great work, *The General Theory of Employment, Interest and Money*, in 1936, was more art than science. Keynes argued that governments must actively use fiscal (taxing and spending) and monetary (interest rates, supply of money) policies to govern the economy. But the theory, and its practice, had its problems, primarily that giving government vast powers does not grant the wisdom to use them. Regardless, these measures made the NRA codes look amateurish in comparison.

Perhaps the most controversial enactment of the Second New Deal, the Public Utility Holding Company Act of 1935, a.k.a. the Wheeler-Rayburn Act, empowered the SEC to break up electricity companies that operated in more than one state and had more than one corporate tier. The

New Dealers based this severe intrusion into the public utilities market on a Federal Trade Commission investigation, along with a report of the National Power Policy Committee FDR had formed, in June 1934, largely in reaction to the Samuel Insull scandal. Senator Wheeler and FDR believed fervently that electricity should be provided by public, that is government-operated, entities. For example, the TVA operated across almost all of the Southeast, but, because it was an agent of the national government, that passed their review. De-monopolizing and promoting government-operated utilities also fit the Second New Deal's commitment to enlarging political authority over economic matters. In short, they were too important to be left to the market, the same mentality behind the NRA.

While the Senate had little difficulty passing the legislation, the House received a flurry of telegrams, letters, visits from unregistered lobbyists, and a print and radio campaign opposing the so-called death clause for interstate utilities. The death clause supposedly would have bankrupted those companies like today's ultimate sanction against college football programs, in which they lose all their scholarships, albeit briefly, for violations. Under the weight of this supposed public hostility, the House removed the "death clause." Suspecting a corporate sabotage of the bill, FDR tapped Senator Hugo Black, Democrat from Alabama, to lead an investigation into the lobbying against the bill. The Black Committee managed to document that almost all of the opposition had come from public utility companies, using practices that ranged from faking telegrams, advertisements, and letters to arranging with board members of media companies to create hostile coverage. With an American public now firmly behind the law, to punish the discredited utilities, the House reconsidered then passed the "death clause." FDR signed it into law on August 26, 1935.

The Revenue Act of 1935 not only constituted the last major legislation of the Second New Deal; it also embodied the new approach to reordering American society: redistribution of wealth. Its critics called it the "soak the rich" plan, and with some justification. Although progressive income taxation was not new, the steep progressive tax rates topped off at over 70 percent of income in the top bracket, a marked departure from the Republican years under Treasury Secretary Andrew Mellon (at the time still under prosecution for tax evasion). This kind

{ *Chapter Four* }

of taxation takes income based on ability to pay, while government services, especially under the New Deal, are given to the public either regardless of income or to help middle- and lower-income people more than upper-income people.

The tax brackets were "progressive" because each level of income was taxed at a higher rate than the one below it. Steep progressive taxation has been a pillar of liberalism ever since. It was no coincidence the redistribution also favored rural and agricultural areas over urban, industrial, and developed areas. As such, the Revenue Act cemented the major elements of what scholars call the New Deal coalition: organized labor, rural areas, the progressive left, and the at-risk poor and/or elderly. With the Jim Crow South solidly Democrat, FDR and his would-be successors could dominate national politics for years to come unless something threatened these and other enactments. They were also a philosophical rebuke of *Schechter* and its supposed conservative brethren. The cases faced in the Court's 1935–1936 session gave very strong signals of trouble.

Year of Decision

In the autumn of 1936, there was another major US election, including a presidential election. It also saw what many people perceived as the height of the US Supreme Court's negative scrutiny of the New Deal. President Roosevelt and his supporters became increasingly alarmed about the Second New Deal's prospects as the Court dismantled substantial pieces of the First New Deal. In reality, the vast majority of the First New Deal had not been seriously challenged. The regulatory agencies hummed away, producing rules that would govern America well into the next century. Even *Butler*'s voiding of the AAA was temporary, and *Ashwander v. TVA* had gone the administration's way.

In response to *Butler*, Secretary of Agriculture Henry Wallace and his legal team swiftly drafted a new statute that omitted the processor fees and licensing provisions. The government would simply pay farmers, if they wanted, to reduce their output while purchasing the surplus. President Roosevelt signed the Soil Conservation and Domestic Allotment Act into law on February 29, 1936. Its educational provisions encouraged farmers to plant tree breaks in the fields, use crop rotations, and limit their tilling of the soil, particularly in the Dust Bowl–ravaged Great Plains. Eventually, the crop subsidies went into effect, and people watched with amazement as the US government created vast store-houses of surplus cheese, grains, and other items while many Americans and people around the globe remained ill fed.

Another major effect of the subsidies stemmed from the payments being based on acreage held. The disproportionate assistance to larger holdings not only reduced the number of family farms over the following decades but also dealt a death blow to sharecropping—the land tenancy system in the South since the end of Reconstruction. The large land-holders used their newfound gains to mechanize their operations. Also, their need for tenant farm labor fell precipitously, and many tenants found their leases terminated. Almost all of them were African American. When World War II increased the demand for their labor in the industrial areas of the North and Far West, the Second Great Migration began in earnest, transforming Black America from a largely southern and rural population to an urban one. This was another example of the law of unintended consequences—a warning to those who think mea-sured actions will be confined to their immediate subject matter.

Behind the Scenes

While Congress patched the holes the Supreme Court's cases created, Attorney General Homer Cummings's office continued to conduct a "secret investigation" into how to deal with the Court's and the fed-eral bench's hostility to the New Deal that had begun in 1933. President Roosevelt, running for a first term, had referred to the overwhelmingly Republican judiciary unfavorably in an extemporaneous remark. He ig-nored the resulting criticism from Hoover and others about his tenden-cies toward authoritarianism. After victory in 1932, Roosevelt anticipated the opposition of judges and justices to his ambitious program. He tasked his attorney general, who shared his views, with addressing this issue, given the judiciary's power of judicial review. The *Schechter* decision, among others, only increased his sense of urgency.

In addition to Special Assistant Carl McFarland, who worked on the *Schechter* appeal, Justice Department attorneys Alexander Holtzoff,

Warner W. Gardner, R. C. MacCutcheon, and others tried to find ways the administration could thwart the Court's anticipated opposition to the New Deal. They considered eliminating the Supreme Court's appellate jurisdiction, limiting its ability to review certain laws, and amending the Constitution. None seemed feasible. There is also no evidence they seriously considered telling the president that the laws had simply been poorly drafted, ill-conceived, or a combination of the two. Perhaps spending more time on making the legislation constitutional and less time trying to thwart judicial hostility would have been a better use of their limited resources. Instead, over the course of 1936, they shifted to a different solution.

After "Black Monday," Congress and public pundits entertained notions that something needed to be done about the US Supreme Court. While most of the proposals members of Congress made centered on how to remove jurisdiction, on Senator George Norris's proposal that the Court need to be unanimous to overturn congressional enactments, or on requiring a seven-justice majority to overturn acts of Congress, the criticism focused on how out of touch the justices were. Frequently, editorial writers mentioned the fact that six of the justices were over seventy years old. While today some would refer to this kind of analysis as ageism—a prejudice against someone based on their age—lifespans were shorter and there was little in the way of a lobby for the elderly. In early 1936, Attorney General Cummings wrote a memo to Roosevelt suggesting a constitutional amendment forcing justices to retire at age seventy. Though the amendment idea did not survive, the notion of an age limit for judges had traction.

Perhaps the reason the amendment process received so much attention in the corridors of executive power stemmed from the successful enactment of two amendments to the US Constitution right before and during FDR's first term. Congress approved the Twentieth Amendment in March 1932 and the states ratified it in January 1933. It moved presidential inaugurations from March to January, had Congress convene earlier, on January 3rd, and provided for presidential vacancies between elections and inaugurations. Ratified by the states on December 3, 1933, the Twenty-First Amendment repealed the Eighteenth Amendment, which had inaugurated the country's "great experiment" with Prohibition. The Democrats had been opposed to this largely Republican project since its enactment in 1919. New York's Al Smith had campaigned against it as the party's nominee in 1928, and Roosevelt renewed the push for repeal in 1932. After these relatively easy victories, it seemed that if deficiencies in the Constitution could be so easily fixed with these two amendments, perhaps the Supreme Court's supposed hostility to the New Deal could be rectified in the same way.

For FDR, the only person whose views truly mattered, the problem with the Court's rulings had not been the Constitution. Indeed, a constitutional amendment would have been a tacit admission that the justices had been correct about the unconstitutionality of the New Deal legislation. In this, the *Schechter* case appears to have played an outsized role in the president's thinking. Even the liberals had voted to invalidate his favorite solution to the Great Depression. Because he believed he had been right about the NIRA, the justices were the problem, not the Constitution. He needed to replace or overcome these justices with ones who were his people. In other words, Roosevelt viewed Supreme Court appointments like any other in at least one regard. They were part of the spoils system that Andrew Jackson had inaugurated when he first became president, and the first Democratic one at that. Nevertheless, there was still an election to win.

As the Supreme Court had completed its rulings in *Tipaldo*, the political campaign season began in earnest. Having blundered with several outward criticisms of the Court, FDR stuck with his newly formed Second New Deal coalition. His opponent, Governor Alf Landon of Kansas, surprised almost everyone by supporting a constitutional amendment and the intent of the New Deal reforms, concluding that only their execution was at fault. This strategy made sense in that, if Landon could avoid being associated with the discredited businessmen the public blamed for the Depression, he could play the moderate to Roosevelt's radical.

After the nominating conventions, FDR took to the seas off New England for his usual summer vacation, swimming and fishing, leaving the campaign to his subordinates. Landon took advantage with an active speaking tour where he managed to convince many newspapers to endorse him and his moderate platform. Roosevelt returned in September to tour the West and Northeast, giving a fairly combative speech in Madison Square Garden in October. Scrupulously avoiding the unpopular

Supreme Court and its baffling decision in *Tipaldo*, he emphasized the New Deal's accomplishments. Disturbingly, he also made the issues personal. He welcomed the "hatred" of the "economic royalists" he had condemned at the Democratic National Convention, because it made him seem like a tribune of the people from the Roman Republic. While newspaper editorials condemned the supposedly Fascistic or Stalinist overtones, its alleged Caesarism was good political theater. In addition to offering a set of memorable lines, well delivered as usual, FDR demonstrated his mastery of newsreels and radio—the new media of American politics. His critics, including Al Smith, failed to moderate their tone to account for the effect of the new technology. Instead of landing sharp blows, their actual voices sounded shrill and petulant.

While American unemployment remained stuck in double digits, international affairs deteriorated into Italian, German, and Japanese aggression, and bigotry reigned supreme against Black Americans and Latinos, FDR and his New Deal were popular with most Americans. In the November elections, the voters gave Roosevelt and the Democrats an overwhelming victory. They held on to their massive House majority and picked up six Senate seats, to bring them to seventy-five out of ninety-six. Roosevelt received a little over 60 percent of the popular vote and won every state except Maine and Vermont. If anything demonstrated a public mandate for the New Deal and FDR, the 1936 election decided the issue with resounding support.

Unfortunately for them, it was still possible to misinterpret the meaning of the mandate—just like a prophecy from the Oracle at Delphi. "If I go to war, will I win?" the king asks the Oracle. She replies, "If you go to war, a great kingdom will fall." The king understands this to mean he will achieve victory. Instead, it is his great kingdom that falls as a result of the war. Along these lines, almost immediately after his great victory, FDR accelerated Cummings's secret investigation into what to do about the supposedly hostile Supreme Court. He also broadened it to include constitutional law experts like Edward Corwin at Princeton University. Without the moderating influence of his longtime adviser from New York, Louis Howe, who had died on April 18, 1936, President Roosevelt drifted away from his Brain Trust to his new coalition. With their support, he believed, even the Court would not be able to stand in his way.

The Plan

At this point, it might be useful to pause and reflect on why so many people, including lawyers and law professors like Felix Frankfurter, had become convinced that something needed to be done about the US Supreme Court, regardless of that notion's wisdom. After all, the Court had upheld several New Deal laws including the highly questionable TVA. *Tipaldo* had been a shock, it is true, yet even that case held a key to future victory: New York had not mounted enough of a challenge to *Adkins*. If it had, allegedly, it was certainly possible, if not likely, that both Chief Justice Hughes and Justice Roberts would have joined the dissenters for a majority. Massive blows like *Schechter* had been unanimous because the weight of legal opinion doubted the constitutionality of the legislation from its inception. Then there was the very fact that several of the justices on the right were close to retirement or death, as well as the aged Brandeis. That would give Roosevelt several appointments to the Court, something he had been lacking in his first term. Why go through the effort of adding justices to the bench, denying the Court appellate jurisdiction, or considering amending the Constitution when it was not necessary?

Several theories come to mind. The first is that American politics is subject to the issue cycle. Some new, emotional news story comes to the forefront with expert opinion, the media, and the public calling for action. Politicians listen. The public discourse fills with debate on the topic. The politicians either act or do not, depending on the state of public fervor. A new news story comes to light, and the cycle begins again. It is not that the political system actually solved the underlying problem, if there was one. It is just that public attention is limited. It is entirely possible FDR, his inner circle, and the New Dealers became wrapped up in an issue cycle of Court rejection of congressional action. It did not matter whether the Court needed reform or if the New Dealers just needed to draft better legislation. Their emotional involvement overrode their objectivity.

Another theory stems from human psychology. People tend to discount information, advice, and analyses that contradict their entrenched world views—a phenomenon known as cognitive dissonance. Instead of reevaluating their ideas, people will do the reverse, and become more committed. A mental process known as confirmation bias works in the opposite way. People will look for, overemphasize, and/or more readily accept reports that support their views. President Roosevelt, for example, disproportionately emphasized the negative rulings, focused on the supposed antiquated interstate commerce jurisprudence, and overemphasized his choices over those of the Court. Attorney General Cummings tended to share this view. That these two experienced politicians would have come to these conclusions when they took office, if not before, seems more like an ideological fixity than a reasoned analysis carefully crafted based on evidence over time.

Adding to and reflecting these phenomena, columnists Drew Pearson and Robert Allen wrote a scathing personal attack on all of the justices, titled "The Nine Old Men," just in time for election season. It contained their usual gossip, innuendo, and scurrilous material, but it did strike a nerve with the public. The idea that the black-robed justices reigning on high from their new building, "a mausoleum of justice," were in truth corrupt, incompetent, tainted, and ludicrously out of touch with America at large found a receptive audience. Though the New Dealers did not express themselves that crudely, they shared the overall impression that the Supreme Court needed to be updated.

A third possible explanation of this unchecked desire to take on the Supreme Court, especially Roosevelt's, is based on presidential politics. Regardless of how one looks at FDR's politics, personality, and background, he was definitely a politician's politician. His correspondence, press conferences, and recollections—and reports of his conversations and actions—show him to be politically astute, self-confident, and morally flexible. His various trial balloons for the Court problem, foreign policy, and domestic issues produced public reactions that altered his plans. At all times, he had his eye on public opinion, electoral votes, and congressional votes. He calculated, planned, and cultivated in order to achieve success. Only in the aftermath of his overwhelming historic victory in 1936 did his political antennae fail him, and not just in terms of public regard for the US Supreme Court.

On December 26th, 1936, at the White House, Attorney General Homer Cummings met with President Franklin D. Roosevelt on a confidential matter. Cummings's secret investigation ordered by the president had reached its end. He now had a plan that would solve the administration's problems with the US Supreme Court's conservatives. Unlike the amendment Chief Justice Taft had favored in his memoir and Professor Edward Corwin wanted, a judicial reform act would use Congress's power to appoint additional justices and judges with a simple majority. Federal judge William Denman had recommended the appointment of additional lower court judges to help clear the federal docket, especially in the rapidly growing states of New York and California. Cummings combined this genuine reform with the idea that judges and justices over seventy needed help in order to justify additional justices on the US Supreme Court.

According to Cummings's secret diary, the only account we have of this meeting, the need for more federal district and circuit court judges covered their actual objective of overcoming the Four Horsemen. The bill would max out the number of justices at fifteen, with six immediate additional appointees giving the liberals a nine-vote majority. Cummings estimated it would take sixty days at most. This was important given that the Court's docket contained a number of challenges to the New Deal, which were expected to be supported by the *Tipaldo* majority if not Hughes's sixth vote. Neither FDR nor Cummings liked the idea, given the amount of opposition there might be to "packing" the Court. However, Cummings recorded in his secret diary they both believed they had no choice. They had to act and act soon.

This was how President Franklin D. Roosevelt and his administration arrived at what the opposition and press would call "the court-packing plan." Lawyers and advisers inside and outside of the administration were far from unified about the plan. Most did not know of its existence, let alone the process of arriving at it. While historians like Laura Kalman and William Leuchtenberg find the president wily and shrewd in his planning, and the plan still was a "partial win," the balance of scholarly opinion is that his caution, which he had maintained for so long, had eroded, and the president was rushing into a constitutional crisis. Yet closer reading of the evidence suggests that FDR examined the matter closely almost from the start of his administration. He was fifty-one years old when he became president and an active fifty-four at his second inauguration. Did the justices of the Supreme Court seem crotchety, frail, and obsolete?

According to Alexander Hamilton, in *The Federalist Papers*, in theory the US Supreme Court is "the least dangerous branch" of the US government. It does not declare wars, pass laws imprisoning people, or command the military. It rules only on the "cases and controversies" that come before it and nothing else. Even that role is supposedly restricted under judiciary acts of Congress, codes of judicial conduct, the strictures of the common law, and a healthy respect for their nonpolitical, nonpartisan role.

By the end of 1936, despite these assumptions, many, including the president of the United States, had come to regard the Court as the political opposition, a deeply flawed institution, whose personnel needed alteration if the United States were to prosper. In other words, a constitutional crisis had befallen the nation. A fundamental struggle seemed inevitable between a popular president, with most of the people behind him, and the robed justices of the Supreme Court. How would it end? What would the impact be on the country? And why did it turn out as it did?

Court Packing?

In her 2022 book, *FDR's Gambit*, eminent legal historian Laura Kalman has challenged the traditional account of the "court-packing" episode. "I aim to show that [FDR's] hubris did not explain" his actions. Instead, "he was deploying the same shrewdness that enabled him to win a massive 1936 reelection victory." Nor was the plan an "inevitable defeat." Yet at the end of her story, she concedes that "someone else who studied the court fight might tell the story in a different way." My account is one of those. It begins with a return to the "horse and buggy" press conference at which Roosevelt expressed his dismay, taking his case "to the country," and ends with the demise of the plan in the Senate legal affairs committee. This episode is one of the many important impacts *Schechter Poultry v. U.S.* had on US history and law.

The unanimous ruling in *Schechter* seems to have shocked President Roosevelt and the New Dealers. The US Supreme Court's invalidation of the Agricultural Adjustment Act in *U.S. v. Butler* six months later, among other blows, convinced many in the administration, especially Roosevelt, that the Court, particularly its conservative members, were not only sticklers for constitutional requirements but the principal opponents to the New Deal itself. For these reasons, despite contradictory evidence in *Schechter* itself and favorable rulings like *Ashwander v. TVA*, the president and his attorney general, Homer S. Cummings, put into action a plan to deal with the supposedly hostile justices.

Stating that the problem was an understaffed judiciary, Roosevelt proposed an enlargement of the federal bench, including the Supreme Court. He recommended adding a justice for each current member over the age of seventy and six months, up to a maximum of fifteen justices, immediately giving FDR six new appointments to the Court. Other plans, as well as different analyses of the situation, fell by the wayside in the aftermath of Roosevelt's overwhelming victory in the 1936 election.

With veto-proof majorities (more than two-thirds) in both houses of Congress, a simple majority could enact the legislation. Swiftly, without fuss, FDR and the New Deal Democrats would solve their difficulties with the Court (assuming a swift confirmation process for the new justices) before the existing Court could rule on important pieces of the Second New Deal, including Social Security and the Wagner Act. Afterward, the administration could build on what it had already done with no judicial obstacles. Unfortunately, it did not go as they had planned.

The Rollout

President Franklin D. Roosevelt appears to have believed that the 1936 election served as a mandate not just of the New Deal, his presidency, and his party's right to govern, but also for the purpose of changing the US Supreme Court's interpretation of the Constitution. The so-called judicial procedures legislation would accompany his reorganization of the executive branch in the name of progress, reform, and enacting the will of the people, which he translated as support for his and the New Dealers' view of the US Constitution. While everyone in the Justice Department and the White House staff, with the notable exception of Thomas G. Corcoran, finalized the wording of the legislation, the president kept this major effort a secret from the cabinet, the press, and most of his advisers.

Corcoran, or "Tommy the Cork," as FDR called him, was one of Professor Felix Frankfurter's hot dogs at Harvard Law School. After graduating from Harvard Law School, he clerked for Justice Oliver Wendell Holmes Jr. then engaged in private practice in New York City. He made a name for himself in the Reconstruction Finance Corporation, where he came to President Roosevelt's attention. (By this time, according to James Olson's 2017 monograph, the RFC was pouring a lot of money into the banking system and the railroads.) Along with another of Frankfurter's hot dogs, Benjamin V. Cohen, *Time* magazine's "Gold Dust Twins" wrote early drafts of much of the New Deal that survived judicial review. Yet while Cohen worked on the later drafts of the judicial procedures proposal, Corcoran did not. Corcoran was against the idea and had advised his president not to proceed. Everyone knew that Corcoran had strong ties to Brandeis and the other liberal justices while Cohen did not. Corcoran's opposition signifies that the New Dealers agreed that the Court was a problem but did not agree on FDR's preferred solution.

In the meantime, Roosevelt gave hints, in two of his major speeches, that big things were coming, before the rollout of the bill on February 5th. The first was his State of the Union address on January 6, 1937. Most of the address was a general endorsement of the previous four years and what needed improvement in the future. Contained within it were also several cloaked jabs at the US Supreme Court. First, he asserted that his plan updated the judiciary to align with modern life. "Ours was the task to do more than to argue a theory." No one could miss his reference to the "horse and buggy" jurisprudence of the conservative justices' attitudes. After stating that the outright goal of democratic government was to "assist" everyone, he took on the *Schechter* decision outright. "Sober second thought confirms most of us in the belief that the broad objectives of the National Recovery Act were sound." But "it tried to do too much." Whether he intended it or not, he was misrepresenting the Court's rationale for the decision.

President Roosevelt then devoted an entire section of his address to arguing with the Court about the *Schechter* decision and all of the other cases his administration had lost. First, he posited that states could no longer cope with modern economic issues. It had to be the national government's job. Second, he concluded that the problem was not with the Constitution itself. "Difficulties have grown out of its interpretation; but rightly considered it [the Constitution] can be used as an instrument of progress, and not as a device for prevention of action." To bolster his view that the Court had gotten it wrong, he cited the Preamble and Edmund Randolph, a member of the Constitutional Convention from Virginia and its Committee on Detail, which wrote much of the language. The Randolph quote argued that certain provisions "ought to be accommodated to times and events." FDR's staffers had done their research. However, they had missed important facts, including Randolph's refusal to sign the document.

Having identified the disease—a lack of "harmony" between the presidency and the Court—President Roosevelt laid out the cure. "Means must be found to adapt our legal forms and our judicial interpretation to the actual present national needs of the largest progressive democracy in the modern world." He took no blame for the poor drafting of some of the First New Deal. He did not anticipate that the better drafted Second New Deal would survive judicial review. He did not acknowledge the Court's rightful role in the constitutional order as established under Chief Justice John Marshall in *Marbury v. Madison* (1803). It was as if the president of the United States failed to appreciate how the political branches were checked by the judicial one. After all, James Madison's *Federalist Papers #51's* origination of "checks and balances" was far better known than Edmund Randolph's views.

Republicans and most of the press's editorials criticized FDR for introducing campaign-style partisanship to the State of the Union. His supposedly threatening language to the Court also did not go unnoticed. What the opposition failed to observe was that Roosevelt had addressed the joint session of Congress in person, in front of a microphone and film cameras. They were not the intended audience; the public was. The president was using the newer technologies of radio and movie newsreels to reach Americans without the intervening, interpretive perspectives of the news media. He was fostering a more personal relationship with the American people. He had used this technique successfully thus far, something the justices could not do, due to tradition, role, and, most likely, lack of interest.

FDR's next salvo at the Court came within his second inaugural address on January 20, 1937, the first inaugural address to conform to the Twentieth Amendment's reform of the national government's calendar. The Four Horsemen, who were four of the six over seventy, made a point of attending, while Brandeis kept to his practice of staying at home. Roosevelt's opening summarized his overall philosophy. The US government would master science, America's "complex civilization," and modern ills. "To do this we knew that we must find practical controls over blind economic forces and blindly selfish men." Apparently, Adam Smith's "invisible hand" played no role in the president's understanding of how even a sophisticated economy worked. To make the case that the framers wanted an all-powerful national government taking control over the entire economy, he cited the Constitutional Convention. A generation that had fought against centralized tyranny in what would become known as World War I now fought the Great Depression with command-and-control economic policy.

Sounding like a present-day progressive, FDR made the case for vast new government power. "By using the new materials of social justice we have undertaken to erect on the old foundations a more enduring structure for the better use of future generations." Reverence for, conservation of, and respect for the past's wisdom would now yield to the needs of the present because those needs stemmed from a new social order. He promised "democratic methods of government" in order to meet his redistributive goals. "The test of our progress is not whether we add more to the abundance of those who have much; it is whether we provide enough for those who have too little." Gone was the self-reliance of Hoover. Gone was Coolidge's belief in America as a self-regulating prosperity engine. Now the national government would ensure a benevolent outcome for all. Notably, there was no recognition of the pitfalls of the "progress" governments provided, only FDR's signature optimism.

President Roosevelt delayed his first public disclosure about his plan to reorganize the judiciary until February 5th. He later claimed secrecy about his "big surprise" was necessary in order to prevent opposition from forming in advance of the proposal. This meant he could not tell even his cabinet or the congressional leadership. Like everyone else, his cabinet and the congressional leadership learned of the proposal, his accompanying message, and its details just before he spoke to the White House Press Corps on February 5th. Although news reports, including Pearson and Allen's, predicted court packing, the cabinet, with the exception of the attorney general, and the congressional leadership were taken completely by surprise. In an annual dinner for the justices and key members of the administration on February 2nd, FDR probably enjoyed his clandestine references and little jibes at the Court in front of most of the unknowing justices. It was a little fun before the battle. Unfortunately for FDR, this secrecy did not turn out well for his proposal to enlarge the judiciary.

In the Senate, where the debate would take place, the legislation acquired its official title: "The Judicial Procedures Reform Bill" of 1937. President Roosevelt's accompanying message explained his official reasons to Congress and, by extension, the public for the first time. The central purpose, based on a role the Constitution had given Congress, was to address a problem: "the personnel of the Federal Judiciary is insufficient to meet the business before them." The solution was equally obvious—add judges. This, then, would necessitate more Supreme Court justices. "The attainment of speedier justice in the courts below will enlarge the task of the Supreme Court itself." As for the assertion that this was Congress's role, he provided statistics to document this "heavy burden." Cummings and his secret task force had done its work. Once more, it is important to note that the Constitution gives Congress the authority to create all federal courts (except the Supreme Court), to set the business of federal courts (except the original jurisdiction of the Supreme Court), and to determine the number of federal judges and Supreme Court justices.

If he had stopped there, President Roosevelt might well have gotten away with it. No one could argue with the statistics that reflected the reality of attempting to litigate in the federal courts. The courts were flooded, mostly with a surge in bankruptcy cases. (These had dominated the courts' time since repeal of the Volstead Act had reduced the number of criminal prosecutions for bootlegging.) A bitter critic might have noted that the New Deal may well have been responsible for some of that surge, but it would have been a voice in the wilderness. A modern economy needed modern courts. It was perfectly natural. Yet FDR did not stop there. He noted that many of those judges were "aged or infirm," particularly those, presumedly, over seventy years old. While some of "advanced age" retained their "full mental and physical vigor," others did not. Roosevelt also provided a quote without attribution to describe these "aged or infirm" judges: "They seem to be tenacious of the appearance of adequacy." He had noted the source in his meeting with the congressional leadership—Chief Justice Hughes's 1928 *The Supreme Court of the United States.*

President Roosevelt, America's first—and, as yet, only—disabled president went on to associate being over seventy and a half years old with conservative, thus, out of date, jurisprudence. "A lowered mental or physical vigor leads men to an examination of complicated and changed conditions." Apparently, wisdom did not necessarily come with age. And what of the conservative forty-year-olds? In our present era of sensitivity to ageism, almost everyone would recognize the prejudice Roosevelt's remarks conveyed. However, we should note that many commentators at the time were put off by these assertions. In any case, he insisted it was "obvious" that aged judges and justices needed a "supplement" to "accelerate the work of the court."

In his conclusion, President Roosevelt recommended the immediate creation of positions for new federal judges and justices: one for each judge or justice over seventy, up to a maximum number. He declared: "These proposals do not raise any issue of constitutional law." That much was true. Congress had the Constitution-given authority to do it. However, did the president forget to consider the letter of the law as well as the spirit of the law? Having the ability to do something did not make it right. He did not seem interested in the contradiction. According to his reasoning, modernity would overcome the traditional regardless. It was a kind of Whig progressivism. The old must make way for the new.

Furthermore, Roosevelt recommended that Congress mandate that judges give notice to the attorney general of any pending order affecting national laws so that the government would have the opportunity to be heard. The present system of the Department of Justice having to wait for the appeals process, while federal laws were suspended, created an unacceptable uncertainty. "Thus the judiciary, by postponing the effective date of Acts of the Congress, is assuming an additional function and is coming more and more to constitute a scattered, loosely organized and slowly operating third house of the National Legislature." The process of projection—ascribing to your opponent what you yourself have done or are doing—was obvious here, keeping in mind that *Schechter* had been all about the encroachment of the executive branch on the legislature using slow, complicated, and arguably unfair procedures.

If Congress passed this proposal, President Roosevelt asserted it would forestall the need to consider "any fundamental changes in the powers of the courts or the constitution of our Government." Unknown even to most of the administration, this vague but ominous threat had begun with the Cummings investigation and was only now emerging into the public eye. Then the legislation went to Congress for its consideration.

Though New Dealers dominated the House of Representatives, it still operated under the rules set up after a revolt against Speaker of the House James G. Cannon in 1910. The Speaker of the House still dominated the legislative agenda, but House committee chairs continued to

{ *Chapter Five* }

exercise outsized power, and these chairs were selected on the basis of seniority—the amount of continuous time served in the House. Committee chairs not only ran the hearings in their committees, they also largely determined the schedule. A clever, determined, and knowledgeable committee chair could bottle up a bill indefinitely. In this set of circumstances, the chair of the House Judiciary Committee, Hatton W. Sumners from Dallas, Texas, not only resented being blindsided at the meeting on February 5th; he genuinely believed the bill to be unconstitutional. Keeping in mind this love of the Constitution did not extend to checking his overt racism or his vehement opposition to federal lynching laws, his opposition, which became vocal, meant the bill had to go to the Senate first.

While the large New Deal majority in the House of Representatives could be expected to approve the plan if it ever reached the floor, its passage through the Senate was another matter. Though Democrats dominated the chamber, many of these Democratic members antedated the New Deal. A large number had their own independent power bases in their states. All of them were sensitive to public pressure, but, more importantly, held themselves, their prerogatives, and their distinctly senatorial way of doing things in high regard. They needed management, mustering, coaxing, and, when needed, perhaps a deal, and certainly respect for their elevated status. Most of the senators steadfastly refused to be a rubber stamp for any president, even one who had just gained reelection by a landslide. Roosevelt's secrecy had prevented the Senate leadership from strategizing, campaigning, and bargaining significantly in advance of the hearings and subsequent debate. That was unfortunate.

A Very Public Battle

In his first term, and on other issues during his long presidency, FDR had launched trial balloons to gauge the political winds. He had done little to advance his supposed reform of the judiciary, besides launching criticisms. When he took on the Supreme Court directly in the "horse and buggy" press conference, remarks during the campaign, and his State of the Union and second inaugural addresses, it had elicited criticism, sometimes widespread. The Judicial Procedures Reform plan had no such trial balloon, and it produced a flurry of opposition. This time the letter writing, telegrams, and public reactions flooding the White House, Congress, the newspapers, and the justices may well have been genuine and overwhelmingly hostile to the scheme.

Though presented as both a reform and an aid to the elderly members of the bench, the opposition, which soon included a large majority, referred to the legislation as "court packing." In truth, it was. However, no one was supposed to know that. While Attorney General Cummings tried to advocate for the bill as a reform of the judiciary, both in public speeches and before Congress, his remarks always came back to the Supreme Court's adverse rulings, just as FDR's message to Congress had. Packing the Court was bad enough, but Roosevelt's secrecy and dishonesty packaging the measure did immeasurable damage to the plan's credibility as a genuine reform. There was no mandate for court reform from the 1936 election because, aside from the party platform's plank about an amendment, FDR had made only veiled references. Apparently, he had conflated support for his administration and the New Deal with his opinions on the Supreme Court. He now learned otherwise.

Newspapers were particularly brutal in their take on the proposed legislation. After only a few days, the vast majority called it a "court-packing plan." Editorial cartoons encapsulated the critique best. One of them, published in the *Washington Post* on February 6th, one day after the rollout of "the big surprise," showed FDR presenting his proposal to Congress with six FDR clones sitting behind the current nine justices, chatting with one another and whispering in the ears of the original nine. The editorials did not pull any punches about the allegedly dictatorial move, the reduction of the independent judiciary, and the attack on the Court. With the often hostile print media full of negative reporting, Roosevelt's coalition in the Senate came under intense pressure to not give the president his way. One could posit that the flurry of opposition seemed suspiciously coordinated, over the top (FDR was clearly not a dictator), and a far from disinterested inquiry into the case law. Yet it also seems all too familiar in our social media–dominated discourse.

The organized bar, a much more conservative group than it is today, was almost unanimous in condemning the immediate appointment of six new justices. State bar associations, the American Bar Association, and even the elite Association of the Bar of the City of New York passed resolutions against the plan. Invariably, they argued for an independent judiciary and against the president's overreach. Though they represented a relatively small constituency, the legal profession had an immense influence over the operations of US government. All but a handful of US presidents, including FDR, had received legal training. Congress's largest contingent, if not a majority, were lawyers. As the nineteenth-century observer Alexis de Tocqueville had noted, "There is hardly a political question in the United States which does not sooner or later turn into a judicial one." With the American bar almost uniformly, strenuously, and vocally against the measure, the president's lobby confronted an incredibly difficult task.

Before the president's traditional retreat to Warm Springs, Georgia, he and his aides, including Corcoran and Robert H. Jackson, tried to round up support for reforming the courts. FDR tried working his charm in private meetings at the White House. When that did not work, he tried patronage deals. Cummings let Congress and the public know that the increase of justices the bill would allow would not be permanent. As justices retired, the number of justices would fall back. The opposition was not mollified.

Polling conducted in late February indicated that public opinion was almost evenly divided on the topic. Around 38 percent were opposed. Another 45 percent or so supported the president. The rest were undecided. The Senate was divided as well, with almost all of the southern Democrats, who were waiting to see how public opinion coalesced, among the undecided. That level of popular support was insufficient for the bill to prevail. If FDR was counting on his popularity to garner the undecideds in the Senate, his bill would fail.

Battle Lines Drawn

With the House leadership frustrating alternative proposals from Sumners's Judiciary Committee on instructions from the White House and Sumners's committee returning the favor on the bill from the White House, the battleground shifted to the US Senate. Republicans were uniformly against the plan. However, their leadership also knew that if they spoke out, Democrats were likely to close ranks against them. So they kept quiet despite their inclination as politicians and senators to talk. The key senator opposed to the bill, thus, was a Democrat: Senator Burton K. Wheeler from Montana, a firm progressive who strenuously objected to Roosevelt's plan as a danger to the balance of powers. Wheeler's politics were pro-union and civil liberties, isolationist, and independent-minded. Behind closed doors and in public, Wheeler organized, publicized, and plotted against his president and party with a great deal of success.

Roosevelt's champion in the Senate was Senator Joe Robinson of Arkansas, the minority leader from 1923 to 1933 and the majority leader since 1933. He had been a staunch Wilsonian progressive but had distinguished himself by making deals with Republicans, including Republican presidents. After 1933, Robinson dutifully forwarded, shepherded, and fought for FDR's New Deal. He viewed it as his obligation as a loyal Democrat to serve the leader of his party. Robinson was also known for his temper. The Chevy Chase Golf Club expelled him after he punched a doctor who had asked to play through. In 1920, at the Democratic National Convention, he had punched a guard who had questioned his credentials. On several occasions, he had nearly gotten into fights with his Senate colleagues, including Bob LaFollette and Huey Long. Nevertheless, he retained his iron grip on the leadership, even though his arguments on the floor of the Senate often devolved into red-faced, fist pounding, foot-stomping rants. There was no doubt Robinson would fight for his president's bill to the bitter end.

As battle lines were forming in the Senate, House Judiciary Chair Sumners advanced his own plan to solve the crisis. Learning that Justices Van Devanter and Sutherland wanted to retire but were concerned about their post-retirement salaries being cut as previous justices' had been under FDR's budget cuts, he proposed a bill in which they would retain their judicial status but leave their positions. Thus, their salaries, their "compensation" according to the Constitution, could not be reduced during their lifetimes and would be exempt from the federal income tax. Though his accomplishment was overshadowed by FDR's plan, Sumners managed to secure House approval of the Supreme Court Retirement Act, granting those privileges to justices over seventy. In an about-face, President Roosevelt signaled his support for the bill. It passed the Senate and became law on March 1st. Although some disagree, it may well have played a significant role in the defeat of Roosevelt's bill.

As the opposition, particularly newspaper syndicate owner Frank Gannett, organized to defeat "court packing," aides like Jackson convinced President Roosevelt to change his messaging. The public did not comprehend any of the overcrowded statistics Attorney General Cummings had presented. The federal courts seemed to be operating as normal. If anything, most people thought the courts were doing too much. Roosevelt needed to make a clear, honest, persuasive case for expanding the Supreme Court. If his motivation truly was to protect the popular Second New Deal, which had survived for the time being, he should say so to the American people.

Though he was reluctant to change his message in the middle of the campaign, Roosevelt agreed. Unfortunately, he may well have gone too far. His first fusillade came on March 4th at the Victory Day dinners, which raised money for the indebted Democratic Party. In a tone befitting a political rally, FDR opened fire at the jurisprudence of the interstate commerce clause, which had prevented the national government from dealing with flooding rivers, modern economies, and the popular will. Using the metaphor of three horses pulling a plow to describe the three branches of the federal government, he singled out the Court as not being in line with the other two.

Undeterred by the lack of support following the Victory Day speech, once again FDR turned to his tested mechanism of a fireside chat. Originally pitched as the president entering people's living rooms through the radio, the fireside chats had become a key feature of his presidency. Radio was not a new technology, but turning it into a means of mass public opinion formation was. Previously, one-sided political views came through the print media. Once psychology emerged from its infancy during the 1920s, advertisers could hire mass psychology experts to craft advertising campaigns, not just in print but for radio programs and movies. Hollywood and Madison Avenue in New York City thus combined to produce a potent force for shaping the nation.

The most infamous marriage was the movie studios' deal with Big Tobacco to place cigarettes into the hands of its actors and actresses, not just in movies but in their public appearances. Celebrity culture ensured the cigarette's popularity, especially among impressionable young people—then, as now, a hugely important demographic. They were single urban dwellers, with disposable income and a youthful commitment to luxury spending, usually alcohol and sex-related amusements. Sigmund Freud's identification of cigarettes with phalluses may have been overdone, but the subliminal messaging certainly existed. Cigarettes went from being a boutique, only for women item to a mass consumption one, prevalent throughout American life. Roosevelt's upturned cigarette in its holder in his mouth emblematized all of this newfound emphasis on youth, optimism, and, possibly, sexual arousal.

Whatever the psychological impact, the fireside chats personalized FDR in a way that the occasional speech could not. Moreover, without the filter of the press, this consummate politician could shape public opinion all on his own. His manner was always personable, plain-spoken, and moderate in both language and tone. They were also heavily scripted, wordsmithed, and closely crafted for maximum effect. One could easily label them as highly effective propaganda. His fireside chat of March 9, 1937, on the court reform bill, was no different. Its purpose was to turn the tide of popular opinion from hostility to support. Roosevelt had not thought it necessary to do public relations for the bill. The fireside chats were an exception.

Roosevelt opened with his usual "My friends" and promptly reminded the public how an extraordinary amount of government power had saved the country from the banking crisis . . . by only one vote of the Court. His over-simplification of the Court's decisions had only just begun. According to the president, the Court was threatening to put the country back into the Great Depression unless the Congress did something immediately. "To complete our program of protection in time, therefore, we cannot delay one moment in making certain that our national government has power to carry through." Supposedly, "abuses and inequalities" had caused the Depression. The New Deal had cured them. And yet there was still a threat of depression. If he was aware of the contradiction between having cured the ailment with Supreme Court compliance and the ailment still being there with Supreme Court opposition, he did not seem to notice.

Instead, Roosevelt made the point that somehow the "protection" his program afforded was still under threat from the Court. Calling back to his second inaugural address, "one-third of a nation ill-nourished, ill-clad, ill-housed" apparently still needed national government help the Supreme Court would not allow. Once more he used the plow metaphor. The "three-horse team" was not pulling in unison. The Court needed to be reined in. "It is the American people themselves who are in the driver's seat." Though it was anything but, Roosevelt stated the Constitution "is an easy document to understand when you remember that it was called into being because the Articles of Confederation under which the original thirteen states tried to operate after the Revolution showed the need of a national government with power enough to handle national problems." Again, he called upon the Preamble to support his position that the Constitution supported the creation of a powerful, bureaucratized, and controlling nation-state.

Roosevelt was on sounder ground when he quoted from the dissents of the cases that had gone against his administration. The dissents in the Railroad Pension Act and *Butler* and *Tipaldo* cases were strongly worded in his favor, and he wisely ignored the unanimous Court in *Schechter*. To acknowledge it would have reminded his audience of his most disastrous defeat. Moreover, the American public would have wondered why the legislation was so badly drafted that all the justices believed it violated the Constitution. Maybe President Roosevelt and Congress were the ones pulling the plow in the wrong direction.

Roosevelt said that his plan was only to "save the Court from itself." It was not a court "packing" plan. After all, no "president worthy of his office" would appoint "puppets." He only wanted justices who would not rule "arbitrarily" and would stick to the Constitution. Fixing the retirement age was a widely accepted practice, and this proposal was merely to aid the aged justices. They needed "new and younger blood." He was only doing this out of "necessity." Continuing, he declared that it was not an "attack on the Court; it seeks to restore the Court to its rightful and historic place in our system." He quoted from Justice Brandeis in *Adams v. Tanner* (1917) that the Constitution is "a system of living law." Roosevelt did not mention it was a dissenting opinion.

After dismissing the amendment process as a solution to the problem, as too cumbersome and slow, President Roosevelt repeated his claim that he was a conservative serving progressive aims. "During the past half-century the balance of power between the three great branches of the federal government has been tipped out of balance by the courts in direct contradiction of the high purposes of the framers of the Constitution." He concluded, "It is my purpose to restore that balance." To sharpen the picture for the American people, he reminded them, "You who know me will accept my solemn assurance that in a world in which democracy is under attack, I seek to make American democracy succeed. You and I will do our part." In 1937, with Japan aggressing against China, Hitler's Germany on the march, and Mussolini's Italy extending its overseas empire in Ethiopia, this was no exaggeration. However, there may well have been some question in Americans' minds about whether it was the Court or the president who was threatening the democratic republic.

The Battle Engaged

Behind the scenes, FDR was drawing up a list of senators and representatives who opposed him on the judiciary reform bill. If the carrot of patronage did not work, he would apply the stick of withdrawing national party support for outspoken critics, like Senator Millard Tydings of Maryland, in the midterm elections of 1938. Tydings had been a strong supporter of the New Deal, but he had denounced the court-packing plan as similar to Hitler's and Mussolini's assaults on the political institutions of their nations. Roosevelt's passionate reaction to this charge is understandable. Unfortunately, his growing commitment to purging his party of non-loyalists was unlikely to counter the charge that he had trouble with dissent.

Having admitted outright, publicly, and combatively that the original stated purpose of the legislation—reform—was window dressing, Roosevelt went on his annual vacation to Warm Springs, Georgia. Despite all contrary evidence, he was convinced his personal appeals had persuaded the public to support his war on the Court. The proceedings before the Senate Judiciary Committee, under its chair, Henry F. Ashurst from Arizona, now took center stage. His adjutants continued advocating for "reform," but this meant openly lobbying against the US Supreme Court's adverse majority. The unanimity of the justices in *Schechter* and all other evidence to the contrary dropped out of sight.

On March 10th, the Senate Judiciary Committee heard its first witness, Attorney General Cummings. Robert H. Jackson testified next. Both did well, with Cummings sticking to the need for reform and Jackson focusing on the poor quality of the Court's decisions. Though the opposition harangued them with questions, they were well prepared, remained professional at all times, and came off well. However, Corcoran soon realized that the long list of witnesses for their side was playing into the hands of the bill's opponents. While the testimony was essentially the same, the clock ticked on as their hearings went on for two weeks with only half of the administration's list having testified. The speediness FDR had wanted was evaporating before the opposition's delaying tactics with no one either in the Senate or the public being converted into supporters. On Corcoran's and others' advice, the administration cut the list of witnesses on their side short, hoping that their opponents would be brief. They were wrong.

The most devastating testimony came on Monday, March 22nd, from Senator Wheeler, who produced a letter from Chief Justice Hughes refuting the administration's charge that the Court was overwhelmed and could not handle its business efficiently due to the age and infirmity of the justices. Behind the scenes in the weeks prior, Wheeler had met with Justice Brandeis in his Washington, DC, apartment to ask for justices to testify before the committee. Brandeis objected to this plan as too political and suggested instead that Wheeler arrange to present a letter from the chief justice limited to the assertion that the Court could handle its workload, specifically the certiorari petitions it had turned down as opposed to the few it had accepted. Hughes was likely to take on the task for several reasons, not the least of which was that he had dedicated himself to managing the Court's workload, at least according to Justice Stone among others.

Whether Brandeis's meeting with Wheeler was proper is another matter. The justice regularly reached out beyond the Court, particularly to Harvard Law professor and protégé Felix Frankfurter, for assistance in a variety of matters. He, at least, did not consider the doctrine of separation of powers as limiting his contact with members of the other federal branches. This was a very dangerous maneuver. Possibly, it was a throwback to when some governance took place amiably in private—behind closed doors—while appearing nonpartisan in public.

Wheeler read the letter to the committee to great effect. Hughes and his clerk had done an excellent job mustering the data, from the Solicitor General's office and on their own, about the work of the Court. Contrary to the administration's assertions of inefficiency and being overwhelmed, the justices had cleared their docket completely and rapidly. Moreover, they had actually expanded their review of cert petitions, with most rejections because of technical deficiencies, not for arbitrary reasons or because they did not have the time to review them. Hughes's conduct of the conferences had contributed greatly to a rapid turnaround of the cases they did review, often to the discomfort of Justice Stone, who felt that Hughes was overly managing the Court. Thus, the chief justice was able to weigh in on the legislation without seeming to overstep his role as an impartial arbiter of the law. His letter also made a very good case that Roosevelt's proposed reform was a solution in search of a problem, though there is criticism, to this day, that Hughes's involvement was improper.

As Ashurst let the Senate Judiciary Committee's hearing drag on into April, the administration worked the battle from both angles. While Assistant Attorney General Joe Keenan and Corcoran offered deals to senators, Secretary of Agriculture Wallace, Assistant Attorney General Jackson, and others tried to muster support from farm organizations and organized labor. Both groups had been burned by adverse Supreme Court rulings. Both were avid supporters of FDR and the New Deal. Both had much to lose if the Supreme Court remained hostile. Yet both groups failed to throw their weight behind the legislation.

Wallace reported that farmers were just too "conservative" to back a change to the Court. Many took a wait-and-see attitude. Others could not be bothered to invest much effort in trying to understand why the administration could not pass a subsidy law that would survive judicial review. Organized labor did not rally behind the bill because it was too divided. The Congress of Industrial Organizations (CIO) had broken with the American Federation of Labor (AFL) and was conducting a series of sit-down strikes in the automotive industry. Although very effective at forcing management to consider negotiations, sit-down strikes were unpopular with the public, exacerbated confrontation, and were politically controversial for various reasons, not the least of which was because they were illegal. Even though the Ninth Circuit Court of

Appeals and other federal courts had cast doubts on the legality of the Wagner Act, the enforcement of it, along with the TVA, the SEC, and other New Deal laws, was in a state of limbo waiting for the Supreme Court to rule instead of creating imminent threats. Regardless of the cause, agriculture and organized labor were either hostile or silent on the bill—a loss for the administration.

Perhaps the most devastating witness against the bill was Erwin Griswold, a former member of the Justice Department. He had specialized in tax litigation before the Court and was presently a professor at Harvard Law School. Griswold patiently, thoroughly, and, for many, convincingly tore apart the administration's argument that somehow the changes in number of Supreme Court justices over the preceding century were all analogous to the current situation. The future prominent dean of Harvard Law School explained how the motivations for the judiciary acts of 1862 and 1866 had been in recognition of expansions in the size and population of the country, and neither of them had been because of adverse rulings. Furthermore, he likened the current efforts to a "more gentlemanly way" of changing the Court's personnel as opposed to shooting them. In case anyone had missed his point, Griswold quoted Brandeis in *Myers v. U.S.* (1926), noting that giving the president that level of control was one step closer to dictatorship. Griswold possessed the stature, even at that time, to puncture the testimonies of supporters of the bill, like Princeton professor and constitutional law expert Edward S. Corwin, leaving the measure without the academic gloss it needed to prevail.

Still, it is important to recognize that Griswold's testimony was his interpretation of various judiciary acts governing the number of justices on the Supreme Court and reorganizing the circuits. Today, there is a consensus among historians and general commentators alike that the judiciary acts of 1862 and 1866 "packed" the Court and the federal bench. In the midst of the Civil War, the Lincoln administration and an overwhelmingly Republican Congress passed the 1862 act condensing the South's circuits, expanding the North's, and adding a justice to the Supreme Court specifically to ride circuit for the Far West, especially California, whose population had boomed as a result of the gold rush of 1849. Instead of reorganizing the existing Court, the Republicans, seeing a hostile Democratic majority on its bench, added a justice for Lincoln to appoint as well as several federal judges in the North. At a stroke, a largely southern or southern-leaning Democratic bench became largely Northern and Republican with the new tenth Supreme Court justice, Stephen A. Field, a Unionist Democrat. For a time, the Court had ten justices instead of nine.

During Andrew Johnson's presidency, the number of justices fell back to seven after the anti-Johnson Republican Congress passed another judiciary act, in 1866, allowing the Court to be reduced in order to prevent Johnson appointments. In 1869, after a Republican, Ulysses S. Grant, succeeded Johnson as president, the Republican majority in Congress increased the number of justices to nine. Once again, historians generally agree that these judiciary acts were political, akin to packing or, in the case of 1866, reducing the Court. They consider the Republicans' explanations that population shift and westward expansion made this necessary to be largely window dressing. Either Griswold honestly disagreed with this assessment, taking those Republicans at their word, or he was stacking the deck, in his testimony, against court packing. We cannot know the answer. Both views are plausible.

The Senate Judiciary Committee hearings on the bill to reorganize the judiciary ended on April 23rd. By that time, the hearing room, which was usually filled with national press coverage every day, had witnessed four weeks of testimony from those opposed to the legislation, including the president of Princeton University, the head of the New York bar, and other constitutional experts. They had often gone beyond the legislation to criticize FDR's arguments directly. While some favored an amendment, others counseled patience with the Court. We do not know the effect of this daily lesson in civics on the public, but Ashurst drew the hearings to a close because he had calculated that a majority would vote against it.

Robinson and its other supporters would still bring it to the Senate floor for debate, but any number of actions could lead to its demise, including a filibuster. Though Roosevelt put up a confident face throughout the battle, the only certain result was that his bill had occupied the congressional calendar for most of the spring with prospects for the rest of the season disappearing as well—a lost opportunity for his New Deal supermajorities in both houses.

{ *Chapter Five* }

Switches in Time

When the Court had announced its decision in *Tipaldo* in 1936, voiding New York State's minimum wage law for women and children and seemingly upholding *Adkins*, criticism reached a fever pitch, spurring New Deal Democrats to seek ways of dealing with the Court's supposed conservative majority. It was not just the fact that the "freedom of contract" doctrine had been the bane of state minimum wage laws ever since *Lochner* in 1905, but the stagnation it represented. As FDR had put it at the time: "It seems to be very clear . . . that the 'no man's land' where no government—state or federal—can function is being more clearly defined. A state cannot do it and the federal government cannot do it." Because Justice Roberts had been the deciding vote, *Tipaldo*—more than the unanimous *Schechter*—was a convenient target for the ire of would-be reformers, even though *Schechter* had been the initial spur to action.

All was not as it seemed. Justice Roberts had stated outright in the conference, the meeting to discuss the case, that the time to revisit *Adkins* had not arrived because New York State's attorneys had not raised the issue in their briefs or arguments. Otherwise, he would have voted to overturn *Adkins*. That had been far from the popular impression *Tipaldo* had created. Enforcement of state minimum wage laws throughout the United States had largely ceased, including in Washington State, where the 1913 law remained on the books. Interestingly enough, on December 16th and 17th, 1936, the US Supreme Court heard oral arguments concerning that very same law, but this time the lawyers for Washington State challenged *Adkins* directly. One is also entitled to wonder whether Roberts's justification is genuine given that the attorneys for New York State did raise overturning *Adkins* in their brief. Was Roberts arguing they had not done it often enough?

Nevertheless, by a 5–4 decision, with Roberts as the swing vote, Chief Justice Hughes wrote the majority opinion in *West Coast Hotel Co. v. Parrish* (1937) expressly overruling *Adkins* and upholding Washington State's minimum wage law. He read the opinion on March 29, 1937, before Senator Wheeler read Hughes's letter to the Senate Judiciary Committee. According to some later accounts, Hughes had delayed issuing this opinion of the Court from February, when it was decided, until later in the term in order to assure its impact. Regardless of whether or not these recollections are true, Justice Roberts had reversed his position since *Tipaldo*. The decision in *West Coast Hotel* signaled that the Supreme Court now supported minimum wage laws and had moved away from "horse and buggy" jurisprudence. This decision undercut the rationale for adding more justices to liberalize the Court's jurisprudence. Thus, a myth was born in the press and the public that Roberts had helped save the Court from Roosevelt's court-packing plan—"the switch in time that saved nine." This phrase was based on the old saying that "a stitch in time saves nine" and was coined on April 14th by Cal Tinney, a journalist and quipster with the *New York Post*, according to John Q. Barrett.

The only certainty is that the saying stuck due to its pithiness and this widespread belief. Evidence explaining Roberts's supposed shift was, and is, in short supply because of the tradition of secrecy that governs the Court's activities to this day, the leak that occurred on May 2nd, 2022, of the recent *Dobbs* decision overturning *Roe v. Wade*, being a notable exception. Owen Roberts, like Justice Cardozo and Chief Justice John Marshall, had his papers destroyed after retirement, so the search for answers is that much more difficult.

The question remains whether this "switch in time" is true. Did Justice Roberts switch his vote on the constitutionality of the minimum wage either because of the court-packing threat or because he was paying attention to the election returns in November of 1936? The only document we have explaining his decision is a memorandum Roberts wrote to then Justice Felix Frankfurter at Frankfurter's request for Roberts's reasons for overruling *Adkins* in *West Coast Hotel* but not *Tipaldo*. Frankfurter arranged for the memorandum to be published in the December 1955 issue of the *University of Pennsylvania Law Review*. In it, Roberts answered several questions but left others unanswered.

About his vote in *Tipaldo*, Roberts stated he was against granting cert in the case because New York State was not challenging *Adkins*. When it came up for a conference vote after the presentation of briefs and oral arguments, he noted that New York tried to distinguish the *Adkins* case rather than challenge it directly. "The argument seemed to me to be disingenuous and born of timidity. I could find nothing in the record to substantiate the alleged distinction." As a result, he voted with the Four

Horsemen. Justice Butler received the opinion to write. Roberts had expressed his view to Butler that the opinion should be limited to Roberts's views, "but after a dissent had been circulated he added matter to his opinion, seeking to sustain the *Adkins* case in principle." Instead of writing a concurrence explaining the true situation, he remained publicly silent. Apparently, either the Hughes or Stone dissent, probably Stone's, pushed Butler to write a stronger opinion for the Court than the caution Roberts's swing vote merited.

As for the *West Coast Hotel* case, Roberts's vote was purely a matter of timing. Justice Stone had been seriously ill, "comatose" according to Roberts's memorandum, during the conference discussion of how to resolve the case. Washington State's attorneys had called for the overturning of *Adkins*, and "thus, for the first time, I was confronted with the necessity of facing the soundness of the *Adkins* case." When he voted to overturn it, one of his "brethren" asked another, "What is the matter with Roberts?" It was a good question. The memorandum does not provide his reason for finding fault with the "soundness" of *Adkins*. The vote had taken place on December 19th. Because of Stone's absence, it was 4–4, and the case "was laid over for further consideration when Justice Stone should be able to participate." At the February 6, 1937, conference, Stone cast the fifth vote, and the decision's announcement was scheduled for March 29, 1937.

That is the sum total of Justice Roberts's account of switching his vote from *Tipaldo* to *West Coast Hotel*. He provided little reason for wanting to overturn *Adkins*. He did not explain his lack of concurrence with Butler in *Tipaldo* when Butler's majority opinion went far beyond Roberts's actual views. The only thing he did state with any certainty was: "These facts make it evident that no action taken by the President in the interim had any causal relation to my action in the *Parrish* case." What is more, in conference before the election, Roberts had indicated how he would vote on *West Coast Hotel Co. v. Parrish*. Though this fact plainly disputes the argument that the court-packing plan influenced his vote, it also does not rule out the possibility that the election returns might have stiffened his resolve. The only thing we can be sure of is that *West Coast Hotel* undermined the Roosevelt administration's alleged urgent need to add justices to the Court.

Another question the Court's decision in *West Coast Hotel* raises is whether it truly signified a shift of its jurisprudence, its constitutional interpretation, from *Adkins* and *Tipaldo*. It is entirely possible *Adkins* was the outlier and *Tipaldo* merely a circumstantial outgrowth of *Adkins*.. After all, the Court, in *Muller v. Oregon* (1908), had already made an exception for women from *Lochner*'s days and hours "freedom of contract" restriction. How much of a switch was *West Coast Hotel?* Ben Cohen had drafted the New York law to distinguish it from the DC law that Frankfurter had defended. Only an examination of the opinion in *West Coast Hotel* can shed some light on the matter.

Hughes had several challenges to overcome with his opinion, not the least of which is that he needed to mount enough of an argument to overrule *Adkins* while upholding Washington State's minimum wage law for women from 1903. To do so, he disposed of *Tipaldo*, which he called *Morehead*, using Roberts's explanation for his vote: New York State had not tried to challenge *Adkins*. Hughes proceeded to use *Muller*'s paternalism toward women to good effect. Applying *Nebbia*'s rational basis test, he cited *Muller*'s protection of women, who were vulnerable, and Washington State's use of a commission, originally, to determine a safe wage to secure "the vigor of the race": women's biological function of producing future generations. Thus, he linked a vital state interest—motherhood—with a rational, "neither arbitrary nor capricious," means to achieve it.

As for why the US Supreme Court needed to revisit *Adkins*, Hughes cited the many states that had adopted similar laws, "the close division by which the *Adkins* case was reached," and "the economic conditions which have supervened," as well as the "reasonableness" of Washington State's actions. Apparently, the Court's review process was to take current circumstances, like the Great Depression, into account as well as paternalistic goals. Finally, he dispensed with "freedom of contract" and replaced it with the principle of protecting workers from unscrupulous employers. "But the liberty safeguarded [under due process] is liberty in a social organization which requires the protection of law against the evils which menace the health, safety, morals and welfare of the people." Instead of the analysis focusing on protecting people from the government, government would protect the people unless it could be proven otherwise.

Though he may not have known it, Chief Justice Hughes, alongside Roberts, had announced a major shift in the US Supreme Court's jurisprudence under the guise of safeguarding the supposed "weaker sex" (not his words) from "oppression" (his word). Stone and the other musketeers had already articulated the doctrines after the unanimity of *Schechter* had dissipated. Well-drafted legislation that did not violate the separation of powers, and reasonably intruded into the states' traditional areas, could now advance whether or not they destroyed previous notions of leaving market-based actions in place. The era of the managed economy had arrived, with the Court no longer a bulwark against government encroachment on private decisions. All decisions in the marketplace were now the public's, thus, the government's, business.

The great contradiction at the heart of the *West Coast Hotel* decision was the litigant, the underpaid maid, Elsie Parrish. She fought her employer, against the odds, all the way to the US Supreme Court. This intrepidness belies the vulnerable woman envisioned in the Washington State law, *Muller v. Oregon*, and now the majority opinion in *West Coast Hotel*. Moreover, she was not alone or helpless. She was married and had children and grandchildren, and a community around her. Although the national organizations did not support her appeals to the courts, because they believed *Adkins* and *Tipaldo* made it hopeless, her suit did have support from her locality as well as the Washington State government. What emerges from this contradiction is not only traditional attitudes toward women and family, but a shift in approach to government, from laissez-faire to what some strident critics call the "nanny state," where individuals are not self-reliant in traditional ways but have to yield to the collective good.

Justice Sutherland wrote a dissent for himself and the other horsemen. He unabashedly defended "freedom of contract" and the role of the Court in determining whether a "rational doubt" existed as to the constitutionality of the statute. In other words, the dissenters placed the burden on the state government to overcome the constitutional hurdle, not on the Court or the individual challenging the state government. The Four Horsemen were resisting Hughes's and the Musketeers' shift of the burden of proof, which made it far easier for state governments to pass laws governing people's behavior. Sutherland also raised the standard of review from the lowest level—the rational basis test—to that of reasonable doubt, used in criminal trials. Given that states were fining and/or imprisoning people for violating these laws, he may have had a point. However, all of this was largely moot. The era of laissez-faire had passed away with Roberts's vote.

For what it is worth, Sutherland pointed out key problems in the jurisprudence of the new majority. He declared the judicial restraint policy "ill-considered and mischievous." Judges took an oath to uphold the Constitution, not to withhold judgment in the face of political majorities. As for the idea that "the ebb and flow of events" should influence the Court's reading of the Constitution, Sutherland held that "is to rob that instrument of the essential element which continues it in force as the people have made it until they, and not their official agents, have made it otherwise." There was an amendment process. It empowered the people's representatives to change the words. It was not for the Court to do so. "The judicial function is that of interpretation; it does not include the power of amendment under the guise of interpretation." The Constitution had a set meaning.

Yet this also left the Constitution sadly antiquated in the modern world. How should justices and judges interpret the language for new circumstances not envisioned by the framers? What should they do with wiretaps, electronic surveillance from satellites, and social credit scores administered by private companies at the behest of government authorities? Sutherland did not seem to appreciate that the devil was in the details of interpretation.

Sutherland and the dissenters also disagreed with the majority's application of *Nebbia*'s rational basis test. To the contrary, they found the determination of a healthy wage to be "essentially arbitrary." Interestingly, Sutherland's opinion laid out one of the basic problems in law. The commission, or any governmental agency for that matter, set up rules for all those in a given classification, in this case women. Sutherland points out that individuals vary according to their particular situations. An appropriate wage for Elsie Parrish may be too much or too little for someone else. Under this approach, government command-and-control economics could not substitute for the market in wages.

Furthermore, the Washington State law discriminated against women. "Women today stand upon a legal and political equality with men. There is no longer any reason why they should be put in different classes in respect of their legal right to make contracts; nor should they be denied, in effect, the right to compete with men for work paying lower wages which men may be willing to accept." In other words, the Washington State law, instead of helping women, was actually lowering the number of jobs available to them. Under the strange circumstances of the late 1930s, Justice Sutherland envisioned himself and the other horsemen as the advocates for women's rights while the liberal, progressive majority were upholders of sexism and paternalism. Of course, it did not matter. Sutherland and the other horsemen were in the minority.

That same day, March 29th, 1937, the Supreme Court upheld two more Second New Deal laws. As a result, *West Coast Hotel*'s switch became a trend later known as "White Monday" to contrast with *Schechter*'s "Black Monday" in 1935. In *Virginian Railway Company v. Railway Employees [Federation]*, Justice Stone wrote an opinion for the Court, without dissent, upholding the 1934 amendments to the Railway Act of 1926 creating a labor board governing the interstate railway companies. Because the labor board performed a similar function to the National Labor Relations Board (NLRB) of the Wagner Act, *Virginian Railway Company* signaled the Court's openness to what its supporters called "labor's Magna Carta." The Court had long recognized that interstate railroads, including their labor practices, were a fit subject for congressional oversight, The only novelty was Stone's inclusion of the amendments' justification—labor peace in the railroad industry—as a legitimate object for congressional action under the interstate commerce clause.

In the third case decided that day, *Wright v. Vinton Branch*, Justice Brandeis wrote the opinion of the Court, without dissent, upholding the revised Frazier-Lemke Act the Court had invalidated in *Radford*, decided on "Black Monday" with *Schechter*. Congress was still trying to protect farmers from losing their farms to bankruptcy. This time they made a point of not only addressing the Court's objections in *Radford*: they stated in the *Congressional Record* in clear terms that they were trying to protect farmers, which Brandeis cited approvingly. Everything the previous Court had found objectionable, the Congress had modified. In *Wright*, Brandeis could vindicate Congress's powers over bankruptcy as written in the Constitution without concern that somehow it was destroying contract law, overstepping its bounds, or instituting some newfangled system of credit.

West Coast Hotel, *Virginia Railway*, and *Wright* showed a Court amenable to New Deal legislation and not just by a 5–4 margin. The two latter cases had been unanimous. "White Monday" was the reverse of "Black Monday," with the administration prevailing in all three cases. Solicitor General Stanley Reed had been busy, and so had the New Deal lawyers. Their able interventions had salvaged the legislation, turning unconstitutional majorities into unanimous affirmations. Though victorious, FDR emphasized what Robert H. Jackson had told the Senate Judiciary Committee before "White Monday." The one-vote victory in *West Coast Hotel* was too slim a margin.

Unexpected Victories

On April 12th, 1937, the US Supreme Court ended the anxiety surrounding the Wagner Act, which established the NLRB, with a series of decisions upholding the law. Justice Roberts wrote the decisions, many of them nearly unanimous, covering the newspapers and transportation. Both were clearly covered under the interstate commerce clause. But Chief Justice Hughes reserved for himself the opinions upholding the legislation for manufacturing. Under the *Carter Coal* case, Hughes and Roberts had voted with the Four Horsemen that the interstate commerce clause did not apply to coal mining because it had only a secondary effect on interstate commerce. In *NLRB v. Jones & Laughlin Steel Corp.*, they switched their votes and endorsed the Cardozo dissent in the *Carter Coal* standard—the degree of the effect on interstate commerce. As much as *West Coast Hotel*, this switch defined the Court's shift on the New Deal.

Hughes's opinion centered on whether Jones & Laughlin, hence its labor relations, substantially affected interstate commerce. Contrary to the finding in *Schechter*, he and the majority determined that the NLRB had successfully investigated and documented the entity's interstate character, despite the specific labor dispute being located in one state. Though his opinion did not state it outright, it appears the key difference between *Jones & Laughlin Steel* and *Schechter* was Congress's use of a commission-like agency to carry out the particular objectives of the legislation instead of the ad hoc, indeterminate methods of the NRA. Although relying on the "direct burden" standard, Hughes and Roberts likely needed the Progressive Era commission to legitimate congressional authority over an industry.

Hughes's opinion did not stop there. He virtually applauded the purposes of the Wagner Act. "Discrimination and coercion to prevent the free exercise of the right of employees to self-organization and representation is a proper subject for condemnation by competent legislative authority." He might well have been quoting from the Democratic Party platform of 1936. What was more, he enshrined the "right to organize" in the Supreme Court's case law. Instead of having a judicial system that had flattened organized labor since the nineteenth century with only a few exceptions, the United States was now a pro-union jurisdiction. As much as anything else, this was a momentous change in US law and a major departure from the voiding of wage and hours provisions in *Schechter*.

In case there was any doubt as to the preferences of the new majority, Hughes's opinion closed by supporting the legislation's value with the highly speculative proposition that somehow enshrining collective bargaining in federal law would promote peace between labor and management. "Experience has abundantly demonstrated that the recognition of the right of employees to self-organization and to have representatives of their own choosing for the purpose of collective bargaining is often an essential condition of industrial peace." An impartial observer might suggest that the reason Hughes did not cite any source for this assertion was that there was no source. In fact, there is unlikely to be any demonstrable relationship between independent unions and the absence of strikes. Company unions and successful employment of anti-union tactics are far more likely to eliminate strikes than the widespread presence of organized labor. Regardless, a factual determination was not the issue for the Hughes majority, only the legitimacy of what Congress had concluded. And the majority was no longer disposed to second-guess Congress's imposition of unionization throughout the United States.

Justice McReynolds wrote the dissent for himself and the other horsemen in the NLRB cases, specifically *NLRB v. Friedman-Harry Marks Clothing Co.* He pointed out that Hughes's majority had overruled not only *Carter Coal* but also *Schechter* and all the preceding cases that established the difference between interstate commerce and manufacturing.

He also noted the problem for federalism inherent in such a shift. Under the "stream of commerce" justification, whereby everything that substantially affects or is affected by interstate commerce is subject to regulation by Congress, there is nothing left for the states. "Almost anything—marriage, birth, death—may in some fashion affect commerce." On the basis of the Tenth Amendment alone, the Wagner Act overstepped constitutional restrictions.

In the end, McReynolds and the dissenters had to lament the demise of "freedom of contract" as a legal doctrine. Employers and property owners no longer had absolute rights to run their businesses as they pleased so long as it did not harm anyone else. The concept of "free labor, free men," which had galvanized the creation of the Republican Party in 1855, was now fading away in the aftermath of the Great Depression's empowerment of New Deal Democrats. "The right to contract is fundamental, and includes the privilege of selecting those with whom one is willing to assume contractual relations," McReynolds wrote. "A private owner is deprived of power to manage his own property by freely selecting those to whom his manufacturing operations are to be entrusted. We think this cannot lawfully be done in circumstances like those here disclosed." The dissenters objected to national government–sanctioned unionization. Hughes's and Roberts's new views made those concerns obsolete.

When it came to the Social Security cases, the FDR administration racked up two more victories. Argued on April 8th and 9th and announced on May 24th, 1937, the last day for decisions, instead of Hughes writing for the new majority, Justice Cardozo had the honor of distinguishing *Butler*'s destruction of a similar plan for agricultural subsidies and the Agricultural Adjustment Act and the United States government taxing and spending for old age pensions and unemployment and disability insurance. *Steward Machine Co. v. Davis* dealt with several major issues, but the key point concerned congressional authority to collect and spend taxes in an area traditionally reserved for the states. Using the Great Depression as the background, Cardozo's majority saw no harm or impingement of state governments, even though state taxes were to be collected, held, and distributed through the US Treasury Department. Once again, Roberts's and Hughes's votes gave the musketeers their majority.

Again, Justice McReynolds dissented for himself and the other horse-men. He lamented the collapse of federalism. "Apparently the States remained really free to exercise governmental powers, not delegated or prohibited, without interference by the Federal Government through threats of punitive measures or offers of seductive favors. Unfortunately, the decision just announced opens the way for practical annihilation of this theory, and no cloud of words or ostentatious parade of irrelevant statistics should be permitted to obscure that fact." Much later, analysts of the massive power the US government had over the states referred to the problem as one of "unfunded mandates." In 1984 the US government could impose a minimum age for alcohol purchase of twenty-one by threatening to withhold federal highway funds, for example, even though that was purely a matter for state law. All of the states needed the federal highway money so much they changed their laws to comply by 1988. Technically speaking, this has led to the US government's control over almost all of higher education, public schools, and a host of other matters. *Steward Machine Co.* was the start.

The companion case, *Helvering et al. v. Davis*, gave Cardozo a more re-sounding victory. With only two dissents, from Butler and McReynolds, he wrote for the majority that his interpretation of the general welfare clause was now the law of the land. The justification? The teachings of the Great Depression. "The purge of nationwide calamity that began in 1929 has taught us many lessons. Not the least is the solidarity of interests that may once have seemed to be divided. Unemployment spreads from State to State, the hinterland now settled that, in pioneer days gave an avenue of escape." As in almost all Supreme Court opinions, Cardozo did not explain how exactly he had arrived at those two conclusions. Economic events do not teach anything. People may draw lessons from them, but those are the workings of a human mind, not the phenomenon.

Then there was the "frontier thesis" of historian Frederick Jackson Turner's Columbian Exposition address in 1893, which Cardozo appears to have referenced. Upon the closing of the American frontier, according to the US census, that is, Native American lands had fallen under complete US jurisdiction, Frederick Jackson Turner argued that, unlike any other time in US history, there was no "safety valve" of open land for the dispossessed of the cities to settle. During the previous centuries, an economic downturn like a recession or depression would lead to migration of the unemployed to the supposedly empty land out west. That process allowed the United States to avoid the class strife affecting Europe and other Western societies.

Historians have almost universally rejected Turner's thesis. After all, factory workers newly unemployed are highly unlikely to migrate west in order to set up a farm. Then there is the idea that the frontier was "empty" and untamed. In reality, the West had inhabitants who had settled there long before—the Native Americans. Nevertheless, Turner's thesis dominated academic circles during Cardozo's time, so it was not unexpected that this now-debunked view should find its way into a Supreme Court opinion. Despite these criticisms, the new majority upheld the Social Security Act, contrary to Roosevelt's fears.

––––––

One might have thought these victories before the US Supreme Court would have dampened enthusiasm for court packing. It did, at least in the public's mind. It also virtually eliminated organized labor's support for Roosevelt's plan. Yet FDR remained committed to his "reform" of the judiciary. For him, the votes remained too close. His holy grail was to nominate appointees to the Court, and he would settle for nothing less. In some ways it resembled another Democrat, Andrew Jackson, and his "war" against the Bank of the United States in the 1830s. A popular president, who ran against the establishment, sought to imprint himself and his political program on the nation come hell or high water. Perhaps, FDR should have taken Jackson's war as an example. Although Jackson won a large victory for reelection, his king-like actions with his "pet banks" spurred the creation of the Whig Party—a viable opposition.

CHAPTER 6

Aftermath

As the US Supreme Court wrapped up its term in the spring of 1937, President Franklin D. Roosevelt's Judicial Procedures Reform Bill, more commonly known as his court-packing plan, still rested with the Senate Judiciary Committee. The Court's recent rulings in *West Coast Hotel*, NLRB, and the Social Security cases signaled a major shift in its stance toward the New Deal, in particular the Second New Deal—the supposed "switch in time that saved nine." However, the president was adamant that the 5–4 rulings were not sufficient. There needed to be new "blood" on the Court. Popular support had ebbed with the Court's switch, yet the president still had veto-proof majorities in Congress. Would Democrats defy their president? Would the Court grant them more ammunition in the argument that adding justices was unnecessary? What would the future hold?

Then there is the overriding question of how these developments affected the *Schechter* story. The unanimous Court certainly disappeared as did doctrines like *Lochner*'s skepticism of business regulation, close scrutiny of legislative actions, and a deep concern for federalism. Did anything remain of *Schechter* besides the non-delegation doctrine? If not, how was alleged court-packing part of the *Schechter* story? It may have prompted the effort, yet that was a long time ago in jurisprudential terms. For the answers we must examine the aftermath in the next generation, as it were, of the shock of "Black Monday."

Final Blows

In late April and early May of 1937, between administration victories before the US Supreme Court, President Roosevelt's Judicial Procedures Reform Bill's prospects went from bad to worse. Bracketed by the double blows of needlessness the Court had delivered with its recent decisions, these few weeks witnessed a bizarre spectacle as the once massively popular president, who had won reelection with overwhelming support, with veto-proof majorities in both houses of Congress, scuttled any chance for success in packing the Court. Though he later claimed in his reminiscences that no chance for compromise had been presented to him, actually he had rejected any kind of give and take. His legislative aides provided carrots and sticks, he personally called and met with reluctant senators, and public messages issued forth relaying the president's desire to fight it out.

Perhaps the most astounding meeting Roosevelt held occurred at the White House in late April with Senator Joseph O'Mahoney, a Democrat from Wyoming, and Harvard economics professor William Z. Ripley. At that meeting, Roosevelt's guests were stunned by the president's view of the ideal relationship between the presidency and the judiciary. FDR wanted "friendly and approachable" justices with whom he could consult, like the members of the Court of Appeals of New York, New York State's highest court, when he was governor. He recounted how he had tried to establish this relationship with Chief Justice Hughes, but Hughes had insisted on an "independent" judiciary. "You see," the president observed, "he wouldn't cooperate." Not only had Roosevelt not taken the hint, but he had also misinterpreted its origin in a long-standing understanding of the operations of the US Constitution.

Also, this exchange possibly explains a great deal about why FDR committed so many errors during the Court fight. Aside from the idea that O'Mahoney had completed law school (Georgetown Law School, as it was then known) and Roosevelt had not, experience and mindset play a role in shaping historical actors' decisions. Roosevelt was drawing upon his extensive knowledge, training, and work in state government in Albany, New York. His experience with Washington, DC, had been limited to his term as assistant secretary of the navy, who has only occasional dealings with Congress. Then there is Roosevelt's well-documented record, from his childhood at Groton to Harvard College, as a convivial, charming, and not particularly intellectually inclined student. After all, someone who has succeeded at politics to the point where they won a landslide reelection victory as president of the United States is going to be a people person more than a scholar, and have the confidence of a

Harvard cheerleader and editor-in-chief of *The Crimson*, Harvard's daily newspaper.

In addition, there was a significant result of the passage of the judicial pension law earlier in the court-packing fight. On May 18th, Justice Willis Van Devanter let the public know he planned to retire in early June, giving Roosevelt his first appointment to the Court and a replacement for one of the horsemen, albeit not the most conservative. It was highly unlikely Van Devanter left for political reasons. He had reached retirement age and was concerned about his pension. After all, former justice Oliver Wendell Holmes Jr. had retired only to have his pension reduced as part of Roosevelt's cost cutting at the start of his administration. With a guaranteed pension, he could be assured of a significant salary in his declining years. If FDR was grateful for the gift given by Congressman Sumner's law in the form of a Supreme Court appointment, he certainly did not show it. After all, it undercut support for the judicial reform bill by removing one of the critical reasons for its passage.

Also on May 18th, the Senate Judiciary Committee held a series of votes that led to the committee reporting adversely on the Judiciary Procedures Reform Bill by 10–8 margins. Ultimately, on June 14th, the majority report for the committee reached the rest of the Senate as well as the public. It was a stinging indictment of the legislation in plain language. In effect accusing President Roosevelt of deception, unconstitutional overreach, and poor judgment, it declared the bill a threat to the independent judiciary, a foundation of the constitutional order. Its closing lines were unequivocal: "It is a measure which should be so emphatically rejected that its parallel will never again be presented to the free representatives of the free people of America." To make matters worse, these words came from seven Democrats as well as three Republicans.

With the outcome in serious doubt, Senate Majority Leader Joe Robinson of Arkansas prevailed upon Roosevelt to compromise. In a White House meeting in early June, the adverse report of the Judiciary Committee aside, Robinson steadfastly believed that he could arrange for a positive Senate vote. As the heat and humidity of Washington, DC's, notorious summer took hold, his confidence was welcomed. Possibly adding to the majority leader's optimism was Roosevelt's long-standing promise to make Robinson his first Supreme Court appointment. His Senate colleagues were certainly behind the potential nomination, and some said so openly after Van Devanter's announcement of his retirement. However, Robinson's age, sixty-five, and his likely conservative southern views worked to his disadvantage in the minds of northern New Dealers, including Roosevelt himself. Nevertheless, a deal was a deal. Without the expected announcement of being named to the Court, Robinson toiled into early July attempting to work out a compromise that would gain Senate approval and still give Roosevelt the win he so desperately wanted.

Despite FDR's charm offensive, on an island in the Chesapeake, with Democratic members of Congress, opposition to the newest compromise measure—the Hatch-Logan bill—remained solid with the debate on the Senate floor yet to proceed. Beginning on July 6th, Robinson and the leadership opened the most raucous few days the Senate had experienced for decades. The nays hectored Robinson and his co-presenters so effectively Robinson clearly lost his temper on several occasions. He had to take the next day off with chest pains but returned on the eighth to continue the fight. Using his experience and what he was owed after many years as leader, Robinson managed to restrict debate before any attempt at a filibuster, including keeping the Senate with no break from January to the sultry temperatures of Washington, DC, in July. This aroused the ire of many, but there was little they could do.

As the opposition took the floor, Senator Bailey persuaded some of the waverers with a well-argued and well-delivered speech. Robinson had to excuse himself and returned to his un-air-conditioned apartment. On July 14th, a maid discovered him on the floor in his pajamas with his glasses in one hand and a copy of the *Congressional Record* in the other, the victim of a massive heart attack. With the Senate debate paused for the majority leader's funeral train back to Arkansas and the funeral, various events combined to end what was left of support for the legislation. First and foremost, Robinson's IOUs had died with him. Free to vote their consciences, the undecideds turned into opponents. Second, President Roosevelt misjudged the mood of the Senate by not making the trip on the funeral train and sending a letter to acting leader Senator Alben Barkley of Kentucky, later known as the "Dear Alben" letter, urging a continued fight for the bill. Despite its wording, senators objected to not only the inappropriate politicking the day after Robinson's death but the apparent support for Barkley in the forthcoming election of a new majority leader. This looked like White House interference in the Senate's internal operations.

Third, Robinson's death brought Vice President John Nance Garner back from his vacation in his home state of Texas for the funeral and the return trip of the train full of senators from Little Rock, Arkansas. Although a firm supporter of the New Deal, Garner was a skeptic of court packing as well as a former senator with a great deal of knowledge of his colleagues. By the time the train arrived back in Washington, DC, Garner had found a solid majority against the bill. On July 21st, Garner arranged for the Senate Judiciary Committee to recommend a recommitment of the legislation to the committee for revisions, including eliminating any changes to the Supreme Court. Though Roosevelt made last-ditch efforts to convince supposed stragglers to support his bill, the majority of the Senate was now firmly opposed.

All the president's allies could do was to try to avoid an outright defeat for the administration. On July 22nd, with Garner presiding, the Senate considered the Judiciary Committee's motion to recommit the proposal. Only the procedural reforms—including Department of Justice notification and involvement on any suits involving the constitutionality of federal legislation—remained. Making sure the record of the proceedings contained an admission of the administration's defeat, the opponents openly cheered. With overwhelming bipartisan majority support, but not the leadership's, the Senate ended any chance for FDR to get his compliant appointees onto the bench.

For 168 days, the US Senate had fought over Roosevelt's plan to "reform" the judiciary, which many rightly believed was mainly to gain additional appointments to the US Supreme Court and ensure a friendly majority on the nation's highest tribunal. We do not know how much money Frank Gannett, founder and publisher of the eponymous newspaper and magazine media empire, and other opponents of the plan spent on their National Committee to Uphold Constitutional Government or how much its proponents spent on their efforts. What we do know is that much of the first session of FDR's New Deal Congress, elected in 1936, had been wasted on a Court fight, with a great deal of damage done to the president's reputation, his legislative agenda, and Democratic Party unity. And there was more bad news to come.

Roosevelt's Revenge

Seeking revenge for the demise of his judiciary bill and cleaning up the Democratic Party of its southern conservatives came together for FDR after the fractiousness of those 168 days. With the Van Devanter vacancy yet to fill, the president attempted to salvage his political agenda. The wages and hours bill presented by Senator Hugo Black of Alabama did not make it out of committee. Senator Wagner's housing bill made it into law, but the conservatives loaded it with restrictive amendments in order to deny urban areas aid that would have come at the expense of the rural areas. Congress passed a Neutrality Act in the face of a deteriorating situation between Nazi Germany, fascist Italy, and the rest of Europe. Roosevelt objected to the dismemberment of Czechoslovakia as well as the annexation of Austria, but he did very little to stop it. Instead, he turned his attention to domestic politics.

To general surprise, on August 11th, FDR nominated Senator Hugo Black to Van Devanter's seat. Black had little to no judicial experience, did not have a jurist's temperament, and did not have a reputation as a great legal thinker. Still, he did possess a strong voice in support of the New Deal, openly criticized the Court for its laissez-faire reading of the Constitution, and had vehemently supported the judicial procedures reform bill over all objections, even from his own constituents. These factors endeared him to the president for several reasons, not the least of which was that the Senate had expected a less political choice. Nevertheless, Black's status as a senator helped him win the support of the Judiciary Committee and a large majority of his fellow senators' votes, but there were objections to his confirmation. Interestingly, none of them concerned his membership in the Ku Klux Klan during the 1920s.

The second Ku Klux Klan had arisen after the popularity of the D. W. Griffith blockbuster Hollywood movie, *Birth of a Nation*. The "nation" to which the title referred was the Klan of Reconstruction. Its domestic terrorism included murder; destruction of homes, businesses, and churches; and hooded intimidation of African Americans and supporters of civil rights. In the film the Klan was portrayed as defenders of innocent white women against bestial African American men portrayed by white actors in blackface. The original title, from the novel by Thomas Dixon on which it was based, was *The Klansman*. The first Klan had fallen after successful prosecution in federal courts, in some areas, or being supplanted by Democratic white militias in others. When post-Reconstruction Democratic white supremacists "redeemed" the South with segregation, the systematic abuse of African Americans, and the accompanying denial of the vote through racist administration of poll taxes and literacy tests for voting, the first Klan disappeared. The second Klan was a slightly different beast.

Instead of confining their hatred to African Americans, the second Klan added Jews, immigrants, and Catholics to their list. This broadened their appeal for a time during the late 1910s and into the 1920s such that they became a national organization with "klaverns" (clubs) in the North and Midwest as well as the South. While scandals involving their leadership's propensity for teenage girls and secret abortions funded by Klan money diminished their reach by the late 1920s, they remained a powerful organization in the Democratic South, where only the all-white primary mattered. Klan endorsement was a necessity for any aspiring officeholder, and Hugo Black from northern Alabama needed just that. From 1922 to 1925, Black was a member in good standing of America's largest terrorist organization. However, it was only after the Senate had confirmed him for the Court that the press brought up the issue.

Justice Hugo Black later claimed that, in his chat with Roosevelt at the White House regarding his appointment to the Court, the president said that he knew about Black's Klan membership and that it was not a problem. FDR told the press he had not known, and it did not matter all that much. Either account makes sense. After all, Roosevelt spent a great deal of time in Warm Springs, Georgia, in the Deep South. Segregation and the Klan were everywhere. In 1924, in support of what became the Immigration and Naturalization Act, restricting immigration from "undesirable" places like Eastern Europe, the Klan had marched down Pennsylvania Avenue in Washington, DC. FBI Director J. Edgar Hoover had watched approvingly from his balcony, and he kept all his presidents, including FDR, well-informed about the Klan and everything else the FBI's wiretaps and electronic surveillance reported. Though Roosevelt wanted a purge of the Democratic Party's conservatives, most of whom were from the South, he did not seriously consider using their ties to a domestic terror organization against them. The Klan was an accepted part of American life in the South, irrelevant to FDR's desire to put his people on the US Supreme Court.

The second prong of Roosevelt's revenge plan required a purge of the congressional conservatives, largely southern, who had thwarted his judiciary bill. With the by-election primaries underway for 1938, FDR threw his support to challengers. This process of removing incumbents from the party's ballot is now known as "being primaried," and it seldom leads to good results for the president. By-elections are notoriously bad for sitting presidents, and the vast majority turn on local issues rather than whether the president supports or opposes the candidate in question. During this period, presidential endorsements mattered even less, especially since Roosevelt picked conservatives who had strong bases in their states.

He also widened his break with the Southern Democrats, who controlled much of Congress thanks to the seniority system's determination of who became chairs of the committees. In a speech in Gainesville, Georgia, on March 23, 1938, he stated: "When you come right down to it, there is little difference between the feudal system and the fascist system. If you believe in one, you lean to the other." It was unlikely anyone missed the implication that the Jim Crow South was feudal and, therefore, one step away from fascism. If FDR had wanted to take on the many violations of federal elections laws and Klan Enforcement Acts his opponents in the South were committing, he certainly could have, but it would have required a concerted effort with orders to the US Attorneys. Given that the federal judiciary and US Attorneys were all from the Jim Crow system, this was likely to fail. Therefore, one may charitably interpret Roosevelt's Gainesville words as mere campaign rhetoric.

As such, it had little effect on the outcomes of the primaries and caucuses. None of FDR's challengers won their races. What was more, Roosevelt had solidified the rift in the party. His presidential agenda would either be subject to substantial compromises or not move at all. The fight over the judiciary had done lasting damage to his presidency. Hubris from the 1936 election victory may have caused this gross miscalculation. Yet the suspicion lingers that the blow the US Supreme Court delivered on Black Monday, in particular the destruction of his New Deal centerpiece, the NIRA, in *Schechter* had left a lasting mark that Roosevelt wanted avenged. FDR well knew that his personal popularity and his ability to forward his agenda went hand in hand. Whether it was *Schechter* or anything else, politics was at least partly perception. A vulnerable president was a weak president.

Another blow hit FDR's reputation when the US economy entered a recession over late 1937 and into 1938. US unemployment skyrocketed back to the atrocious 25 percent mark from around 17 percent at the height of the New Deal. Roosevelt had predicated his presidency, further New Deal reforms, and his need to reform the judiciary on the success of the New Deal. Now the Supreme Court had sustained the entirety of the Second New Deal as well as many of the reforms of the First, but the economy still suffered from fragility. FDR got caught in a trap of his own making. One cannot take responsibility for the economy's successes and not be blamed for its downturns.

As for the actual cause or causes of the so-called Roosevelt Recession, even today we still do not know. Keynesian economists, or ISLM or "Saltwater School" (because it is centered at MIT and the University of California–Berkeley), argue that Roosevelt's budget cutting at the behest of Treasury Secretary Bernard Baruch, who wanted a balanced budget, reduced the fiscal stimulus the economy still needed. (One might note that Johnson, the future first director of the NRA, had assisted Baruch at the World War I–era War Industries Board.) Others blame the Federal Reserve Board for raising interest rates prematurely to fight inflation. The monetarists, or "Blue Water School" economists (because they are centered at the fresh lake University of Chicago and University of Minnesota), assert that the administration's income tax, anti-monopoly, pro–labor union, and general anti-business policies undermined business confidence. (Federal anti-monopoly laws go back to the Sherman Antitrust Act of 1890 and the Clayton Antitrust Act of 1914, neither of which the Court overturned.) That, in turn, supposedly reduced investment, leading employers to cut workforces, which then led to a crisis in consumer confidence. With less spending, the economy fell back and unemployment rose. Regardless of the cause, the midterms went poorly for FDR's New Dealers, making the New Deal's prospects of continuation grim.

Although all of the New Deal relief agencies and a more expansive agenda met their demise in the next few years, the last New Deal Congress did pass the Fair Labor Standards Act, establishing, among other things, a federal minimum wage and amendments to the National Housing Act of 1934, leading to the creation of the National Mortgage Association of Washington (NMAW), later known as the Federal National Mortgage Association, or Fannie Mae. The NMAW created a secondary market in essentially government-guaranteed mortgages, dramatically lowering the mortgage rate for American home buyers with qualified mortgages. The key word is "qualified." Local offices of the Federal Housing Administration, created by the National Housing Act of 1934, often used their power to reinforce segregation and "redlining"—the practice of denying mortgages to African Americans because they were supposedly not economically viable.

Fannie Mae and the Federal Housing Administration (FHA) also created criteria for home mortgages that furthered the New Deal goal of turning urban dwellers into suburbanites. Financed homes had to be single-family, single-use, free standing structures. Housing developments in the suburbs, where everyone needed an automobile, was the intended result. After all, the same motivation that undergirded the NIRA and produced the *Schechter* case still underlay much of what the New Deal and Roosevelt administration did. The US economy, technology, and society supposedly had reached its final stage. The Depression was the result of abuse by monopolists and Roosevelt's so-called economic royalists. The national government needed to step in and fix the market's oversupply and underspending. Suburban housing forced Americans to become extensive spenders rather than intensive users of products and resources. The entire point was to hollow out cities in favor of these new "ideal" managed communities. Casual bigotry simply accompanied the execution of these policies.

Another piece of the New Deal puzzle for the new economy has largely gone without notice, obscured by its larger global successor, the General Agreement on Tariffs and Trade (the GATT), the predecessor to the World Trade Organization. The Reciprocal Tariff Act of 1934 extended a lower tariff rate than any negotiated with a subsequent partner so long as the other party reduced their tariff rate to the same level. The Democratic Party had opposed tariffs ever since its formation in 1828 as a southern, non-industrial alliance with northern workers and immigrants. FDR's secretary of state, former Tennessee congressman and senator Cordell Hull, took the opportunity to work for this new system after the disastrous reputation of the Smoot-Hawley Tariff, which had spurred a trade war worsening the Great Depression. For a country that was already an industrial leader and expected to remain at the pinnacle, the regime made perfect sense. With the Court's traditional deference to foreign policy, it was unlikely to face serious review, even though it served all of the objectives of early New Deal thinking.

The actual enactment of this massive reworking of American society and the economy had to wait until after the Depression (and the coming war) to take effect. When it did, it did so with a massive impact. The FHA literally changed the landscape of the country in favor of the suburbs and the automobile. National government regulation of banks, commerce, industry, and income expanded tremendously, largely according to the planning of the early New Deal. The further development of reciprocal tariff reductions led to the hollowing out of American industries under the weight of foreign competition by the late 1960s. Regardless of these future developments, the newest Second New Deal legislation still seemed at risk. Those measures required the time, space, and acclimation of the American people to this new national government to do their work. In the meantime, they needed a friendlier Court to ensure their survival.

A Transformation of the Court

President Franklin D. Roosevelt had failed to supplement the conservative, aged justices with his own supportive, younger ones through judicial reform legislation. Yet, over the next three years, retirements and deaths gave him the appointments the defeat of his bill had denied him. These justices had little to no difficulty with his more expansive view of the national government's powers over the country. As a result, the alleged laissez-faire precedents of *Schechter* and its predecessors largely fell by the wayside (although non-delegation doctrine is alive and well, and *Schechter* has never been explicitly overruled). FDR's appointment of Justice Hugo Black was only the beginning of this transformation.

Justice Sutherland announced his resignation from the Court on January 5, 1938. Roosevelt rewarded his second solicitor general, Stanley Reed, who had successfully argued many of the cases following Black

Monday and *Schechter*, with the seat. The Senate approved by voice vote that same month. From that point on, the Four Horsemen were no more. The president could be assured of his majority. When Justice Cardozo died in July 1938, Roosevelt consulted Professor Frankfurter for potential nominees. Instead of those suggestions, he took the highly unusual step of nominating a law professor, Frankfurter himself. Frankfurter had extensive service in the War Department, but, more importantly, his at times fawning correspondence made him a sure vote for Roosevelt as well as someone who would work collegially with the president. After his nomination in January 1939, the Senate confirmed him through voice vote later that month.

Roosevelt gained yet another appointment when Justice Brandeis retired in March 1939. His nominee and Brandeis's choice for a successor was Washington State's William O. Douglas (at least according to Douglas's memoir). Douglas had participated in the judicial reform bill effort from his seat as chair of the SEC. He gained confirmation from the Senate in late March by a vote of 62–4. When the sole Catholic on the Court, Butler, died, FDR nominated former Michigan governor, attorney general, and Catholic New Dealer Frank Murphy. Once again, the Senate confirmed the nominee by voice vote, in January 1940. The following year saw the retirements of McReynolds and Hughes. Roosevelt nominated Stone to be chief justice, and Attorney General Robert H. Jackson and Senator James F. Byrnes of South Carolina for the two vacancies. Thus, by the summer of 1941, the Four Horsemen were gone, and the Court was almost entirely Roosevelt appointees. All it had taken was a little time and Roosevelt's unprecedented third term as president after he won reelection in 1940.

As for the Court itself, the New Deal–affirming majority now had to distinguish *Schechter* and its accompanying decisions from the congressional actions it would now affirm. Their requirement of commissions with quasi-judicial procedures was a good start, but there needed to be a standard they could invoke for the lower courts to follow. A system built on precedent required this kind of signature case in order to function smoothly. Oddly enough, Justice Stone found the formula but buried it in his majority opinion in *United States v. Carolene Products Co.* on April 25, 1938. McReynolds dissented impotently. Butler wrote a brief concurrence. Black agreed with all but the third part of Stone's opinion.

Cardozo and Reed did not take part. Roberts, Hughes, and Brandeis sided with the majority.

The statute in question, The Filled Milk Act from 1923, prevented companies from shipping "milk" products with non-milk substances via interstate commerce. A previous majority might have wondered about the substance of what Congress was doing, given that there were no effects other than bad labeling at stake, but Stone, in his opinion for the Court, did not particularly care. The Court would henceforth defer to Congress, which embodied the democratic will of the people. Stone used the *Nebbia* rational basis test to prevent further investigation into the law's constitutionality. As long as there was a legitimate state interest and a reasonable means of achieving it, the government could do what it thought best. After all, Stone noted that Congress had spent some time investigating the topic, and that was good enough.

The template came easily enough. Produce enough testimony in congressional hearings and engage in floor debate so the Court could tell the legislature was serious and it would be a legitimate state interest, probably in the interest of public safety. Then claim in the legislation itself that this was a limited way of achieving that goal. The work was done. Yet there was that lingering question of whether *Buck v. Bell*, permitting sterilization procedures without consent, could pass the test. Tying someone down to a table, forcibly administering anesthesia, and cutting them open to remove their reproductive organs was considered a reasonable way to prevent genetically disabled people from producing children that would become tax burdens. Did the liberal majority behind the Second New Deal have an issue with eugenics? Surely they did, given how they voted in *Skinner v. Oklahoma* in 1942, striking down a state law that allowed the state to order sterilization as a punishment for crimes of "moral turpitude." Yet that particular analogy did not arise in what was clearly considered an economic matter.

Stone and the majority had to address this issue indirectly, as it was not raised specifically in the case. While the Four Horsemen might have declared that depriving someone of their livelihood and bankrupting them while subjecting them to imprisonment and fines for putting vegetable oil into milk was a violation of fundamental rights embodied in the Fifth Amendment, the liberals did not. Only something else would trigger their concern: "it is of such a character as to preclude the assumption that it rests upon some rational basis within the knowledge and experience of the legislators." Then footnote four appeared. A casual reader might well have missed it or ignored it, but that footnote proved to be the most important part of the decision, not for what it did in *Carolene Products* but for what became of it.

The note opened with an exception to the low level of scrutiny the rational basis test first announced in *Nebbia*: "when legislation appears on its face to be within a specific prohibition of the Constitution, such as those of the first ten amendments." It went on to describe the kind of legislation that would receive this higher level of review: "legislation which restricts those political processes which can ordinarily be expected to bring about repeal of undesirable legislation." In other words, the Court expected powerful groups like adulterated milk producers to be able to get legislatures to act in their favor. Therefore, what kinds of groups would not be able to do so and would have to rely on the courts as a last resort? Stone's answer went to previous precedents with one exception. "Restrictions on the right to vote," "restraints on dissemination of information," "interferences with political organizations," "prohibition of peaceable assembly," "statutes directed at particular religious . . . , or national, or racial minorities" had all elicited Supreme Court decisions.

At the end of this remarkable footnote came a statement suggesting the future direction of the Court's Roosevelt majority. "Whether prejudice against discrete and insular minorities may be a special condition, which tends seriously to curtail the operation of those political processes ordinarily to be relied upon to protect minorities, and which may call for correspondingly more searching judicial inquiry" was left open. That is, "discrete" and "insular" minorities were vulnerable to legislatures, thus, government power. Therefore, any legislative action affecting them and their rights might well receive a higher level of scrutiny. "Discrete" means definable, belonging to a describable category. "Insular" means set apart from others and isolated, generally without political power of any kind.

Though the footnote did not expressly state which laws would be subject to this stricter scrutiny and what "discrete and insular" minority groups might be the targets of these laws, there was a clear and obvious answer with its most visible location in the American South. By the time of *Carolene Products'* footnote four in 1938, the United States had an international reputation for racial segregation, which served as a model for apartheid South Africa and Nazi Germany's Nuremberg Race Laws of 1935, segregating Germany's Jewish population from the rest, stating that Jews were a "race" and needed to be quarantined. In the aftermath of the nearly unanimous US Supreme Court decision in *Plessy v. Ferguson* (1896) and subsequent decisions, the South, as well as other parts of the United States, had enacted state laws dividing their populations into "white" and "colored" races, from birth until death, such that dining, schools, theaters, cemeteries, and hospitals all discriminated, always adversely, on the basis of race. This made a mockery of the equal protection clause of the Fourteenth Amendment with a domestic terror organization, the Klan, just one of the more vicious elements of a racial police state.

So why did Stone's opinion relegate this important signal of a needed shift in the Court's jurisprudence to a footnote? If obiter dicta is the portion of the opinion that does not have the impact of the ratio decidendi, the reason for deciding the case, then a footnote is the dicta of the dicta. Why was the Roosevelt majority so skittish about signaling the new standard for legislation? After all, the Scottsboro Boys case had highlighted the legal problems with the segregated South. Harvard Law graduate and Dean of Howard University Law School Charles Hamilton Houston had begun his litigation, on behalf of the NAACP's Legal Defense Fund, against *Plessy*, but it had not reached fruition. A full US Supreme Court shift on civil rights was on the horizon, and just that.

Final Victory

After the bruising Senate fight on Roosevelt's Judiciary Procedures Reform Bill, one enactment stood out both as a rejection of part of the Court's unanimous ruling in *Schechter* and as action on the part of what remained of the defiant New Deal Congress's commitment to what they regarded as a reform of the US economy—the Fair Labor Standards Act of 1938. It was the result of decades of lobbying, a negotiation process as long as the New Deal itself, and a hail Mary throw by legislators concerned about the Court's skepticism of mandatory minimum wages and hours restrictions. The very same provisions that had failed in *Schechter*'s poultry code came to fruition in the FLSA.

While today people advocate for a "living wage," meaning the current minimum wage is too low, the FLSA Congress enacted their mandatory minimum wage on the same grounds. For them, the blame for low wages, long work weeks with no overtime, and lack of records requirements for federal oversight rested solely with the employers. Federalism allowed states to conduct a race to the bottom, undercutting one another with ever-lower restrictions on employers, and nefarious employers were taking advantage. Congress did not concern itself with the labor cycle, in which wages and hours rose and fell on the basis of market forces, nor the progress labor could make through the Wagner Act. They also did not notice the long trend of the economy toward better wages and hours for an ever more skilled workforce. Government had to step in because the Great Depression was the result of market failure, bad businessmen, and a lack of stewardship. But how would the Court react now that Roosevelt had his appointees instead of the Four Horsemen?

On February 3rd, 1941, a unanimous US Supreme Court ruled, in *United States v. Darby Lumber Co.*, that the federal minimum wage and maximum hours law, the FLSA, was a constitutional exercise of the interstate commerce power, even though the business at issue operated wholly within the state of Georgia. Justice Stone's opinion for the Court stated that "a substantial effect" on interstate commerce was sufficient, expressly overruling *Hammer v. Dagenhart* (1918). The Court agreed that allowing businesses within states to operate outside of national standards would undermine the commerce of the nation. In so doing, they laid to rest one of the pillars of *Schechter, Carter Coal,* and others that there were limits to congressional regulatory power under the Tenth Amendment, based on an original understanding of the framers' intent to create a federal government of limited powers with the states exercising the greatest control in their respective spheres.

Even more than the Wagner Act and Social Security cases, *Darby Lumber* marked the new era of Supreme Court jurisprudence. Behind the decision was Stone's language about the economy of the nation as it approached midcentury. Markets were no longer local. The national government was no longer constrained by "horse and buggy" doctrines, as FDR had put it in reaction to *Schechter*. Electricity powered by federal government dams, localities connected by federally funded roads, and federal government–regulated railroads funded by practically universal income and wage taxes had created a new economy not fit to be divided by mere state government choices. Henceforth, the national government would proscribe wages, hours, and contracts as it saw fit, provided these provisions could pass the increasingly lenient rational basis test.

Buried within this application of "commerce" to manufacturing lay the objective of the law. Congress sought, according to Stone's likely accurate reading of the legislation, to prevent "conditions detrimental to the maintenance of the minimum standards of living necessary for health and general wellbeing" anywhere in the United States. No greater rejection of laissez-faire can be found. Prior to *Darby Lumber* and embodied in cases like *Schechter*, only progressives would have thought to use government, let alone national government, power to take over labor contracts, shifting this responsibility from the people directly involved, management and labor. From the framers to the *Lochner* Court, liberty and autonomy had been presumed. The idea that government would assume this type of authority on behalf of labor would have been laughed off as some kind of bizarre socialism. Yet, in *Darby Lumber*, the justices unanimously voted in its favor. What had happened?

Justice Stone answered this question in the opinion itself, although it requires some unpacking. First and foremost, he distinguished *Hammer* by referring to how narrow it was and how the Court had recently begun to chip away at it. He never mentioned *Schechter*'s unanimous finding. Second, his rational basis test did what it was supposed to do. The legislature is presumed correct in all its findings, whether factual or constitutional. Third, the "evils" and "substandard conditions" spoke for themselves. He never questioned whether it was a well-founded conclusion. Fourth, he found the "means" to be "so related to the commerce" that it was beyond questioning. Only a Court immersed in a post–New Deal mindset could have found this normal.

Chief Justice Hughes and Justice Roberts had survived the court-packing fight. They had witnessed Franklin D. Roosevelt's unprecedented three victories in subsequent presidential elections. Popular support for the New Deal's vast alteration of the balance between the national and state governments in favor of large federal government programs, powers, and responsibilities had not wavered. Instead of meeting in the Old Senate Chamber in the Capitol, the US Supreme Court had occupied its "marble temple" of justice since 1935. Marble monuments to Lincoln and Jefferson announced the national capital's arrival alongside the headquarters of the Federal Reserve Board and a host of permanent government bureaucracies. Who were they to stand in the way of this administrative revolution?

———

Triumph at All Costs

On July 7th, 1937, Japanese and Chinese troops clashed, in what would become known as the Marco Polo Bridge Incident, outside Beijing, China. Imperial Japan used it as a pretext to launch a wider invasion of China. On September 1st, 1939, Nazi Germany invaded Poland. A few days later Britain and France declared war on Germany in defense of Poland. With the third member of the so-called Axis powers—Benito Mussolini's Fascist Italy—in tow, the United States found itself astride the Second World War. FDR had broken with George Washington's two-term precedent and run for a third term. He defeated Wendell Willkie, a lawyer and former head of the Commonwealth and Southern Power Company, which FDR's New Deal had dissolved, with a large majority of both the popular and Electoral College vote. Americans trusted Roosevelt possibly because of his statement, "I have said this before, but I shall say it again and again and again; your boys are not going to be sent into any foreign wars." We cannot know whether this was an outright lie or he meant it at the time, but Roosevelt was already aiding the British and initiating severe sanctions on Japan for its actions in China.

On December 7th, 1941, a Sunday, Japanese naval and air forces attacked the US Pacific Fleet and Army Air Force fields in and around Pearl Harbor, Hawaii, in a sneak attack, hours before their ambassador could deliver the message initiating hostilities to Secretary of State Cordell Hull. This attack led to a US declaration of war against Japan. Shortly thereafter, Hitler declared war on the United States, and the United States recognized a state of war between itself and the Axis powers: Japan, Germany, and Italy. Although the Roosevelt administration had begun a rearmament program, the US military, the public, and the

{ *Chapter Six* }

economy were not prepared for the shock of the blow at Pearl Harbor or the U-boat attacks on US shipping just off the Atlantic coast.

Added to these sudden jolts to American confidence, there was a reservoir of racism on the West Coast, particularly in California, against Japanese and Japanese American residents. They had suffered similar restrictions to those of the Chinese and Chinese Americans, leading to the Chinese Exclusion Act of 1882 (which barred Chinese immigration for ten years, followed by the Geary Act of 1892, extending the ban for another ten years, followed by a permanent ban in 1902). In 1907, President Theodore Roosevelt reached the Gentleman's Agreement with Japan to exclude Japanese immigrants. Like many other immigrant groups to the United States, Japanese Americans had a number of success stories in business, farming, and commerce. And, as with other successful immigrants, this success often generated jealousy and resentment among the rest of the population.

Organizations like the Native Sons of the Golden West, as well as some labor groups, lobbied the state government of California and the national government for more restrictive laws on immigration generally, and against Asian groups in particular. This suspicion of Japanese Americans reached a boiling point after the attack on Pearl Harbor, when assertions of disloyal Japanese Americans having contributed to the attack gained credence without any supporting evidence except suspicion and rumor. Congress and President Roosevelt eventually responded with a gross violation of civil liberties, due process, and human rights. (There was never any evidence of Japanese American collusion with the Imperial Government of Japan.)

At the behest of the War Department, particularly Lt. General John L. DeWitt of the West Coast Command, President Roosevelt, under his Article II war powers, issued Executive Order 9066 on February 19, 1942. It authorized elements of the War Department, the US Army, to "relocate" any individual or group of individuals deemed to pose a threat of sabotage or espionage within their military districts. With only a brief discussion, Congress passed Public Law 77-503 enacting this order on March 21, 1942. Pursuant to these instructions, DeWitt oversaw the forced relocation of over 110,000 Japanese Americans from the West Coast to "relocation centers" in the plains states—effectively prison camps for men, women, and children—merely on the basis of their ancestry. The civilian War Relocation Authority carried out the removal, transportation, and internment of these people with no procedures, no trials, and no inquiry other than their ancestry and ethnicity. The US government had interned and dispossessed over a hundred thousand people, most of whom were American citizens, based on the decision of a general with the express delegation of authority by Congress to the president—although like Lincoln, with the blockade of the Confederacy in 1861, the president acted first, and Congress followed.

All of the elements were in place for the US Supreme Court to void these atrocious actions under the non-delegation doctrine of *Schechter*, the Fifth Amendment's due process clause, and a failure to meet the strict scrutiny standard of *Carolene Products'* footnote four, although eminent legal scholar Mark Tushnet, among others, believes probably rightly that *Schechter* was distinguishable. After all, the United States was not at war in 1935. The War Relocation Authority created its procedures, bureaucracy, and rules with far less procedural care than the NRA. The poultry code from the NRA, at issue in *Schechter*, should have looked constitutionally perfect by comparison. The internees were deprived of their liberty and property with no due process at all. Finally, according to some accounts, the US Supreme Court would be using the strict scrutiny standard from footnote four of *Carolene Products* for the first time, as these Japanese Americans were clearly being subject to this deprivation of liberty and property without due process on account of their ethnicity alone, for they were surely an isolated and insular minority.

Despite these possible objections, the Supreme Court unanimously upheld a curfew order in *Hirabayashi v. U.S.* (1943), in an opinion by Chief Justice Stone. It also unanimously upheld, by a 6–3 majority in *Korematsu v. U.S.* (1944), in an opinion by Justice Black, the "exclusion" orders that had removed Japanese Americans from the West Coast and interned them in Relocation Centers—the War Relocation Authority's camps. With the exception of Justices Jackson, Murphy, and Roberts in *Korematsu*, FDR and New Deal justices upheld this substantial violation of human rights and the US Constitution. The liberalization of the Court's majority and the concern for minority rights in *Carolene* did not prevent the Court from giving the president what he wanted.

Of course, it is almost too easy to distinguish *Schechter* from *Korematsu*.

One was in time of peace, one in time of war. One relied on the expertise of hastily assembled code framers, the other on the expertise of the armed forces and local authorities. And *Korematsu* was clearly driven by racism, which was ubiquitous in American society. Justice Black's later comment that "one Jap looked like another" demonstrates that prejudice in the general population also exists in the courtroom. Outside the courtroom, the "othering" of the Japanese was so prevalent that army brochures prepared in 1945 told GIs how to spot the difference between the Chinese and the Japanese based on the alleged primitiveness, barbarity, and subhuman qualities of the Japanese. It was not difficult for the Court, and America in general, to produce such racism. After all, it had been producing it for African Americans since its inception, along with anti-Catholic, anti-Irish, anti-French, and anti-Muslim bigotry, and occasional bouts of anti-Semitism. Native Americans are in a very specialized category of discrimination apart from these other groups because they existed as "wards" of the US government according to the Constitution.

The Japanese internment cases, *Hirabayashi* and *Korematsu*, were not a question of whether the United States government can draft people into the armed forces or declare martial law in a war zone. They were about the delegation of discretion to an agency with few guidelines or standards. Internment was carried out solely on the basis of ethnicity and ancestry. At best, it was a shortcut for easing fear of an internal fifth column of enemy agents. Yet the law's protections for civil rights and liberties exist for the very purpose of preventing such hasty, error-ridden, and abusive government actions. During wartime, the courts' examination of these topics should be more skeptical, not less. Of course, *Schechter* and the NRA were not wartime episodes.

What was even more shameful is that the Justice Department's lawyers knew DeWitt's evidence of Japanese disloyalty was false. Reports of smoke signals and signals conveyed by lanterns, in houses on the coast, to enemy ships had been investigated by the FBI and found to be without foundation. Homeowners were burning leaves in their backyards and using lanterns to go upstairs to bed at night in their homes, which did not have electricity. The Justice Department presented these false reports to the US Supreme Court under orders from their superiors in the White House and the administration. A more conscientious Court, properly using the strict scrutiny test from *Carolene Products'* footnote four, would have seen through this smoke screen, but that would have violated the deference New Deal justices were supposed to exhibit toward the political branches

In *Ex parte Mitsue Endo v. U.S.*, decided on December 14, 1944, on the same day as *Korematsu*, a unanimous Supreme Court—in an opinion by Justice William O. Douglas—issued a narrow ruling in favor of a Japanese American woman, Mitsue Endo, who had filed a habeas corpus petition against her detention in a War Relocation Authority center. Once again, the Court largely deferred to the War Relocation Authority's system of detention, but it found that Mitsue Endo had met their criteria for being a provably loyal citizen. Endo had been born in the United States, spoke no Japanese, and had lived her life as the American that she was. Douglas seemed unfazed by the fact that the War Relocation Authority had, nevertheless, detained her and denied her application for release and return to the West Coast.

Moreover, Douglas's opinion bent over backward to reconcile the fact that *Korematsu* upheld her exclusion from the West Coast based on ethnicity, which had been determined by an executive agency with no due process. After all, it was war time. "In interpreting a war-time measure, we must assume that their [Congress and the president] purpose was to allow for the greatest possible accommodation between those liberties and the exigencies of war." To translate this judicial reasoning into plain language, Douglas and a majority of the Court presumed the political bodies restrained by the Constitution would be acting in a constitutional manner, despite the Constitution's express limitations on their actions and despite knowing they could act in an unconstitutional manner. After all, that was why the 1787 Constitution received the first ten amendments shortly after the meeting of the first Congress. To their credit, Justices Murphy and Roberts wrote concurrences that agreed only with the result—Endo's release—but disagreed completely with the reasoning.

Endo, instead of being a resounding victory for individual rights and liberties, was a cowardly retreat. The FDR Court had signaled the end of the internment of Japanese Americans but set a precedent for the national government abusing its power during wartime, a period when people's rights and liberties require the highest level of protection from the political branches. Roosevelt learned of the *Endo* decision in advance of its announcement. Shortly afterward, he issued another executive order ending internment. By January of 1945, Japanese Americans could return to the West Coast, but their hastily taken and sold possessions, including their homes and businesses, were lost. Just like the Schechters, they had their day in Court and still forfeited their economic wherewithal in the process.

The Administrative State

The story of *Schechter* and the New Deal's constitutional history has an ironic coda. It is the rise of the administrative state—a veritable fourth branch of the federal government. Administrative agencies with rulemaking power predated the twentieth century and grew in number during the Progressive Era. They proliferated during the New Deal. They survived Black Monday and multiplied during World War II. Though many of the latter were dismantled, permanent additions to the executive branch of the US government continued their work. Centralization and nationalization were now enshrined in US law through statutes, regulations, and court cases. There would be no retreat from the administrative state.

European nations had led the way. The term "administrative state" originated there during the late nineteenth century to describe a national government that exerted power over its territory through hierarchical power structures, what others might call the bureaucracy—rule by officialdom. The term "bureaucracy" originated earlier in the nineteenth century from the French term for a filing cabinet—the stuff of clerks the world over. Political scientist Dwight Waldo popularized the term "administrative state," with his book of the same name, in 1948. The idea that there was a remote, powerful group of officials running everything through arcane rules and regulations had been developing long before *Schechter* dramatized it in 1935, but many believed the post–World War II state needed restraining.

The major reform in the United States, the Administrative Procedure Act of 1946 (APA), stemmed from the opposition of the American Bar Association (ABA) Special Committee on Administrative Law to unfettered regulatory expansion beginning in 1933. It continued with a

White House effort that began in 1938 under Solicitor General, later Attorney General, Robert H. Jackson to rein in the federal bureaucracy. The purpose of the APA was to restore executive control. One of the outcomes was the Reorganization Act of 1939, which, among other things, allowed FDR to create the Executive Office of the President. He transferred the Bureau of the Budget to this newly created office, moving it from the Treasury Department to the White House. The APA also gave the president additional advisers to oversee the sprawling officialdom. At the same time, after the "switch in time," opposition to the New Deal's centralization and planning shifted from the US Supreme Court to legislation.

Often the rhetoric that advocates deployed repeated the charges during the court-packing fight. Roscoe Pound, dean of Harvard Law School and one of the originators of courses on administrative law, chaired the Administrative Law Committee of the ABA and co-authored its 1938 report on administrative law reform. Its central section was titled "Administrative Absolutism" and denounced unrestrained regulation as "a Marxian idea much in vogue now among a type of American writers." Given that there were House and Senate committees on "Un-American Activities," a.k.a. Communism, this was a serious charge. New Dealers occasionally responded with denunciations of such rhetoric as Fascist. Thankfully, unlike in the Spanish Civil War, which was nearing its bloody conclusion, the debate did not lead to violence.

Republicans and Southern Democrats passed the Walter-Logan Act in 1940 to limit the power of the New Deal's regulatory agencies and provide a less cumbersome review process for the subjects of agency regulations, like the Schechters fighting against the Poultry Code of the NRA. It provided for a special administrative appeals court, restrictions on agency discretion, and expanded review of regulatory challenges by the courts. FDR vetoed the bill, later referring to it as "A Bill for The Relief of Unemployment Among Lawyers." Just as with the court-packing controversy, Roosevelt framed the debate as those in favor of the New Deal and government versus the lawyers and big business. With Democrats looking at FDR's 1940 reelection for a third term, the House and Senate failed to override the veto then began the long work, severely interrupted by World War II, of creating a compromise.

The Roosevelt administration's conduct of World War II impacted the debate over the administrative state in two important ways. First, the early chaos and arbitrary conduct of Roosevelt's wartime agencies diminished public trust in regulatory agencies in general. Second, that dissatisfaction led to an increased number of anti–New Deal Republicans and Democrats in Congress. Besides eliminating New Deal agencies, Congress looked for a way to stem the tide of regulation through legislation after the war was over. The sheer length of Roosevelt's presidency also meant conservatives could no longer rely on the courts for strict review of agency actions. They were almost all FDR-appointed New Deal liberals.

The result was a small victory for the New Dealers and a substantial concession by Republicans and conservative Democrats—the Administrative Procedure Act of 1946, the "bill of rights for the new regulatory state." It established a quasi-judicial, multi-staged process of review for regulations within each regulatory agency overseen by administrative courts. This supposedly allowed individuals and entities to participate in hearings, appeal decisions, and receive notice without obstructing the agency's regulatory work. President Harry S. Truman's involvement led to the passage of this reform, but on the side of the regulatory or administrative state. In theory, the Schechters would have been able to receive proper notice, be heard, and appeal the NIRA's rulings.

Ironically enough, the Administrative Procedure Act would not have aided a small business like the Schechters'. They did not have representation in Washington, DC. They could not afford the lawyers necessary to make the proper presentations at the hearing or use the appeals process. In fact, no individual or small business was likely to be able to use the APA at all. So what purpose did the APA serve other than window dressing for the vast growth of the administrative state with the accompanying violation of the non-delegation doctrine, as decided in *Schechter*?

Most likely, even New Deal liberals like President Truman recognized the need to pass some kind of measure to govern the sprawling administrative state. Until the First New Deal illustrated the problem, Harvard professor Erwin Griswold's suggestion, in a law review article, that regulations needed to be published struck many as overwrought. First, after the Second New Deal, Congress required the publication of new regulations in *The Federal Register* without substantial debate. By the time of the Truman administration, those regulations filled multiple volumes of the *Register* with the pace ever accelerating. Second, the once conservative and skeptical ABA saw the light as to the possibilities administrative law opened up for professionally trained lawyers. We might well call the APA an employment act for lawyers.

In one more important way, *Schechter* and related cases influenced the passage of the APA, which Truman signed into law on June 11, 1946: its manufactured legislative history. Because the legislation resulted almost entirely from compromises, everyone involved knew that its express purpose of scientifically providing fair and impartial procedures for the adoption of regulations did not have any support in the record, either in the committee hearings or in the debates preceding the unanimous support for the bill. As a result, both sides filled the *Congressional Record* with their materials so that they could give the courts, especially the US Supreme Court, the ability to sustain the act. Its ambiguity, like that of the US Constitution, enabled everyone to support it with the hope the courts would read it in their favor. In this way, *Schechter* still lived, albeit surreptitiously.

The last significant US Supreme Court cases dealing with the non-delegation doctrine, which helped decide *Schechter*, came many years later, in 1989, in *Mistretta v. U.S.* and *Gundy v. U.S.* (2019). The Stone Court had given way to the Vinson Court, then to the Warren Court, then the Burger Court. During that time the justices had initiated, then backed away from, the so-called Civil Rights Revolution—a period during which the Court supported desegregation, alleged criminal rights, and reproductive rights (according to its supporters). Beginning during the Burger Court and reaching its apogee after conservative Republican president Ronald Reagan appointed staunchly conservative justice William H. Rehnquist to the center chair in 1986, the US Supreme Court seemed to back away from the New Deal and the civil rights liberalism of the past. In *Mistretta*, the two sides, except for Justice Antonin Scalia, found common ground in upholding Congress's delegation of power to the United States Sentencing Commission—but not without later controversy.

Justice Harry Blackmun wrote the majority opinion for the Court. He used the *J. W. Hampton* decision as the standard and relegated *Schechter* and *Panama Refining* to being exceptions. The "increasingly complex society" allowed Congress to delegate its powers provided it "is sufficiently specific and detailed to meet constitutional requirements." The US Sentencing Commission met the standard. How could it not? The "constitutional requirements" came from the Court, and the Court deferred to Congress so long as Congress created a sufficient evidentiary record to support their creation of a judicial body that was not a court but governed the judiciary's sentencing of convicted criminals in federal courts, rather than Congress setting the penalties itself. He also managed to square the circle of a body within the judiciary not being a court but also not being a political branch. If the Sentencing Commission had none of the qualities of a court, either procedurally or substantively, then how was it a part of the judiciary other than because Congress stated it was so?

Justice Antonin Scalia's dissent expressed a degree of frustration with this effective burying of the non-delegation doctrine. As he was wont to do when not writing the majority opinion, Scalia was dismissive of the idea that Congress could create this judicial agency, which he derided as a "junior-varsity Congress." What was more, Scalia rejected "the regrettable tendency" to treat the Constitution's requirements as mere guidelines. Although he did not state it, *Korematsu* certainly loomed in the background. Once the Bill of Rights had gone the way of the interstate commerce clause and the separation of powers, what was left to safeguard the rights and liberties of those within a republic of law?

In *Gundy*, non-delegation was again mentioned, but it was not central to the decision. The question concerned the Sex Offender Registration and Notification Act (SORNA) of 2006: did delegation of authority to the US attorney general to issue regulations violate the non-delegation doctrine? The Court, in a 5–3 decision, found that the act did not give the attorney general unrestrained discretion to do with offenders as he wished. Though a *Schechter* Court might have disagreed, or at least looked more closely at the matter, the political branches could still rely on judicial restraint.

Something of a pushback on the vast expansion of the national government's authority occurred with *United States v. Lopez* in 1995. By that time, regulatory agencies of the administrative state had expanded into workplace safety, environmental protection, traffic and automobile safety, and effective national control of—or at least influence over—grade school and higher education for both civil rights and health and safety purposes.

Federally funded programs such as Medicare and Medicaid extended this influence into health care. Counter to this trend, the presidency of Bill Clinton witnessed some revived concerns about the administrative state, particularly its voluminous nature. Vice President Al Gore's National Performance Review, which became the National Partnership for Reinventing Government program in 1998, was intended to increase efficiency within the national government. Though various recommendations became law, the sprawling administrative and national security state had powerful backers in Congress, who resisted the cost cutting and tried to preserve their areas of authority.

Nevertheless, in an opinion by Chief Justice Rehnquist, a 5–4 majority took issue with the Gun-Free School Zones Act of 1990. Concerned with gun violence at or near public schools, Congress had passed legislation making it a federal crime to possess a firearm within a thousand feet of a school. They based this power on the interstate commerce clause. To their minds, this was little different from the now long line of cases deferring to Congress and the president on regulatory issues. As for how guns near a school related to interstate commerce, they probably assumed the Court would not look all that closely. Rehnquist proved them wrong.

As is customary, Chief Justice Rehnquist laid out the permissible before pointing out the impermissible. Congress could regulate three areas: the "channels" of interstate exchange, the "instrumentalities" (persons or things), and the activities that "substantially affect" or "relate" to interstate commerce. He and the majority could find no such link between possession of a firearm at or near a school and interstate commerce. The primary dissent, from Justice Stephen Breyer, rightfully pointed out that firearms derive from interstate commerce, the firearm was purchased using US currency, and firearms disrupting public schooling certainly has an effect on interstate commerce.

Rehnquist replied that if the Court upheld the legislation, there would be nothing left of police power for the states. This violated the purpose of having a government of limited, enumerated powers, a design the Tenth Amendment reinforced and the unanimous Court had held in *Schechter*. Breyer and the other dissenters applied the Holmesian judicial restraint and deference theory. Congress was right unless *Carolene Products'* footnote four was at issue. (As a sidenote, there were two concurrences and two additional dissents making it very difficult to determine what the Court had decided and why. This became a common feature of the very fractious Rehnquist Court.)

A final, significant case concerning the interstate commerce clause, which was one of the substantial topics of *Schechter* and other New Deal cases, stemmed from congressional passage of the Violence Against Women Act (VAWA). Among other things, it allowed people who had been sexually assaulted, or subjected to gender-related violence according to the VAWA, to sue their attackers in federal court. In *United States v. Morrison* in 2000, Chief Justice Rehnquist again wrote for a 5–4 majority. He held that provision unconstitutional as an overextension of Congress's authority to regulate interstate commerce. Citing *NLRB v. Jones & McLaughlin Steel* (1937) as well as *Lopez*, Rehnquist concluded that violence on account of gender was too indirectly related to commerce. Moreover, once again, Congress was trampling on both limited government and federalism, embodied in the Tenth Amendment.

Rehnquist also rejected the argument that Congress could pass the legislation under its authority to enforce the equal protection clause of the Fourteenth Amendment. He cited favorably the *Civil Rights Cases* (1883), which had established the doctrine that the Fourteenth Amendment's provisions required "state action." Private parties like the ones aided by the VAWA were not states that the Fourteenth Amendment covered. The dissents declared this to be another trip back to the bad old days of *Lochner* and *E. C. Knight* as well as a refusal to uphold the equal protection clause of the Fourteenth Amendment, and they had a point. Nevertheless, the supposed "new federalism" did embody the small but influential backlash against the ever-larger national government.

Though advocates for women denounced the decision as "patriarchal" and sexist, there was a major undercurrent to the VAWA that cut both ways. Why was VAWA framed as violence against someone on account of gender when it was clear from the title that this was about providing another means of compensation for women who had been sexually assaulted? Just as *Mueller v. Oregon* and *West Coast Hotel* had upheld special protections for women because they were women and assumed to be in need of protection, the VAWA appears to have stemmed from a form of adverse discrimination. The concept of women as victims is widely understood in gender theory to be an excuse for patriarchal—that is, sexist—rule over women. An egalitarian society for the genders would have no need of protections particular to women. Women would have the same protections as men.

In addition, the VAWA was only one of many pieces of legislation in which the national government assumed responsibilities previously left to state and local governments. As such, one can trace its origins to FDR's New Deal. For example, the New York metropolitan poultry market at issue in *Schechter* was already the subject of state and local health and safety standards when the NRA promulgated its code. After all, what was the need for the Sentencing Commission at issue in *Mistretta* if not for the President Nixon–initiated "War on Crime"? Starting small in the early twentieth century with cocaine and marijuana, America's drug war had expanded into a vast regime of crimes, law enforcement activities, prosecutions, and imprisonments. By the late twentieth century, thanks in part to nationalization of crimes, the United States incarcerated more people per capita than any other nation on Earth.

———

Schechter's prompting of FDR's hostile relationship to the judiciary had mixed results. The very public fight over "court packing" did a great deal of damage to his second-term agenda. His reputation also took a beating, which did not revive until his leadership during World War II. Judging from the results of subsequent elections, it also appears to have helped Republicans recover from the devastation of their loss in 1936. Ultimately, through retirements and death, FDR did get the Supreme Court he wanted. Roosevelt's appointments soon took over the Court. In ensuing years, they reshaped US Supreme Court jurisprudence in order to fit his vision of the interstate commerce clause, the non-delegation doctrine, and federalism, in direct opposition to the previous justices' unanimous ruling in *Schechter*.

Also, there were significant legislative accomplishments that forestalled an anti–New Deal backlash. Roosevelt's successful veto of the Walter-Logan Act eventually led to a more New Deal–friendly Administrative Procedure Act of 1946 under Roosevelt's successor, Harry S. Truman. The administrative state became a fixture of American life, creating a foundation for expansion in the ensuing decades, from Medicare and Medicaid, to national health and safety regulations, to the War on

Crime. *Schechter* did live on to an extent in the Rehnquist Court's checks on national government expansion, but public acceptance of a more powerful, wide-ranging national government meant its legacy would be extremely limited.

CONCLUSION

The journey to and from *A.L.A Schechter Poultry v. United States* (1935) and the journey from *Schechter* to the voiding of the Violence Against Women Act was long and twisting. The story of how a group of immigrants operating a kosher chicken business became the center of a massive fight about the future of President Franklin D. Roosevelt's New Deal does not lack for complications. At one time or another, the resulting US Supreme Court case involved politicians from around the country, academic opinion, the news media, and larger ideas about the US Constitution. The US Supreme Court had to decide not just the fate of Jewish American butchers, but, in some ways, the direction of the nation.

Although the Court was unanimous, the justices had to sift through decades of precedent in multiple areas of jurisprudential concern. *Schechter* was not decided solely on the non-delegation doctrine, but federalism and the interstate commerce clause as well. Chief Justice Hughes wrote the majority opinion that invalidated the National Industrial Recovery Act—the signature piece of legislation in the New Deal—alongside two other cases on what became known as "Black Monday," May 27th, 1935, which also rejected President Roosevelt's attempts to reshape American government according to his new conception. Roosevelt and his supporters viewed it as a clash of worldviews, the old justices versus the New Dealers, who wanted not only to end the Great Depression but to rework America into their modern model.

The First New Deal was only a beginning, and the NIRA and its executive agency, the NRA, which were involved in *Schechter*, were only a beginning of the new welfare state. Former general Hugh Johnson, head of the NRA, was to spearhead the New Deal's reworking of the inefficient, outdated market-driven economy that had caused the Great Depression. Government experts and expertise would manage the nation through associations and the codes they would produce. Small businesses would disappear in favor of the large, therefore efficient, mega-producers. The national government would also oversee labor, bestowing good wages, hours, and working conditions. Subsidies would prevent overproduction in agriculture. Regulatory agencies would set the rules for all business activities. Centralized national institutions like the Federal Reserve

Board and its chair in Washington, DC, would control entire sectors of the economy with the greater good in mind at all times. National government programs would rework American society into one of consumers and suburban dwellers, while the corrupt, crowded cities would diminish. Rail would be replaced by the technological marvels of the age—the automobile and the airplane. All would be well.

Schechter and its accompanying cases threatened the whole enterprise. As early as 1933, Attorney General Homer Cummings, with the support of President Roosevelt, contemplated doing something about the obstructionist, antiquated US Supreme Court. According to their way of thinking, the problem lay not with the hurriedly drafted legislation, or the poor litigation on the government's behalf, or the concepts underlying the approach, but with the justices. Something needed to be done. Eventually, after discarding several proposals, from an amendment to the Constitution to various pieces of legislation, Cummings and Roosevelt settled upon a plan to reshape the US Supreme Court. After his overwhelming reelection victory in 1936, Roosevelt set about upending well-established ideas about the nature of the US government.

Miscalculating the effect of his subterfuge, FDR and his agents portrayed the Judicial Procedures Reform Bill as a much-needed reform for the overworked judiciary. No one missed the provisions providing the president an immediate appointee for every justice over seventy, allegedly in order to lighten their workload. Conservative Democrats and Republicans worked with anti–New Dealers to destroy the plan. Instead of an easy win that would protect the Second New Deal, including Social Security and the National Labor Relations (Wagner) Act, the first legislative session of 1937 witnessed a largely intraparty brawl between the New Dealers and the moderates and conservatives who were wary of what increasingly became known as "court packing." For 168 days, the Senate hosted hearings, fractious debates, and furious machinations while the public witnessed a flurry of charges and countercharges that seemed to touch on whether the United States was to remain a democratic republic with an independent judiciary, at least according to journalist Joseph Alsop's immensely popular *168 Days*. Behind the scenes, it was even worse as President Roosevelt alternated between charming and threatening, determined to get his own way come hell or high water.

In the middle of this political maelstrom sat the justices of the US

Supreme Court, who were having their own intense debate about what limits the Constitution imposed on both congressional and presidential authority. Despite the unanimity of *Schechter* and the other like-minded cases, they too were divided. Although the press and New Dealers dubbed them "the Four Horsemen," Justices Butler, McReynolds, Sutherland, and Van Devanter did not forecast or represent the forces of the apocalypse. They were straightforward laissez-faire conservatives who differed among themselves on whether New Deal measures were constitutional. Even a reliable conservative like Justice McReynolds or Sutherland could produce an opinion concerned with civil rights and liberties. It was true they dated from before the Progressive Era's jurisprudential shift, but they were not extremist in their views.

On the other side were the "Three Musketeers," who constituted the Court's liberal wing. Justices Brandeis, Cardozo, and Stone definitely disagreed with the Four Horsemen on the key issue of what standard of review to use concerning congressional authority. Yet here, too, the divisions were more complex than simple left versus right, conservative versus liberal, old versus new, and right versus wrong dichotomies. After all, they all voted with the Four Horsemen on the *Schechter* case, among others. They agreed on various constitutional matters. They also had substantial disagreements with each other about federalism, civil rights and liberties, and the proper reach of the national government.

Then there were Chief Justice Charles Evans Hughes and Justice Owen Roberts. Although Roberts's supposed "switch in time" has elicited the most attention, Hughes's shift away from cases like *Panama Refining* and *Schechter* to support of large portions of the Second New Deal, which seemed to contradict his earlier efforts, also deserves attention. Roberts moved from the Four Horsemen to the Musketeers, and Hughes from *Tipaldo* to *West Coast Hotel v. Parrish*, on the minimum wage, but Roberts later excused his vote in *Tipaldo* arguing New York State failed to propose the idea of overturning *Adkins*. Roberts never did explain why he thought *Adkins* should be overturned. What caused this shift in the Court away from *Schechter* to a slim majority in favor of the administrative state?

The original explanation, as illustrated by the "switch in time" label, gave credit to FDR's court-packing plan. The evidence for Roberts's shift shows decisively that he had changed his vote in December—several weeks before Roosevelt announced his until-then-secret plan to enlarge the Court in February. Was it the November election that proved overwhelming national support for the New Deal and Roosevelt? Did the vastly improved work of Solicitor General Stanley Reed over his predecessor's make the difference? Was Congress's more deliberate, copiously documented, and legally expert drafting, tailored to meet constitutional requirements, what made the difference? Maybe it was simply the zeitgeist (spirit of the times) had changed. We will never know.

What we can know is that the shift in the Court's standard of review, as announced in *Carolene Products*, from skepticism to deference to Congress and the president signified a major shift in the nation's governance. Due to retirements and deaths, FDR gained the Supreme Court appointments the failure of his court-packing bill had denied him. The switch of 1937 became permanent. With it the expansion of the national government's power and the rise of an administrative state to govern it proceeded apace. Long after the stain of the Japanese internment cases faded into distant memory, the New Dealers' Court had given its seal of approval to far-reaching regulatory regimes governing everything in the United States, for good or ill. The *Schechter* precedent faded into relative obscurity.

As for the Schechter brothers, they faded from the scene just as quickly as they had entered it. Despite their victory at the nation's highest tribunal, their business failed, the lawyers' bills overwhelmed them, and they went their separate ways. In many respects, their story was the story of the New Deal. While the NIRA and the NRA disappeared, the rest remained, permanently altering the American way of life. The US population shifted from a producer society to a consumer one, an urban and rural one to a suburban one, and a country of limited government to one of a behemoth. Large corporations furthered their dominance of the American economy by mechanisms old and new.

There was little room for smaller concerns like the Schechters', not merely because the supposedly modern economy could not accommodate them, but because belief in their future dissipated. Highways and airports need not have displaced railroads, but government policy certainly showed no regard for rail. Rail was old, like small businesses. The new captured the imagination, while the old grudges against the railroads set the New Deal coalition against them. Small business would have to become a lobbying organization so that they too could become part of the client state the New Deal had ushered into existence. Just as labor would get the Wagner Act, the retirees Social Security, and farmers crop subsidies, small business would have to play Washington's power game or be left behind.

Receiving far less attention was the switch's abandonment of *Lochner* and the minimum wage and hour requirement portion of the decision in *Schechter*. The *Lochner* era witnessed the birth of the selective incorporation of the Bill of Rights against the states. Its use, largely post–World War II, to destroy de jure segregation and Jim Crow is much celebrated and rightfully so. The abandonment of the "freedom of contract" and economic rights portion post-1937 is also rightly celebrated. States lost the ability to discriminate on the basis of race but gained immense authority over economic matters and health and safety generally. The development of medical expertise gave the imprimatur of science to state-enforced policies like the eugenics of *Buck v. Bell* before fighting the Nazi mass murderers in World War II discredited terms like "master race." Nonetheless, the principle endured.

While the *Schechter* Court literally laughed at the poultry code's restrictions on how to kill chickens from one side of the crate, post-1937 Courts routinely upheld far more restrictive regulations based on broad statutes the states had passed supposedly grounded in science. It is highly unlikely the justices anticipated state governors using virtually unrestrained authority to impose curfews, "quarantine" people in their homes, locking down businesses that were deemed "nonessential" and arresting people alone on beaches or lakes for violating the lockdowns, as many governors did at the height of the COVID-19 pandemic. It did not matter that medical research, scientific knowledge, and best practices did not mandate these policies, just as placing elderly COVID patients in nursing homes with other vulnerable elderly people was unnecessary. Ultimately, no science or medicine speaks for itself.

It is also worth noting that the COVID lockdowns benefited gigantic businesses like Amazon immensely just as it destroyed a huge number of small businesses. After the enthusiasm for the administrative state had died down in the mid-1970s, economists like Milton Friedman, among others, started to prove that regulation imposed substantial costs on consumers and small producers alike. This contributed to inflation and consumer debt and served as a regressive tax on the urban poor. For those who have studied the intent of the New Deal, particularly in cases like *Schechter*, this should not be surprising. It was the intent of the New Deal, in legislation like the NIRA, to promote exactly these results in order to end the Great Depression, eliminate the possibility of a recurrence, and manage the mature economy. While the *Schechter* Court had a healthy respect for liberty and property rights, what others called economic rights, the liberals of the New Deal were ideologically committed to expert governance rather than economic liberty.

As Chief Justice John Marshall declared in *McCulloch v. Maryland* (1819), "the power to tax involves the power to destroy," so did state and national governments' regulatory authority. Small businesses like the Schechters' could not withstand the poultry code. When the US Supreme Court post-1937 deferred to state and national government authority, they allowed state and national governments to destroy the livelihoods of many. Often, if not always, the administrative state's regulations were intensive, paperwork heavy, and inflexible. While large businesses could employ staff to deal with these regulatory regimes, small businesses could not afford it. Small farms, proprietorships, and family businesses bore the brunt of this new era, forever diminishing the diversity of America's economic landscape.

In another of the New Deal's ironies, the free trade policies, embodied in the GATT, that were meant to preserve America's industrial preeminence, coupled with pro-union and pro-labor policies, eroded that preeminence almost into nonexistence. The overturning of *Lochner* and the reversal from *Schechter*'s skepticism of regulatory agencies led directly to the federal minimum wage law, in the Fair Labor Standards Act of 1938, and support for the CIO organizing semi-skilled labor under the supervision of the NLRB. Though Taft-Hartley would undermine the Wagner Act, the GATT, minimum wages, and well-intentioned but poorly executed regulations, both federal and state, combined to create a witch's brew for US manufacturing from the late 1960s through the early 2000s. With Asia being the largest winner with Latin America not far behind, the New Dealers' managed, mature economy turned out to be not as well-managed or mature as they envisioned.

The same can be said for the rest of the administrative state overseeing health and public safety that emerged after the switch in time.

Cars are safer and so are most consumer products. The air and water are cleaner, though still threatened and polluted in places. Dangerous pesticides like DDT are no longer destroying ecosystems and poisoning people as they used to do. Yet it has come at a significant cost, especially for the impoverished. Overall pollution throughout the planet is probably as bad if not worse than it was, thanks to free trade. Similarly, while international efforts to combat the production of carbon dioxide from fossil fuel use, under the widely agreed upon theory of anthropogenic greenhouse gas causing climate change, have made measured progress, the production and disposal of green energy tools such as wind turbines and batteries present their own challenges.

The story of *Schechter v. United States* is also a local story. The Jewish American immigrant brothers, their Jewish workers, their Jewish neighborhood, and their Jewish customers all lived in Brooklyn, New York City, while Franklin D. Roosevelt came from upstate and could trace his ancestry to the Dutch settlers of New Amsterdam and New Netherland, the city and colony, respectively, that preceded New York, New York. Brooklyn and New York City had a wealth of immigrants who lived in widely varied circumstances, but few like Roosevelt in Hyde Park, New York. In some respects, the case is the embodiment of the interaction between these two worlds with their contrasting worldviews. The Schechters voted Democrat and supported the New Deal, yet FDR did not share their perspective on where the nation should go. He wanted the world to be more like Hyde Park and less like corrupt, poverty-ridden, and chaotic New York City.

As things often do in the United States, these conflicting viewpoints found their way into the court system. Yet instead of this conflict being resolved before the highest tribunal in the land, the powerful president continued his fight long after his beloved NRA crumbled into dust. As Justice Robert H. Jackson wrote in a concurring opinion in *Brown v. Allen* (1953), "we are not final because we are infallible, but we are infallible only because we are final." The US Supreme Court may or may not be wise; however, their decisions do have meaning even when they are rendered largely moot, as with *Schechter*. While the non-delegation doctrine, interstate commerce jurisprudence, and federalism case law superseded *Schechter* long ago, the case still reverberates to this day.

Questions about the scale and scope of the national government are perpetual. So are misgivings over what scholars have termed "the imperial presidency." Most date its origins to Theodore Roosevelt and Woodrow Wilson, with their free-wheeling diplomacy, ready use of military power, and successful recentering of the US government onto the presidency rather than Congress. As such, Franklin D. Roosevelt was an inheritor of a philosophy of government instead of the prime agent. He did make a sizable contribution though. Despite the Court's rejection of his advancement of the imperial presidency in *Schechter* and other cases, FDR's subjugation of the judiciary, with few exceptions, seems to be permanent. *Schechter* appears to have been more of a last gasp of the constitutional order than a harbinger.

Lost amid the fanfare of the Civil Rights Revolution of later years, when the Court led the nation into a better legal environment, is the world of *A.L.A Schechter Poultry v. United States*, "the Sick Chicken Case," left behind for good or ill (though never overruled). No one longs for the Great Depression, bank failures, and unregulated financial markets. Nor do we want to return to the days of poultry most foul. Yet we did lose something on the march to the administrative state, the imperial presidency, and the rule of the supposed experts. Only when we look back to the way things were can we begin to understand what, if anything, that was.

Unfortunately, widespread dissatisfaction with the US Supreme Court's decisions in recent years, most recently its overturning of *Roe v. Wade* (1973), which established a constitutional right to an abortion, in *Dobbs v. Jackson Women's Health Organization* (2022) and the nomination of Justice Brett Kavanaugh to the Court in 2018, which was highly controversial due, in part, to fears that the Court would overturn *Roe*, has reopened public discussion of the Court's role and its membership. There have been several proposals in Congress to enlarge the number of justices in order to reverse its conservative tilt after three nominations by the often fervently disliked President Donald J. Trump. Accompanying these proposals are detractors on both sides of the political aisle wondering how to rein in what is often called "judicial activism" or "judicial supremacy."

In a 1984 case that was beyond the scope of this book, *Chevron v. Natural Resources Defense Council*, the Court ordered federal judges to defer to regulatory agencies' interpretations of unclear statutes. It is highly likely that the poultry code involved in Schechter would have survived under this standard. In 2024, just as this book came out of copyediting, a Court largely composed of President Donald Trump appointees overturned this foundation of the administrative state in *Relentless v. Department of Commerce* and *Loper Bright Enterprises v. Raimondo*, replacing it with a much more restrictive review process. Although the long-term impact of this new precedent is unclear, there is little doubt it has contributed to the calls for a restructuring of the US Supreme Court. The Sick Chicken Case appears to be a case for the ages.

Mark Twain is reputed to have said "History doesn't repeat itself, but it often rhymes." While there are major differences between the United States of 1937 and the 2020s, there are also many parallels, or rhymes if you will. Americans are still divided over many issues. They still wrestle with topics large and small. They both agree and disagree over the nature of law and society in the United States. While some celebrate the nation, others find much to criticize if not lament. There is still no certainty about the proper role of government in American life nor the judiciary's part in it. Though *Schechter* may be distant history, "the Sick Chicken Case" still resonates if only as a distant echo from our past.

March 4, 1929	Herbert Hoover sworn in as president of the United States.
October 24, 29, 1929	Black Thursday, Black Tuesday, the Stock Market crashes; the Great Depression begins.
March 4, 1933	Franklin D. Roosevelt sworn in as president of the United States. The Great Depression has swept the country and threatens the entire banking system.
June 16, 1933	President Franklin D. Roosevelt signs into law the National Industrial Recovery Act, which creates the National Recovery Administration, as part of the First New Deal.
April 13, 1934	President Franklin D. Roosevelt signs into law the Code of Fair Competition for the Live Poultry Industry of the Metropolitan Area in and about the City of New York.
July 26, 1934	Federal Grand Jury for Brooklyn, New York City, New York, indicts the Schechter brothers for multiple violations of the Code and the NIRA. They are arrested, charged, and put on trial.
August 29, 1934	Federal District judge Marcus B. Campbell issues his ruling in *U.S. v. Schechter* and dismisses nineteen counts of the indictment, but upholds forty-one.
October 14–31, 1934	The Schechters are tried. Judge Campbell dismisses eight charges for insufficient evidence and instructs the jury on the remaining thirty-three charges.
November 1, 1934	The jury convicts the Schechters on nineteen counts, leading to prison terms and fines.
January 7, 1935	Amid dissatisfaction with the NRA and its codes, the US Supreme Court issues its decision in *Panama Refining Co. v. Ryan*, invalidating the "hot oil" section of the NIRA.
April 1, 1935	The Second Circuit issues its 2–1 decision against the Schechters' appeal in *U.S. v. A.L.A. Schechter Poultry Corporation et al.*

May 27, 1935	On "Black Monday," a unanimous US Supreme Court rules against the Roosevelt administration in three cases including *A.L.A. Schechter Corporation v. United States*.
November 3, 1936	After many adverse rulings and few favorable decisions on the First New Deal from the US Supreme Court, President Franklin D. Roosevelt and the Democrats win an overwhelming victory in the election.
February 5, 1937	Roosevelt announces and submits to Congress his "Judicial Procedures Reform" bill, which includes an additional appointment to the Court for every justice over seventy. The battle over the "court-packing plan" begins.
March 29, 1937	In a decision known as "the switch in time," Justice Roberts votes with the liberals in *West Coast Hotel v. Parrish*, upholding Washington State's minimum wage law and reversing the decision in *Adkins v. Children's Hospital* (1923).
June 2, 1937	Justice Willis Van Devanter retires, giving FDR his first appointment to the Court. This is probably due to Congress having recently passed a guaranteed salary for justices who retire.
July 14, 1937	US senator and majority leader Joe Robinson dies after fighting for Roosevelt's "court-packing" plan. Support for the controversial plan evaporates soon afterward.
April 25, 1938	After approving the Second New Deal in multiple cases, Chief Justice Stone and several other new Roosevelt appointees initiate the rational basis test for regulation of the economy, but with a notable exception for "discrete and insular minorities" in footnote four of *Carolene Products v. United States*.
December 7, 1941–1945	US enters World War II, with national mobilization of the economy, and the internment of Japanese Americans is upheld by FDR's Supreme Court in the Japanese Internment Cases.

{ *Chronology* }

June 11, 1946	President Harry S. Truman signs into law the Administrative Procedure Act of 1946, inaugurating the formalization of the administrative state.
January 18, 1989	In *Mistretta v. U.S.*, the US Supreme Court reaffirms the deferential standard for the non-delegation doctrine in upholding the United States Sentencing Commission.
April 26, 1995	In *U.S. v. Lopez*, the US Supreme Court issues its first limitation on Congress's authority under the interstate commerce clause since the New Deal.
June 20, 2019	In *Gundy v. U.S.*, the US Supreme Court reaffirms the Congress-gave-an-"intelligible principle" precedent for avoiding the non-delegation doctrine.

Looming over my narrative is the brooding omnipresence (to borrow a phrase from Justice Louis Brandeis borrowed from Justice Oliver Wendell Holmes, Jr.) of Professor Mark Tushnet's nearly 1300-page history of the *Hughes Court from Progressivism to Pluralism, 1930–1941*, volume II in the *Oliver Wendell Holmes Devise History of the Supreme Court* (New York: Cambridge University Press, 2022). It appeared in print after I had finished and submitted my manuscript to the press, but in revision I have found it indispensable. Although I cannot see it being assigned to undergraduates, it is a reference work emphasizing legal doctrine that bears the distinguishing marks of a long career in teaching and writing about constitutional law.

Historian Laura Kalman's lively and provocative *FDR's Gambit: The Court Packing Fight and the Rise of Legal Liberalism* (New York: Oxford University Press, 2022), also appeared after I submitted my manuscript, but in time for me to include it in the revised version of chapter 5, on the court-packing fight. Kalman's use of primary sources is exemplary. The quotes from the book in chapter 5 are from pages x and 258.

Primary Sources

The vast bulk of primary sources for this work are the cases. All of them are available online from various publicly accessible databases. Central are J. W. Hampton, Jr. & Co. v. United States, 276 U.S. 394 (1928); Local 167 of International Brotherhood of Teamsters, Chauffeurs, Stablemen & Helpers of America et al. v. United States, 291 U.S. 293 (1934); Nebbia v. New York, 291 U.S. 502 (1934); United States v. Schechter, 8 F. Supp. 136 (E.D.N.Y. 1934); (The Gold Clause Cases) Norman v. Baltimore & Ohio R. Co, United States v. Bankers Trust Co., Nortz v. United States, Perry v. United States, 294 U.S. 240; Panama Refining Co. v. Ryan, 293 U.S. 388 (1935); United States v. A.L.A. Schechter Poultry Corp., 76 F.2d 617 (1935); Railroad Retirement Board v. Alton Railroad Co., 295 U.S. 330 (1935); Humphrey's Executor v. United States, 295 U.S. 602 (1935); A.L.A.

Schechter Poultry Corp. v. United States, 295 U.S. 495 (1935); Louisville Joint Stock Land Bank v. Radford, 295 U.S. 555 (1935); United States v. Butler, 297 U.S. 1 (1936); Ashwander v. Tennessee Valley Auth., 297 U.S. 288 (1936); Jones v. SEC, 298 U.S. 1 (1936); Carter v. Carter Coal Co., 298 U.S. 238 (1936); Ashton v. Cameron County Water Imp. Dist. No. 1, 298 U.S. 513 (1936); Morehead v. New York ex rel. Tipaldo, 298 U.S. 587 (1936); Labor Board v. Friedman-Harry Marks Clothing Co., 301 U.S. 58 (1937); NLRB v. Jones & McLaughlin Steel Corp., 301 U.S. 1 (1937); Virginian Railway Co. v. Railway Employees, 300 U.S. 515 (1937); West Coast Hotel Co. v. Parrish, 300 U.S. 379 (1937); Wright v. Vinton Branch, 300 U.S. 440 (1937); Helvering v. Davis, 301 U.S. 619 (1937); Steward Machine Co. v. Davis, 301 U.S. 548 (1937); Steward Mach. Co. v. Collector, 301 U.S. 548 (1937); United States v. Carolene Products Co., 304 U.S. 144 (1938); United States v. Darby, 312 U.S. 100 (1941); Ex parte Endo, 323 U.S. 283 (1944); Mistretta v. United States, 488 U.S. 361 (1989); United States v. Lopez, 514 U.S. 549 (1995); and United States v. Morrison, 529 U.S. 598 (2000); Gundy v. United States, 588 U.S. 432, 139 S. Ct. 2116.

The records and briefs of the Second Circuit are available on microfilm, call number: 93/10002 (LL), from the Library of Congress. The briefs and oral arguments for *Schechter* come from *Landmark Briefs and Arguments of the Supreme Court of the United States: Constitutional Law*, Philip B. Kurland and Gerhard Casper, eds., volume 28 (Arlington, VA: University Publications of America, Inc., 1975). Newspapers, particularly the *New York Times*, provided both local and national coverage. The fireside chats, inaugural addresses, and interviews with President Roosevelt are publicly available online from the Library of Congress, the National Archives, and the Avalon Project at the Yale University Law School Library. The National Constitution Center website, among others, also maintains public records relating to the Constitutional Crisis of 1937 and *Schechter* along with other key cases.

Many of the key players in the New Deal wrote memoirs. Hugh Johnson published his autobiography soon after he left the NRA: *The Blue Eagle: From Egg to Earth* (New York: Greenwood Press, 1935, 1968). It contains valuable information but with a decidedly exculpatory spin. Some items, like Justice Roberts's memorandum to Frankfurter, are posted online independently, but all are referenced in whole or in part in the secondary literature. On occasion, a blog will testify to a relevant detail such as the origin of the disclaimer in television shows, Herbork, "Borky Invents TV Disclaimers," *Herbork: A Writer's Site*, January 16, 2014, https://herbork .com/2014/01/16/borky-invents-tv-disclaimers/, but also provide key details on a Justice Department lawyer involved with *Schechter*. Herbert Borkland Sr., Joseph Alsop, and Turner Catledge, *The 168 Days* (Garden City, NY: Doubleday, Doran & Co., 1938), is a contemporary account by two journalists of the protracted debate on Roosevelt's court bill in Congress in 1937. Additional materials come from websites dedicated to particular issues. Because the information on these sites was unverified, I used them with caution.

A final area for primary sources is within the secondary literature. Biographers, law review articles, and books on individual topics have provided a substantial number of quotations from the participants in this story that are accessible only in archives. This work is indebted to these scholars for their enormous efforts to gather, analyze, and disseminate the select content of those archives. See below for secondary sources.

Secondary Sources

There are several books on the Constitutional Crisis of 1937 along with Kalman's. Foremost among them is Marian C. McKenna, *Franklin Roosevelt and the Great Constitutional War: The Court-Packing Crisis of 1937* (New York: Fordham University Press, 2002). It is a comprehensive, meticulously researched volume. It also has a complete listing of the secondary literature as of 2002. William E. Leuchtenburg, *The Supreme Court Reborn: The Constitutional Revolution in the Age of Roosevelt* (New York: Oxford University Press, 1995) is a collection of essays rather than a monograph, but it is well-sourced and a seminal work on the topic. Barry Cushman, *Rethinking the New Deal Court: The Structure of a Constitutional Revolution* (New York: Oxford University Press, 1998) is a thought-provoking, sophisticated re-examination of the topic. His "The Hughes Court and Constitutional Consultation," *Journal of Supreme Court History* 79 (1998): 79–111 (quotation in text on page 84) was also useful. G. Edward White, *The Constitution and the New Deal* (Cambridge: Harvard University Press, 2000) is a work by a preeminent legal historian at the height of his powers. It concentrates on doctrine, jurisprudence, and the threads of intellectual argument for the internalist position. John Q. Barrett, "Attribution Time: Cal Tinney's Quip 'A Switch in Time'll Save Nine,'" *Oklahoma Law Review* 73 (2021): 229–242, offers one source for the phrase.

Daniel R. Ernst, *Tocqueville's Nightmare: The Emergence of the Administrative State in America* (New York: Oxford University Press, 2014) places *Schechter* into its wider context. The best combination of history and case law, it is a foundational work from one of the foremost scholars, if not the foremost scholar, in the area. Although it is more of a reference work, in a series of books on the Courts divided by chief justice, Michael E. Parrish, *The Hughes Court: Justices Rulings, and Legacy*, ABC-CLIO Supreme Court Handbooks (Santa Barbara, CA: ABC-CLIO, 2002) devotes a great deal of material to the rulings, the controversy, and the biographies of the justices involved. It is an indispensable resource.

The New Deal has a voluminous body of literature. One should start with the magisterial David M. Kennedy, *Freedom from Fear: The American People in Depression and War, 1929–1945* (New York: Oxford University Press, 1999) for a comprehensive list of the literature as of publication as well as a magnificent history of the era. A friendlier rendering of Roosevelt's early presidency is Frank Freidel, *Franklin D. Roosevelt: Launching the New Deal* (Boston: Little, Brown and Company, 1974). For the complete opposite side of the political spectrum, with a detailed rendering of the *Schechter* case, its origins, and outcome, consult journalist Amity Shlaes, *The Forgotten Man: A New History of the Great Depression* (New York: Harper Perennial, 2007). Daniel Fusfield's *The Economic Thought of Franklin D. Roosevelt and the Origins of the New Deal* (New York: Columbia University Press, 1956) places FDR's approach squarely within progressivism. Who am I to disagree? For the predecessor to the NRA under President Hoover, see James Stuart Olson, *Saving Capitalism: The Reconstruction Finance Corporation and the New Deal, 1933–1940* (Princeton: Princeton University Press, 2017).

For volumes pointing out the complex nature of the New Deal's impact, there is James Gross's *The Making of the National Labor Relations Board: A Study in Economics, Politics, and the Law, 1933–1937* (Albany, NY: SUNY Press, 1974); Christopher L. Tomlins's *The State and the Unions: Labor Relations, Law, and the Organized Labor Movement in America, 1880–1960* (Cambridge, UK: Cambridge University Press, 1985); Richard Rothstein's *The Color of Law: A Forgotten History of How Our Government Segregated America*

(New York: Liveright, 2019); and Jason Scott Smith's *Building New Deal Liberalism: The Political Economy of Public Works, 1933–1956* (Cambridge, UK: Cambridge University Press, 2006). All three show the law of unintended consequences. As with any substantial change, the New Deal's legacy defies easy characterization.

In addition to the many biographies of Roosevelt, almost all of the key figures have biographies, including the individual justices. For the lawyers who did not receive individual biographies, there are two books of note. Peter H. Irons, *The New Deal Lawyers* (Princeton: Princeton University Press, 1982), takes a left of center approach. Ronen Shamir, *Managing Legal Uncertainty: Elite Lawyers in the New Deal* (Durham: Duke University Press, 1995), is a political theory–centered take on the topic. Neal Devins, "Government Lawyers and the New Deal: Review of William Leuchtenberg, *The Supreme Court Reborn,*" *Columbia Law Review* 96 (1996): 237–267, *Faculty Publications*, 438, https://scholarship.law.wm.edu/facpubs/438, is an in-depth exploration of the area with copious footnotes to sources both primary and secondary.

There are no books specifically on *Schechter*, but Frank Friedel, "The Sick Chicken Case," in *Quarrels That Have Shaped the Constitution*, John A. Garraty, ed. (New York: Harper & Row, 1962, 1963, 1964), is a book chapter that provides a detailed history of the case and its impact. It is a must read. As noted above, all comprehensive histories of the New Deal cover the *Schechter* case to a greater or lesser extent. Also of note is the contemporary review of the NIRA, largely favorable, by Milton Handler in *The American Bar Association Journal* 19, no. 8 (August 1933): 440–446, 482–483. Handler went on to a distinguished career primarily in writing about anti-trust law. His dispassionate analysis of the NIRA accepts there are limits on government during an emergency, even in war, with the NIRA likely to survive the scrutiny. Gerald Berk, *Louis D. Brandeis and the Making of Regulated Competition, 1900–1932* (Cambridge, UK: Cambridge University Press, 2009); Ellis Hawley's *The New Deal and the Problem of Monopoly: A Study in Economic Ambivalence* (Princeton: Princeton University Press, 1966); and Laura Phillips Sawyer's *American Fair Trade: Proprietary Capitalism, Corporatism, and the 'New Competition,' 1890–1940* (Cambridge, UK: Cambridge University Press, 2017) examine the NIRA's place within the convoluted history of anti-trust policy.

There are also a great many articles, almost entirely in law reviews, on the Constitutional Crisis of 1937. Lisa Schultz Bressman, "Schechter Poultry at the Millennium: A Delegation Doctrine for the Administrative State," *Yale Law Journal* 109, no. 6 (April 2000): 1399–1442, is a thoroughly researched retrospective. Judge Glock, "Unpacking the Supreme Court: Judicial Retirement, Judicial Independence and the Road to the 1937 Court Battle," the *Journal of American History* (June 2019): 47–71, places the retirement salaries for the justices center stage. David B. Green, "This Day in Jewish History: 1935: U.S. Government Loses 'Sick Chicken' Case to Jewish Slaughterers," *Haaretz*, May 27, 2016, Updated April 10, 2018, https://www.haaretz.com/jewish/1935-u-s-loses-sick-chicken-case-1.5387888, is a well-done popular article from the Jewish American perspective. Then there is Kevin Brewer, "Ten-Dollar Bills and Letters of Congratulation: The Unlikely Journey of the Sick Chicken Case," *American Path[o]s: Kevin Brewer's Blog for History, Mystery, Opinion, and Personal Reflection*, October 19, 2020, https://kevinterral brewer.com/sickchicken/, a blog post that reproduces a very well-done paper on the Schechter case with immense detail. For an excellent overview, consult Laura Kalman's "The Constitution, the Supreme Court, and the New Deal," *American Historical Review's Forum*, 110, no. 4 (October 2005): 1052–1080.

The National Recovery Administration has its own literature. Bernard Bellush, *The Failure of the NRA* (New York: W. W. Norton & Company, 1975), focuses on labor and the NRA. Donald R. Brand, *Corporatism and the Rule of Law: A Study of the National Recovery Administration* (Ithaca, NY: Cornell University Press, 1988), analyzes it from a political theory perspective. James Q. Whitman, "Of Corporatism, Fascism, and the First New Deal," *American Journal of Comparative Law* 39 (1991): 747–778, places Hugh Johnson and Donald Richberg's NRA squarely in a fascist-adjacent zone.

There are also a great many articles on the administrative state and subsidiary topics that involve *Schechter* in some way. Daniel R. Ernst, "The Shallow State: The Federal Communications Commission and the New Deal," *University of Pennsylvania Journal of Law & Public Affairs* 4, no. 3 (May 2019): 403–458, is a comprehensive, well-researched foray into the topic. Todd C. Neumann, Jason E. Taylor, and Jerry L. Taylor, "The Behavior of the Labor Market Between *Schechter* (1935) and *Jones & Laughlin* (1937)," *Cato Journal* 32, no. 3 (Fall 2022): 605–627, adopts a law and economics approach to the issue. Aaron L. Nielson, "Confessions of an 'Anti-Administrativist': Responding to Gillian E. Metzger, *The Supreme Court, 2016 Term—Forward: 1930s Redux: The Administrative State Under Siege*," *Harvard Law Review* 131 (November 2, 2017), https://harvardlawreview.org/2017/11/confessions-of-an-anti-administrativist/, is an overview of the subject from the perspective of someone who is skeptical of its benefits. Alasdair Roberts, "Should We Defend the Administrative State?" University of Massachusetts—Amherst, Forthcoming in *Public Administration Review*, February 14, 2020, https://ssm.com/abstract=3441123, is a retrospective. Howard D. Samuel, "Troubled Passage: The Labor Movement and the Fair Labor Standards Act," *Monthly Labor Review* (December 2000): 32–37, examines the history of the Fair Labor Standards Act of 1938, which established the federal minimum wage and maximum and minimum hours requirements.

On the later history of the administrative state, there is even more. George B. Shepherd, "Fierce Compromise: The Administrative Procedure Act Emerges from New Deal Politics," *Northwestern University Law Review* 90, no. 4 (1995–1996): 1557–1683, is a definitive revisionist history of a vital piece of legislation concerning the legalization of the administrative state. Robert L. Stern, "The Commerce Clause and the National Economy, 1933–1946," *Harvard Law Review* 59, no. 5 (May 1946): 645–693, is an old, almost contemporary rendering of the topic. As for the Japanese American internment cases, there is a fair amount of scholarship. The essential secondary source remains Peter Irons, *Justice at War: The Story of the Japanese American Cases* (Berkeley: University of California Press, 1983).

On the specific topic of the interstate commerce clause, there is an immense amount of legal scholarship. Although the *Schechter* case and those that followed it during the New Deal are the focus of this book, its rendering of the history is heavily dependent on that literature, which is too voluminous to mention here. For a wonderful examination of the jurisprudence on the interstate commerce clause, there is a series of articles in the *Arkansas Law Review 55* (2003), a discussion between expert scholars Barry Cushman and Richard D. Friedman, laying out the debate voluminously and with panache.

deference theory, 180
democracy: laboratories of, 4, 74, 94;
 success of, 136
Democratic National Convention, 17,
 117, 132
Democratic Party, 133, 149, 157, 162;
 cleaning up, 158, 159
Denman, William, 120
Department of Agriculture, 71, 95, 96
Department of Labor, 71–72
DeWitt, John L., 171, 173
Dickinson, John, 23
direct burden standard, 148
disability insurance, 110
discrimination, 5, 146, 149, 167, 173,
 181, 188
Dixon, Thomas, 159
*Dobbs v. Jackson Women's Health
 Organization* (2022), 142, 191
Douglas, William O., 164, 174
Dow Jones Industrial Average, 12
Dred Scott (1857), 93
drugs, 40; underground economy
 of, 11
due process, 36, 37, 48–49, 50, 51, 62,
 75, 106
DuPont, 44
Dust Bowl, 12, 15, 56, 95, 114

Eastern District Court, Brooklyn, 32
East Texas Reservoir, 22
Eccles, Marriner, 111
E. C. Knight & Co. v. U.S. (1895), 51,
 89, 181
economic issues, 14, 21, 25, 52, 53, 56
economic recovery, 45
economic rights, 73, 95, 189
economics: classical, 14; command-
 and-control, 125, 146; laissez-faire,
 111; market-based, 10
economic theory, 14, 47, 52

Eighteenth Amendment, 115
Eighth Amendment, 38, 62, 67
Electoral College, 170
Emanuel, Rahm, 66
Emergency Relief Appropriation
 Act, 107
Empire State Building, 44
Endo, Mitsue, 174
equal protection clause, 167, 181
Espionage and Sedition Act, 4, 41
Executive Order 9066 (1942), 171
Executive Office of the President, 176
Ex parte Mitsue Endo v. U.S. (1944),
 174–175

Fair Labor Standards Act (FLSA)
 (1938), 161–162, 167–168, 189
fair trade, 54, 79
fascism, 3, 9, 10, 17, 24, 29, 53, 66, 81, 117,
 160, 170; cartels and, 8
FBI. *See* Federal Bureau of
 Investigation
FCC. *See* Federal Communications
 Commission
FDIC. *See* Federal Deposit Insurance
 Corporation
FDR's Gambit (Kalman), 122
Federal Bureau of Investigation
 (FBI), 19, 29, 70, 173
Federal Communications
 Commission (FCC), 11, 92
Federal Deposit Insurance
 Corporation (FDIC), 20, 111
Federal Emergency Relief Agency, 18
Federal Grand Jury for Brooklyn, 193
Federal Housing Administration
 (FHA), 162, 163
federalism, 42, 65, 89, 94, 102, 103, 151,
 168, 181; case law, 190; violation of,
 97
Federalist Papers, The (Hamilton), 121

{ *Index* }

National Mortgage Association of Washington (NMAW), 162
National Partnership for Reinventing Government, 180
National Performance Review, 180
National Power Policy Commission, 112
National Recovery Administration (NRA), 6, 24, 25, 26, 32, 38, 39, 40, 44, 49, 55, 57, 67, 78, 79, 82; 83, 107, 112, 124, 148, 161, 172, 173, 176, 182, 184, 190, 193; codes of, 31, 54, 58, 111; compliance board, 68; disappearance of, 187; enforcement bureaucracy for, 29; evaluation by, 71; FDR and, 43, 59; leadership of, 52–53; opposition to, 60; popularity of, 43; *Schechter* and, 2; slogan of, 28; striking down; 87, 94; workforce of, 27
National Relief Agency, 22
National Youth Administration, 108
Native Sons of the Golden West, 171
natural laws, 3, 14, 143
Naval Arms Limitation Treaty (1925), 76
Nazis, 9, 53, 65, 81, 101
Nebbia v. New York (1934), 36, 37, 42, 70, 92, 104, 106, 107, 146, 165, 166
Ness, Eliot, 67
Neutrality Act (1939), 158
New Deal, 4, 6, 7, 17–22, 29, 41, 42, 43, 49, 53, 54, 57, 58, 62, 67, 69, 74, 76, 88, 94, 104, 108, 113, 115; AAA and, 95; agencies of, 177; Black Monday and, 60; challenging, 60, 120; coalition for, 116; court packing and, 187; economy and, 162; FDR and, 4, 16, 18, 19, 20, 31, 44, 46, 56, 61, 65, 81, 107, 109; 110, 116, 123, 132, 138, 157, 161, 169, 172, 182, 184, 187, 194; Four Horsemen and, 186; ironies of; 189; legislation during, 2, 118; NRA

and, 3; opposition to, 114, 177; relief agencies of, 161; Supreme Court and, 5, 95, 99, 100, 113, 119, 164
New Freedom, 73–74
New State Ice Co. v. Liebmann (1932), 94
New York Court of Appeals, 77
New York Post, 142
New York Stock Exchange, 13
New York Times, 32, 42, 58, 87
"Nine Old Men, The" (Pearson and Allen), 119
Nineteenth Amendment, 65
Ninth Circuit Court of Appeals, 138–139
NIRA. *See* National Industrial Recovery Act
Nixon, Richard, 182
NLRB. *See* National Labor Relations Board
NLRB v. Friedman-Harry Marks Clothing Co. (1937), 149
NLRB v. Jones & Laughlin Steel Corp. (1937), 148, 181
non-delegation doctrine, 1, 7, 36, 38, 45, 46, 47, 55, 88, 94, 178, 179
Nordic race theory, 9
Norris, George, 115
Norris-LaGuardia Act (1932), 26
Nuremberg Race Laws (1935), 167

Obama, Barack, 22, 66
Ocasio-Cortez, Alexandria, 4
Olmsted v. United States (1928), 75
Olson, James, 123
O'Mahoney, Joseph, 154
168 Days (Alsop), 185
Open Market Committee, 111
"Origin and Scope of American Constitutional Law, The" (Thayer), 36
Owens, Jesse, 9

{ *Index* }

Rivera, Diego, 108

Roberts, Owen, 7, 36, 37, 50, 76, 77, 78, 91, 97, 98, 103, 118, 141, 142, 143, 148, 150, 165, 169, 172; 174, 186, 187, 194; *Adkins* and, 105; Hughes and, 144; opinion by, 96, 104; *Schechter* and, 51; *Tipaldo* and, 144; *TVA* and, 99

Robinson, Joe, 132, 140, 155–156; death of, 156–157, 194

Roe v. Wade (1973), 86, 142, 191

Romeo and Juliet (Shakespeare), 83

Roosevelt, Eleanor, 17, 18

Roosevelt, Franklin Delano, 10, 35, 42, 50, 55–56; ageism and, 127; ancestry of, 190; balance of power and, 132; bank holiday and, 18; Black and, 159; Brain Trust and, 23, 117; bureaucracy and, 69; campaign of, 15–16; character of, 185; Code of Fair Competition and, 27; Constitution and, 135; court packing and, 7, 122, 127, 128, 130, 132–133, 135–136, 152, 186, 187, 194; Cummings and, 117; death of, 16; economy and, 21, 161; election of, 122, 169, 176, 193; *Endo* and, 174–175; executive branch reorganization and, 57; FBI and, 70; first hundred days of, 17; gold standard and, 21, 49; Great Depression and, 4, 22; Guffey-Snyder and, 88; Japanese American relocation and, 171; Japanese Internment Cases and, 194; Johnson and, 29; judiciary reform and, 136–140, 167, 153–154, 185, 195; Klan and, 159; New Deal and, 4, 16, 18, 19, 20, 31, 44, 46, 56, 61, 65, 81, 107, 109, 110, 116, 123, 132; 138, 157, 161, 169, 172, 182, 184, 187, 194; newsreels/radio and, 117; NIRA and, 6, 53, 58, 87; NLRA and, 108; non-delegation doctrine and, 55; NRA and, 2, 28, 43, 59; O'Mahoney and, 154; politics of, 56; 118, 119, 129–131, 156, 166; poultry code and, 33; progressive democracy and, 124–125; *Schechter* and, 52–53, 68, 82, 87, 88, 93, 124, 168–169, 182; SEC and, 170; Social Security and, 51, 52, 152; State of the Union address by, 124, 125; Supreme Court and, 58, 114, 116, 125, 129–131, 166, 182, 185, 187, 194; World War II and, 176–177; youth of, 21

Roosevelt, Theodore, 16, 54, 171, 191

Roosevelt Recession, 161

Rural Electrification Administration, 20, 108

Russian Civil War, 9

Saltwater School, 161

same-sex marriage, 5

Say, Jean-Baptiste, 14

Say's Law, 14

Scalia, Antonin, 178, 179

Schechter, Aaron, 30

Schechter, Alex, 30, 32

Schechter, Joseph, 30, 32, 87–88

Schechter, Martin, 30

Schechter brothers, 24, 37, 42, 60, 62, 80, 93, 175, 187; appeal by, 35, 47; arguments for, 63–64, 67; brief for, 65, 68, 70; defeat for, 35–36, 49; fines for, 34; indictment of, 32, 193; NIRA rulings and, 177; poultry business of, 29–33; trial of, 47, 57

Schechter Poultry, 11; interstate commerce and, 78–79

Scott, Dred, 93

Scottsboro Boys, 167

Sears & Roebuck, 64
SEC. *See* Securities and Exchange
Commission
Second Circuit Court of Appeals, 35,
38, 42–49, 48, 70, 193
Second Great Migration, 114
Second New Deal, 7, 88, 94, 107–113,
123, 161, 165, 185, 194; legislation of,
125, 147, 163; regulations and, 177;
Schechter and, 186; Supreme Court
and, 133
Securities and Exchange Act (1934), 100
Securities and Exchange Commission
(SEC), 18, 20, 50, 111, 139, 164, 179;
autocracy of, 100; FDR and, 170;
function of, 101; Supreme Court
and, 100–101
segregation, 159, 162, 167, 168
Selective Service System, 25
Senate Judiciary Committee, 5, 131,
136–137, 138, 148, 153, 155, 157, 158;
court packing and, 140
separation of powers doctrine, 1, 4
Seventeenth Amendment, 74
sexism, 147
Sex Offender Registration and
Notification Act (SORNA) (2006), 179
sex trafficking, 40
Shakespeare, William, 83
sharecropping, 114
"Share Our Wealth Plan" (Long), 44
Share Our Wealth Society, 44
Sherman Anti-Trust Act (1890), 31, 35,
79, 89, 161
Sick Chicken Case, 192; naming of, 1,
33, 63, 191
Simpsons, The, 98
Sixteenth Amendment, 52, 97
Sixth Amendment, 67
Skinner v. Oklahoma (1942), 165
Smith, Adam, 125

Smith, Al, 16, 43–44, 116, 117
Smith, Gerald L. K., 44
Smoot-Hawley Tariff (1930), 13, 163
socialism, 17, 25, 169
social justice, 126
Social Security, 2, 51, 52, 109, 123, 150,
153, 168, 185, 188; contributions to, 110
Social Security Act (1935), 109, 152
Social Security Administration, 51
Soil Conservation and Domestic
Allotment Act (1936), 113
Solicitor General, 57, 68–69, 138
Southern Pacific Railroad, 63
Soviet Union, 9, 19
Spanish Civil War, 176
Special Committee on Administrative
Law (ABA), 175
Square Deal, 16
Stalin, Josef, 9, 10, 53, 65
Stalinism, 117
Standard Oil, 64
Stanford, Edward Terry, 76
State Department, 74
states' rights, 73
statutory construction, rule of, 46
Steffens, Lincoln, 10
Stephens, Harold M., 35, 68
Stern, Robert L., 68
Steward Machine Co. v. Davis (1937),
150, 151
Stock Market crash, 14, 193
Stone, Harlan Fiske, 37, 52, 57, 75, 76,
80, 85, 86, 91, 94, 98, 106, 109, 138, 164,
165, 166, 167, 169, 172; 186, 194; *Butler*
and, 97; *Darby Lumber* and, 168;
dissent by, 97, 107, 143; *Nebbia* and,
107; *Tipaldo* and, 104–105; *Virginian
Railway Company* and, 147; wages
and hours and, 87; *West Coast Hotel*
and; 143
straight killing, 27, 32, 80

126; interstate commerce clause and, 39; limits by, 186; ratification convention, 81; Reconstruction and, 65
US House of Representatives, 74, 129
US Pacific Fleet, 170
US Senate, 131
US Steel, 64
US Supreme Court, 4, 24, 25, 31, 35, 38, 39, 40, 41, 44, 50, 57, 62, 65, 69, 76, 78, 79, 89, 96, 102, 105; 114, 115, 116, 117, 118, 121, 123, 124; *Adkins* and, 104; Agricultural Adjustment Act and, 122; appeal to, 49; circuit courts and, 139; civil liberties and, 46; civil rights and, 167; constitutional crisis and, 93; court packing and, 5, 152; dissatisfaction with, 191; expanding, 133; FDR and, 58, 114, 116, 125, 129–131, 166, 182, 185, 187; government authority and, 189; Guffey-Snyder and, 88; *Hammer* and, 70; *Hampton* and, 38; increasing size of, 126–127; jurisprudence shift for, 144–145; *Korematsu* and, 174; legalism of, 5; *Lochner* and, 48, 98; New Deal and, 5, 95, 99, 100, 113, 119, 164; nondelegation doctrine and, 55, 178; NRA and, 190; obstructionism by, 185; *Schechter* and, 72–78, 108; SEC and, 100–101; skepticism of, 49–52; transformation of, 157, 163–167; Wagner Act and, 147

Van Devanter, Willis, 37, 75, 76, 78, 103, 132, 158, 186; appointment of, 155; retirement of, 194; *Schechter* and, 73
VAWA. *See* Violence Against Women Act
Versailles Treaty, 12

Victory Day, 133
Violence Against Women Act (VAWA), 181, 182, 184
Virginian Railway Company v. Railway Employees [Federation] (1937), 147–148
Volstead Act (1919), 127
von Hindenburg, Paul, 9

wages and hours clause, 86–87, 90
Wagner, Robert, 23, 108, 109, 158
Wagner Act. *See* National Labor Relations Act
Waldo, Dwight, 175
Wallace, Henry, 113, 138
Walter-Logan Act (1940), 182
War Department, 171
War Industries Board, 161
Warm Springs, 131, 136, 159
War on Crime, 182
War Relocation Authority, 172, 174
War Relocation Centers, 172
Washington, George, 56, 170
Washington Merry-Go-Round, 59
Washington Post, 59, 130
Webster, Daniel, 103
Weimar Germany, 9, 12, 13
West Coast Command, 171
West Coast Hotel, 142
West Coast Hotel Co. v. Parrish (1937), 141, 143–144, 145, 147–148, 153, 181, 188, 194
Weston, Charles H., 68
West Virginia Board of Education v. Barnette (1943), 5
Wheeler, Burton K., 112, 132; Hughes and, 76, 137–138, 141–142
Wheeler-Rayburn Act (1935), 111
Whig Party, creation of, 152
White House Press Corps, 126
White Monday, 147, 148
Wiecek, William, 81

Willkie, Wendell, 170
Wilson, Woodrow, 46, 54, 73, 74, 75, 76; diplomacy of, 191
Wood, Frederick H., 60, 63, 64, 67, 78, 85; brief and, 65; interstate commerce and, 81
Works Progress Administration (WPA), 108

World Economic Conference, 21
World Trade Organization, 162
World War I, 4, 12, 23, 25, 41, 49, 92, 111, 125
World War II, 3, 8, 109, 114, 170, 182, 194; FDR and, 176–177
Wright v. Vinton Branch (1937), 147–148